THE
NAPOLEON OPTIONS

ALTERNATE HISTORY
FROM GREENHILL BOOKS

FOR WANT OF A NAIL
If Burgoyne had Won at Saratoga
Robert Sobel

GETTYSBURG
An Alternate History
Peter G. Tsouras

THE HITLER OPTIONS
Alternate Decisions of World War II
Edited by Kenneth Macksey

INVASION
The Alternate History of the German Invasion of England, July 1940
Kenneth Macksey

DISASTER AT D-DAY
The Germans Defeat the Allies, June 1944
Peter Tsouras

THE
NAPOLEON
OPTIONS

ALTERNATE DECISIONS OF THE NAPOLEONIC WARS

Edited by Jonathan North

Greenhill Books, London
Stackpole Books, Pennsylvania

This edition of *The Napoleon Options* first published 2000 by Greenhill Books,
Lionel Leventhal Limited, Park House, 1 Russell Gardens, London NW11 9NN
and
Stackpole Books, 5067 Ritter Road, Mechanicsburg, PA 17055, USA

British Library Cataloguing in Publication Data
The Napoleon options: alternate decisions of the Napoleonic Wars
1. Napoleonic Wars, 1800–1815
I. North, Jonathan
940.2'7

ISBN 1–85367–388–9

Library of Congress Cataloging-in-Publication Data available

Typeset by DP Photosetting, Aylesbury, Bucks
Printed and bound in Great Britain by
CPD (Wales), Ebbw Vale

CONTENTS

ILLUSTRATIONS

MAPS

INTRODUCTION

The Napoleonic Wars recast Europe and the world by turning upside down the established order of politics, society, expectation and geography. No other conflict in history produced so many reverberations and indisputable legacies.

The very importance of that global conflict means that, inevitably, historians have been asking the compelling question 'what if things had been different?' ever since the final shots died away.

That basic question was the genesis of this book. Alternate history is a kind of time travel, which itself has been an inspiration for writers since the eighteenth century – as Samuel Madden's *Memoirs of the Twentieth Century* (published in 1733) and Louis Sebastien Mercier's *Memoirs of the Year Two Thousand Five Hundred* (published in 1771) testify. But instead of going forward, alternate history delights in going back – not looking at how our world *will* be different, but studying how it *might have been* different but for one or two minor brush-strokes on the canvas of history. Alternate history plays on, and exaggerates a little, one of the chief beauties of history – nothing is without consequence. Even a small, seemingly minor, event has meaning – a lost letter, an accident at birth or accidental birth, or a fall downstairs. Speculation on these chances and possibilities produces alternate history and has done so, surprisingly, for more than 150 years.

This book therefore belongs to a strong if neglected genre and follows in the footsteps of a number of enriching images of world history as it might have been. The first alternate history to be of interest to the Napoleonic scholar, and indeed one of the pioneers of the genre, is undoubtedly *Napoleon et la conquete du monde, 1812–1823: histoire de la monarchie universelle* by Louis Napoleon Geoffroy-Château published in 1836. This fascinating book creates a fantasy world in which Napoleon, after defeating the Russians in 1812, conquers the world and imposes universal order and, inevitably, progress. Geoffroy-Chateau cleverly switched reality so that historical facts become fictional fantasies while the alternate versions are presented and accepted as fact. Although not the first alternate history, it was certainly the first of any length.

Of equal importance and interest to the Napoleonic alternate historian are the wide variety of essays and articles – occasionally gathered into anthologies such as *The Ifs of History* (1907) and *If it Had Happened Otherwise* (1931), but frequently published in journals and periodicals – which take a new look at many periods of history. Such writings came into great favour at the end of the nineteenth century in particular. Covering all historical eras, their authors included such eminent scholars as Philip Guedalla (on a Moorish Spain), G.K. Chesterton (on Mary, Queen of Scots), Harold Nicolson (on Greek independence) and Winston Churchill (who wrote a sparkling alternate history of Gettysburg). André Maurois (on a France unchallenged by Revolution), Hilaire Belloc (on Louis XVI's attempt to escape France in 1793), and G.M. Trevelyan (on a Napoleonic victory at Waterloo), among others, covered the Napoleonic Wars.

Recent years have seen a renewed interest in alternate history and this book follows on, to some degree, from the likes of *The Hitler Options* (1995), *Gettysburg: An Alternate History* (1997), *For Want of a Nail* (1973 and 1997) and *What If? Explorations in Social-Science Fiction* (1982).

As with these more recent studies, in *The Napoleon Options* our aim is to present historical scenarios very firmly rooted in historical reality – this is not fiction, but simulated fact. We don't just ask 'what if things had been different?', we actually put the question to the test, make it happen, stand back and watch the results.

The Napoleon Options presents chapters which put to use a broad range of devices to engineer their alternate events: a storm at sea, a well-timed cavalry charge, the speed of a ship of the line, an energetic garrison commander, the sudden death of a key commander. Thus – just as in real history – chance, mishap and accident play as much a role in bringing about alternate events as incorrect strategic decisions, faulty commands and poor leadership at the highest command levels. Most of the chapters involve Napoleon – although he is not always in control – but we have included episodes in which his subordinates or, as with the chapter on Ireland, rivals, play a leading part. Such events were as decisive and as interesting to the historian as the emperor's major campaigns.

We have chosen to focus on the years on either side of the heyday of the Napoleonic empire and especially when the tide of events begins to turn against the greatest captain of his age – there are more potential alternatives when things start to go awry. Looking at the period before the complete domination of Napoleon, Paddy Griffith examines the results of a serious French invasion of Ireland, a very real danger in the closing years of the eighteenth century; and Charles Grant studies the results of a successful French occupation of Egypt and the Middle East, and the impact of this new French empire on the British in India. From the rise of Bonaparte we then jump forward to the period of declining empire: Philip Haythornthwaite refights the battle of Vimiero, a pivotal moment early on in the great Peninsular War; John H. Gill imagines the impact of an early Austrian offensive in 1809; Digby Smith presents an alternate Borodino and its disastrous effect on the Napoleonic world order; the editor examines how the French could have reversed the retreat from Moscow and looks at the possible results of a successful French defeat of Russia; and John Gallaher analyses how the 1813 campaign in Germany might have been different had Napoleon pursued successfully after Dresden.

Waterloo is, of course, one of the most celebrated examples of a military campaign succeeding by the skin of its teeth and a frequently imagined 'what if'; and Waterloo itself, regardless of the results, presents a wonderful opportunity for the alternate history treatment. I therefore make no apologies for including three very distinct chapters on the Hundred Days – one focusing on the beginning of the drama, one on the middle, and one on the end. Peter Hofschröer considers the consequences of an Allied blunder very early on in the campaign; Andrew Uffindell investigates an alternate – and more bloody – engagement on the field of Waterloo itself; and John Elting suggests what could have happened had the French recovered and fought back *after* Waterloo.

Of course, the Napoleonic Wars, and the Revolutionary Wars which immediately preceded and are obscured by them, throw up a wealth of alternate possibilities, but, unfortunately, we are limited by space. For example, there are no Hornbloweresque chapters on the war at sea. Nor are there any chapters examining the consequences of Napoleon being executed as a Jacobin at Antibes in 1794, having been killed by a chance Austrian bullet at the bridge of Arcola, or retiming a visit to the opera on the night of 24 December 1800. Nor do we look at Napoleon evading the British and travelling to America in 1815, or possible rescues of Napoleon from St Helena – by South American renegades, die-hard Bonapartists or American privateers – during his exile. The options are endless.

This is Napoleonic history, and military history, with just a hint of speculation. But then history, by its very nature, is speculative.

Jonathan North, 2000

THE CONTRIBUTORS

John R. Elting, Colonel USA – Retired, was a soldier 1933–68, with a couple of civilian interludes as a high school instructor. Service included the Civilian Conservation Corps; ROTC Instructor; 71st Armored Field Artillery; the Armored School; CCB, 8th Armored Division; the Philippine Scouts; the Armored Forces Information School; J-2 Division, Far East Command; Department of Military Art and Engineering, United States Military Academy; G-2, Washington Military District. Since retirement, he has 'tried to be a historian': author, co-author or editor of fifteen books, including *The Battles of Saratoga, American Army Life, A Dictionary of Soldier Talk, A Military History and Atlas of the Napoleonic Wars, Swords Around a Throne* and *Napoleonic Uniforms*. Colonel Elting's chapter is based on memories of various night operations – especially a German counter-attack in Hürtgen Forest, November 1944.

John G. Gallaher is professor of history at Southern Illinois University. He is the author of the definitive biography of Marshal Davout, *The Iron Marshal*, a history of Napoleon's Irish Legion, and a biography of General Alexandre Dumas.

John H. Gill is the author of *With Eagles to Glory: Napoleon and His German Allies in the 1809 Campaign* and the editor of *A Soldier for Napoleon*, a commentary on the letters and diaries of a Bavarian infantry lieutenant during the Napoleonic Wars. His publications also include several articles on Napoleonic military affairs, papers presented to the Consortium on Revolutionary Europe, a chapter on the Nazi nuclear programme in *The Hitler Options*, edited by Kenneth Macksey, and a chapter on Napoleon's German Allies in Spain in *The Peninsular War*. He received his BA from Middlebury College in 1977 (double major: history and German) and his MA from The George Washington University in 1987 (international relations). A lieutenant colonel in the US Army, he is assigned to the Defense Intelligence Agency as the Assistant Defense Intelligence Officer for South Asia. Lieutenant Colonel Gill resides in Alexandria, Virginia.

Charles Stewart Grant was born in 1948. The son of the late Charles Grant, a well-known pioneer in wargaming and author of various books including *The War Game*, Charles Stewart Grant grew up in an atmosphere of military history and wargaming. He is the author of a number of books including *From Pike to Shot – 1680 to 1720*, *Scenarios for Wargames* and *Wargame Campaigns*, and has continued the family interest. The Napoleonic era has always been his main area of expertise, in particular Bonaparte's campaign in Egypt. He is a serving army officer, married with three children, and, as he nears the end of his military career, he is looking forward to devoting more time to military history and writing.

Dr Paddy Griffith was a lecturer in War Studies at the Royal Military Academy, Sandhurst, before he became a freelance author and publisher in 1989. He is an expert on Wellington and the tactics of the Revolutionary and Napoleonic Wars; but he has also studied the military art of the American Civil War and of the British Army 1916–18, as well as 'the near future' and the equally unknowable Viking age. His hobby is wargaming.

Philip Haythornthwaite was born in Colne, Lancashire, the county in which he still resides, and for many years combined a career in business with historical research and writing. He has written a series of military history reference works, including *The World War I Source Book* and *The Colonial Wars Source Book*, but many of his publications concentrate upon the Napoleonic Wars. These include *The Napoleonic Source Book*, *The Armies of Wellington*, and *Who Was Who in the Napoleonic Wars*, as well as a number of books on the uniforms and equipment of the principal armies, and on various campaigns. For the Greenhill Napoleonic Library series he contributed introductions to *In the Peninsula with a French Hussar* and *Life in Napoleon's Army*.

Peter Hofschröer is a historian and linguist, who specialises in the Napoleonic era and has written on the Prussian and Hanoverian armies for the Osprey *Men-at-Arms* series, as well as on Leipzig 1813 in the *Campaign* series. He has contributed numerous articles to magazines and journals such as *War in History*, *Militärgeschichtliche Mitteilungen*, the *Journal of the Society of Army Historical Research*, *Age of Napoleon* and *First Empire*. His acclaimed *1815: The Waterloo Campaign – Wellington, his German Allies and the Battles of Ligny and Quatre Bras* and *1815: The Waterloo Campaign – The German Victory* were published in 1998 and 1999 respectively. He has contributed *to Napoleon's Marshals*, edited by David Chandler, and is a contributor to the forthcoming *New Dictionary of National Biography*. He has been awarded a Fellowship of the International Napoleonic Society and has twice received the Memorial Medal of the League of Bismarck, once in bronze, once in silver.

Jonathan North, the editor of this book, graduated from Warwick University in 1991 (Renaissance and Modern History). He spent a number of years working in Eastern Europe as a translator, before returning to the UK and a career in publishing in 1996. He is the author of a number of articles on the Napoleonic period and on Eastern European history, and translated and edited Heinrich von Brandt's memoirs, published in 1999 as *In the Legions of Napoleon*.

Digby Smith, a former officer in the British Army, and also known to Napoleonic enthusiasts as Otto von Pivka, is a highly respected scholar of the Napoleonic period and the author of numerous books including *The Greenhill Napoleonic Wars Data Book*, *Armies of 1812*, *Armies of the Napoleonic Wars* and the forthcoming *Napoleon's Regiments*.

Andrew Uffindell is a British author. His first book was *The Eagle's Last Triumph*, a study of Napoleon's victory at Ligny. This was followed two years later by the publication of his study of the battle and battlefield of Waterloo, *On the Fields of Glory*, written with military historian Michael Corum. He has also contributed a chapter to *Napoleon: the Final Verdict* and edited a compilation of essays by the late Jac Weller, *On Wellington*. Among his published articles have been an analysis of friendly fire at Waterloo and studies of the Franco-Austrian War of 1859. He currently edits the *Newsletter of the Society of Friends of the National Army Museum*.

'THAT MOST VULNERABLE, AND, AT THE SAME TIME, MOST MORTAL PART'[1]

BY PADDY GRIFFITH

Lisbon

Today's date is 16 December 1796. It is a solemn morning in Lisbon, where the officers of the newly-arrived British Mediterranean fleet are burying their leader, Admiral Sir John Jervis, whose fragile health has finally given way to the rigours and disappointments of the service. It is a solemn morning: but not entirely a sad one, since many of his captains have had cause to resent his harsh and often idiosyncratic disciplinary methods. Several had even contemplated challenging him to a duel, and now, as they file stiffly along the narrow streets past the shrine of São Vincente to the British cemetery, they are heartily looking forward to a more relaxed and benign regime under his successor, whoever he may be. They are aware that there is a strong desire for reforms throughout the navy. Indeed, a greater consideration for the lot of the common sailor is almost a necessity, if outbreaks of sedition and mutiny are to be averted. Such reforms would never have been tolerated by Jervis, and some of the better-read among his officers now find it particularly ironic that the crusty old martinet should be laid to rest only a few plots away from a diametrically opposite type of personality, the satirical and scandalous novelist and playwright, Henry Fielding, who had been buried there in 1754.

Paris

Meanwhile, in Paris the date of this same morning is '25 Frimaire Year V'. The weather is frostier and foggier than in Portugal; but the five men at the head of the government, the 'Directory', are gathered in the Luxembourg palace to review the state of national strategy. They note that this year's campaigning season began with great promise, even though it now seems to have fallen into the doldrums. It is excellent that the final pacification of Brittany and the Vendée has at last been completed by the young, gifted, yet unusually humane, General Louis-Lazare Hoche. The navy has also at last shaken free from its Revolutionary travails, and has successfully taken to the deep Atlantic ocean once again, with Admiral Richery raiding enemy commerce as far afield as Newfoundland. Then again, Bonaparte has won some dazzling successes in Italy, as has Moreau in Germany – while Spain's

17

long-awaited military alliance with France has finally forced the British out
of the Mediterranean. Prussia has also ended her opposition, and on 5
August she has signed a secret agreement with France which amounts to
rather more than benign neutrality. Best of all, the worthless 'Assignats'
had at last been abolished, and the end of all other forms of paper money
now seems to be a realistic hope for the near future. The harvest has been
the best for a decade, and the price of bread is falling to a gratifyingly low
level.

Only Austria and Britain still remain as blocks to a generalised French
victory; but unfortunately their resistance has recently been stiffening. The
war in Germany was set back badly by Jourdan's defeat at Würzbourg on 3
September, with the French now closely besieged in Kehl, the Rhine
bridgehead opposite Strasbourg. Equally, Bonaparte has been bogged down
in front of Mantua ever since early June, and his hopes of ultimate success
seem to be fading away. Yet still more ominous to the Directors is his
obvious presumption that French foreign policy in Italy is his own personal
preserve, rather than theirs. He has just established a 'Cispadene Republic'[2]
on his own authority and against their wishes, which has rudely re-
awakened old fears of a military coup in Paris. The Directors are therefore
not entirely heart-broken that the supply of conscripts raised by Carnot's
law of August 1793 is now running out, so that the army has fallen to its
lowest total strength in four years.

With the army blighted both numerically and politically, it may now
perhaps be the turn of the navy to take centre stage. There is a widespread
view that the next big French effort should be aimed against Britain rather
than Austria, and this has recently been reinforced by the extension of peace
feelers from London. A British diplomatic mission under Lord Malmesbury
has been conducting talks in Paris since late October, which suggests that
John Bull's resolution is weakening. Now must surely be the moment to
make a desperate all-out effort, to secure the last extra cards needed to finish
off the diplomatic game. The British themselves appear to be doing this,
since they have seized upon Spain's new alliance with France as a wonderful
excuse to purloin Spanish colonies in Buenos Aires, Trinidad, Puerto Rico
and elsewhere. General Abercromby has already sailed with orders to
capture Trinidad. However, this in turn has advised the Directory that
Britain's defences nearer to home may be correspondingly weakened. The
French are experiencing a uniquely strong temptation to strike directly
against the British Isles.

Official French policy during the late autumn of 1796 has therefore been
to hold fast and hope for the best on the Mincio and the Rhine, but to
invade England, Ireland, Scotland and Wales in whatever ways might be
practicable, conceivable or even remotely imaginable. Clearly such invasions
will have to be conducted as quickly as possible, even though that will limit

them to many fewer soldiers than might normally be deemed desirable. For example, one of the 'remotely imaginable' diversionary attacks that has already been attempted, from Dunkirk to Newcastle upon Tyne, had to sweep the gaols and POW camps to find the 5,000 men required, and they got no further than Flushing, in Belgium. But at least the main effort from Brest has been entrusted to the finest, purest and most successful general of the Republic: Hoche. He has been commander of the 'Army of Ireland' since 1 November and, after many irksome delays, and some last-minute second thoughts in Paris, his energy has now readied the fleet to set sail.

Berehaven

Hoche's force left Brest on 16 December. He took a strong squadron of seventeen battleships, thirteen frigates, eight other warships, and eight large transports plus some smaller ones for subsidiary stores; 14,750 of his best troops were embarked, together with thousands of muskets to be distributed to Irish rebels upon arrival. The chief of these rebels was also embarked, travelling under the pseudonym of 'Adjutant General Smith', supposedly a staff officer to General Chérin. In reality he was Theobald Wolfe Tone, the Ulster Protestant leader of the Society of United Irishmen, who believed in total independence for the whole of Ireland. His organisation was expected to raise up to half a million 'sworn Defenders' determined to expel the hated British from Irish soil. The true figure may well have been nearer 50,000, or even less; but against a government field force of around 4,000 cavalry, 2,000 regular infantry, 9,000 fencibles and 19,000 militia – many of whom were themselves believed to be sympathetic to the cause of liberty – the prospects for success still appeared to be excellent.

The departure of the fleet from Brest was fraught with night-time alarms; confusions of orders and navigation; several serious collisions, and the horrific wreck of the 74-gun *Séduisant*, with the loss of 1,265 men, on hidden rocks in the treacherous Raz de Sein narrows. The admiral had chosen this route as a calculated gamble since, although it was certainly more dangerous than the main Iroise channel, it was thought to be unwatched by the British blockading squadron. The chaos was exacerbated by fog, and an impudent gunnery and firework display provided by the one British frigate captain (Sir Edward Pellew) who was in fact at hand to witness the escape. Nevertheless, it was a gamble which largely paid off, and the main mass of the fleet was able to proceed safely on its way. Only nine ships were eventually found to be missing, apart from the *Séduisant*, although it was highly embarrassing that one of them, the frigate *Fraternité*, carried not only the army's war chest, but also its commander – Hoche himself – as well as the naval commander, Admiral Morard de Galles.

This left the main fleet deprived of its leader. However, his second-in-command, Rear Admiral Bouvet, together with the army's second-in-command, General Grouchy, soon succeeded in gathering most of the invasion force together and directing it forward on the planned bearing. The *Fraternité* and three escorts were still out of touch in thick fog on 18 December, and it is now known that her captain, Fustel, had actually accepted the promise of a large bribe from a British secret agent to ensure that it stayed that way.[3] He did everything he could to lose Bouvet and Grouchy; and was encouraged by the fact that Admiral Morard was half blind and pessimistic, while Hoche was a total landlubber. But alas for treachery! The fog lifted miraculously on the 19th, at the very moment when the *Fraternité* chanced to be closest to the main fleet. They could not avoid recognising each other, and so a junction was necessarily made. Captain Fustel promptly ceased his games, for fear of detection, and could never claim his reward.

Thereafter the weather was not at all pleasant during the 250-mile passage to Bantry, and many of the previously brave Republican troops wished that they had been born in some land-locked country that had never heard of either the sea or the wind, let alone such wild ideas as trying to liberate contented green islands from their lawfully-appointed governments. Nevertheless, the fleet arrived at the mouth of Bantry Bay relatively concentrated and unscathed on the 22nd, and General Hoche was incisive in his orders to disembark at the first possible opportunity. If it had been left to Grouchy, who was essentially a staff officer and a waverer, it is probable that nothing would have been done; but the fiery presence of Hoche ensured that the troops evacuated their hated floating penitentiaries as quickly as they could, and regained the solid reassurance of dry, immobile land. There was still, nevertheless, the small problem of an exceptionally fierce easterly gale, mixed with snow, which caused further collisions, loss of spars, and naval trepidation. The fleet could not possibly beat up the length of Bantry Bay itself, but was forced to make landfall near its mouth, in the sheltered water of Bere Haven in the lee of Bere Island. The ships were able to start discharging their men and stores on the afternoon of the 23rd, although worsening conditions would extend the operation over three days.

General Humbert, commander of the vanguard *Légion des Francs*, made the first landing at the head of a small battalion of combined grenadiers. They scrambled ashore over the rocky beach just south-west of the village of Berehaven. Their powder was spoiled by the surf, and eight of their men were drowned. But their invasion was not noticed by coast watchers until after they had reached land and organised themselves into their proper companies. They shook out into a marching column on the main road, complete with unfurled flags for both the French and Hibernian republics. Then, as they advanced, they were met by a dozen yeomanry under the command of Mr O'Sullivan of Cooliah, a Catholic landowner of considerable local importance. He cursed his ill luck that he had been unable to contest

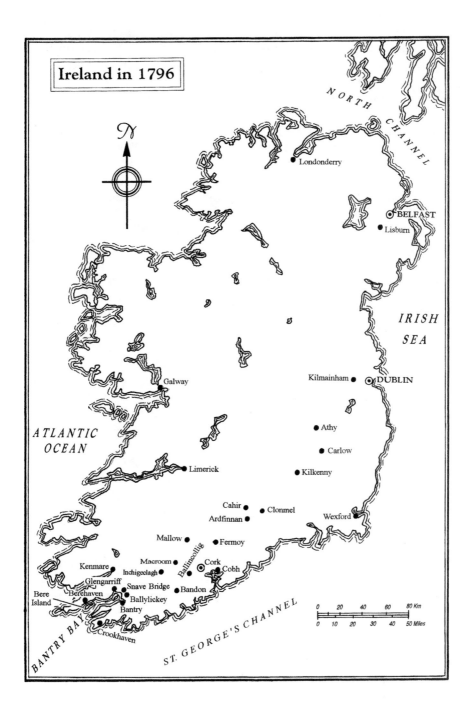

Ireland in 1796

NORTH CHANNEL

Londonderry

⊙ BELFAST

Lisburn

IRISH SEA

Galway

Kilmainham • ⊙ DUBLIN

• Athy

• Carlow

Limerick • • Kilkenny

ATLANTIC OCEAN

Cahir • • Clonmel

Ardfinnan •

Wexford

Mallow • • Fermoy

Kenmare Macroom • Ballincollig

Inchigeelagh • • Cork

Glengarriff Snave Bridge • Cobh

Bere Berehaven • Bandon

Island Ballylickey

Bantry

BANTRY BAY Crookhaven

ST. GEORGE'S CHANNEL

0   20   40   60   80 Km

0 10 20 30 40 50 Miles

the landing itself, when the French would surely have been vulnerable to a determined charge; but now he believed (mistakenly, in the event) that he should play for time. On the previous day, as soon as he had identified the newly-arrived shipping as French, he had already ordered the escape of his own family, and the evacuation of all livestock from the coastal areas. Mr Richard White at Bantry had been alerted – and through him the authorities in Cork[4] – but now a second messenger had to be sent to confirm the fact of a landing, and a third to warn his neighbours to the north-east: Lord Kenmare and Maurice O'Connell (uncle of Daniel O'Connell, then only twenty-three years of age, who would later become a famous patriotic politician). Snapping out instructions for his two most trusted servants to ride off on these missions, O'Sullivan waved a white handkerchief over his head and rode cautiously forward to meet the French. General Humbert halted his grenadiers and accepted the deputation with courtesy, although the essence of his message was uncompromising, and little softened by a well-meaning but nervous interpreter. The whole of County Cork was hereby put under military requisition, and would henceforth owe its loyalty to the newly-founded Hibernian Republic, which was recognised and supported by the full power and majesty of France. O'Sullivan was dryly congratulated upon his good fortune at becoming the very first citizen of the new state; but it was regretted that he would have to be detained, as a guarantee for the good behaviour of his locality. Thus did Berehaven and its diminutive harbour become available for the unloading of the remainder of Hoche's armament.

From the military point of view this was the worst of all possible landing places – some sixty kilometres by execrable roads from Bantry town, which was itself ninety more kilometres short of Cork. It was almost the furthest spot in the whole of Ireland from anywhere of importance, and a landing in the sheltered estuary by Glengarriff and Snave Bridge, at the head of the bay, had been greatly preferred in the original orders. Yet from the naval point of view the almost indecent haste of this disembarkation was embraced with gratitude. The captains were anxious to remove their ships from the dangerously rocky coastline as quickly as possible, not to mention from the expected early arrival of the British fleet.[5] In the event naval opinion seemed to be vindicated by the weather. When the winds had abated on the 23rd there was admittedly a short period during which a landing might otherwise have been attempted a little further to the east – but within twenty-four hours the gales recommenced with even greater ferocity than ever, sometimes reaching hurricane force; and they kept blowing for over a week. If Hoche had not insisted on landing where and when he did, he would either have been swamped in his landing craft, or would have been forced to call off any attempt at a landing at all.

As a strategist he could certainly congratulate himself on getting some 12,000 men and four field-guns ashore as expeditiously as he did; but as a local commander his situation was considerably less happy. His army had to spend Christmas Eve and Christmas Day disentangling itself from the ships and re-acquainting itself with dry land. It could draw few supplies from the fleet, which had been under-victualled from the very start. Its billets in Berehaven were far from ideal and the inhabitants were sullen, incomprehensible and, worst of all, poor. They had little by way of specie, shoes or grain that could be put to the army's use, and the promised 'half million enthusiastic Defenders' were remarkable only by their entire and total failure to materialise. Precisely six could be raised from the village, and even they expressed sorrow that their new comrades in arms were the same atheistic barbarians who had recently pillaged Rome and humiliated the Pope. Very few cattle, sheep or horses could be procured, as a result of the general British contingency plan to evacuate them to the interior as soon as any French ships were sighted. All the horses Hoche had brought with him were required for transport, although the only path inland proved to be a 'butter road', too rough and narrow for any but pack animals and the smallest farm carts. The field-guns and the spare muskets for Irish volunteers had to be left behind by the harbour-side under the guard of an artillery lieutenant and a few soldiers, in the somewhat precarious hope of eventual shipment up the bay in fishing smacks once the weather should improve. Nor could Hoche mount more than a small troop of his cavalry, which was barely enough for the most vital scouting and liaison tasks, leaving no ability to forage widely around the country. He was thus committed to keeping his little army concentrated and mobile, since to stay in one place would surely have led to starvation.

Nevertheless, early on the morning of Boxing Day Hoche and 'Mr Smith' briskly reviewed and harangued the troops, then set them marching out along the awkward little butter road to Bantry, with the mountains rising steeply to their left and the easterly gale flailing sleet into their faces from the front. On the afternoon of the 27th they found some relief in the charming and sheltered vale of Glengarriff,[6] although they also there encountered the first military resistance. Lieutenant Gibbons and Mr White from Bantry had brought forward half a squadron of cavalry and two companies of militia. These boldly opened fire, their optimism unmixed with accuracy, from a collection of stone farm buildings on the outskirts of the town. Humbert, still in the van, took one quick look and sent forward the same grenadier battalion that had arrested Mr O'Sullivan in Berehaven. It now repeated the procedure for Mr White, for a loss of three men killed on each side, and perhaps three dozen injured. Over fifty invaluable horses fell into French hands, and the total number of citizens of the nascent Hibernian Republic was more than doubled from the population of the town. The army enjoyed its first truly comfortable night since it had left Brest, spiced up by its first truly significant pillaging, when it found Mr White's fine castle and summer residence on the far side of the town. To be sure, his renowned wine cellar in Seafield House, Bantry, would remain safe and unscathed throughout the campaign; but the bitterest loss he suffered through his defeat was the cancellation of the peerage that had long been exciting his hopes.

Hoche sternly resisted the pleas of his subordinates for a day's repose in Glengarriff, and by the next evening his army had pressed on past Snave Bridge and Ballylickey crossroads, and inland up the back road heading towards Inchigeelagh, Macroom and, ultimately, Cork. By their third hard day on the road the troops were starting to remember all the little routines, habits and mental attitudes – with their compensations as well as their hardships – which the veteran adopts on campaign. This was their period of retraining and acclimatisation, from which sound morale would quickly be built. They all knew that more testing times lay ahead in the field of military conflict, but it was at least a comfort to know that the very worst physical trials of shipboard transit, bad weather and inhospitable terrain had now been overcome. It had not been without cost – Hoche had already lost the equivalent of a battalion in sick or stragglers since landing – but it was starting to pay dividends in the resilience of those who were left. He was also able to reassure them that in the next few days they would be advancing through rather richer and more sheltered country than the areas they had so far seen.

Cork

The march through Macroom to Ballincollig, 'the town of the boar', was completed by the end of 1 January 1797. The day was celebrated as 'new year' by such Irish adherents as had by now rallied to Wolfe Tone's proud green banner (adorned with a gilded harp); but it was allowed scant significance by the French, for whom 14 July, or even 23 September (the anniversary of the foundation of the Republic) were the true festivals worthy of observance. It was discovered that during the past week a British force under General Dalrymple had been concentrating and fortifying itself first near the depot at Bandon and then, when the more northerly line of the French march had been identified, in Cork itself. For his part Hoche was at last ready to relent in his frenzied onward march, and decreed a two-day period of rest and recuperation. Stragglers were collected and minor deficiencies were made good, although the artillery could not be expected to catch up for many days, if not weeks. Nevertheless, at least the supply services could now be set up on a more workable basis, since the army was starting to overtake the livestock that had been driven inland upon the first news of the invasion. Sufficient horses were also becoming available to mount a more respectable force of cavalry.

Yet Hoche knew that he was still living on borrowed time, since he had not yet captured a town big enough to constitute a solid base. For that, he had to have Cork. In fact he suspected that his whole campaign would live or die on the events of the next few days, during which he would have to attack that city – which was apparently heavily garrisoned – without the benefit of a siege train. He knew General Dalrymple was ready and waiting for him; but he had precious little intelligence about the rest of the strategic situation. The still meagre French cavalry was sent out to interrogate the local people but, lacking in specialised military expertise, their accounts displayed a disconcertingly wide variety of opinion. Some said that Cork had recently been massively reinforced, others that the entire garrison had marched off to join a much larger army assembling in Dublin, or in Limerick, or even in Wexford. They added, by way of reassurance, that everyone in County Cork had particular respect for 'Lord Hoche', because he had brought all of 80,000 men to enforce his will. The cavalry scouts had difficulty keeping a straight face when they heard that – but at least they did establish the fact that the old walls of Cork, which had resisted both Cromwell and King Billy (unsuccessfully in each case), had now decayed into a state of definitive disrepair.

Having rested and fed his troops, Hoche led them forward before dawn on 4 January, in the final approach to the city. One way or another, he believed the day would be decisive; so he had assembled his line of battle with the first real nervousness he had felt in the campaign. In the first wave were Humbert's *tirailleurs* in skirmish order, followed by a line of four battalions with Hoche himself at the centre. On the right flank was Brigadier Mermet's badly understrength 'brigade' of cavalry, while the left flank rested on the River Lee. Behind the vanguard came the first three Demi-Brigades of Chérin's *Corps de Bataille*, while the fourth brought up the rear as a general reserve under the immediate eye of Grouchy and the army staff. It all looked pitifully small by continental standards – it was, after all, less than three months since Hoche had commanded no less than 100,000 men in Western France – but he was gambling that his present 11,000 would appear decisively imposing by the normal standards of internal security 'warfare' within Ireland.

As the French soldiers picked their way towards the city across small, muddy fields, they were at first obscured by the morning mist. Thankfully the wind had abated, although the chill of mid-winter still remained. But when the first wave of *tirailleurs* came to a range of about 200 *toises* (one *toise* = a fathom of six feet) from the city boundary, the first of the defenders' cannon spoke forth, soon to be followed by others. The French light infantry scuttled forward to find cover and return a crackling, irregular volley of

---

ORDER OF BATTLE

First embarkation, mid-December 1796

1re Légion des Francs de l'Ouest (Légion Rouge) (three battalions, one squadron and gunners)

94e Demi Brigade (three battalions)

27e Demi Brigade (two battalions)

Grenadier companies of 81e and 94e Demi Brigades

24e Demi Brigade (three light battalions)

Foreign Brigade – French grenadier cadres, to be completed by Irish recruits after landing:

Regiments (two battalions)	Ferdute	224 men
	O'Meara	143 men
	Le Chatre	155 men
	de Lée	90 men

Chasseurs à cheval de Lamoureux (29 men)

1er Corps Expéditionnaire (124 men)

Attached auxiliary companies (451 men)

7e Chasseurs à cheval (one squadron)

6e Hussards (two squadrons)

10e Hussards (one squadron)

12e Hussards (two squadrons)

Guides (33 men)

Gunners (c.1,000 men)

Second embarkation, planned for late December 1796

27e Demi Brigade (one battalion)

46e Demi Brigade (three battalions)

52e Demi Brigade (four battalions)

81e Demi Brigade (three battalions)

34e Demi Brigade (four battalions)

94e Demi Brigade (one battalion, saved from wreck)

7e Chasseurs à cheval (one squadron)

Volunteer cavalry (five squadrons)

Colonel Tate's force, embarked February 1797

2e Légion des Francs de l'Ouest (Légion Noire) (twelve companies, including two of grenadiers)

---

musketry in reply. Meanwhile the four vanguard battalions immediately behind them flinched, but did not stop marching forward. The officers shouted encouragements, threats, all sorts of patriotic nonsense and exhortation, and to their great relief the line kept marching on towards what was increasingly perceived as a weakly built and weakly defended rampart. When the range had closed to twenty or thirty *toises* these fortifications erupted with an additional roar of musketry, as the British infantry played their part; but to this the French replied with their own, somewhat more political, counter-roar of 'Vive la Liberté! Nous Sommes Invincibles!' Not stopping to discharge their muskets or discard their packs, they rushed forward, straight over and into the enemy defences. The British were caught in the act of reloading, and instantly ran away in terror. The French shot and bayoneted quite a few of them in the back, and within moments had cleared the area of St Finbarr's (Protestant) cathedral and the appropriately-named French's Quay; only to be brought up short by the formidable water obstacle of the South Channel of the river. There the vanguard sought shelter from fire coming from the far bank, and rested until the remainder of the army could catch up. They had lost around 130 killed and wounded, the latter including General Humbert, who had need to seek medical attention to his hand; but they had captured five heavy cannon and counted some hundred enemy dead or prisoners.

It transpired that the victory had been won against only a light screen of militia troops, while the remaining 4,000 militia and fencibles were being gathered in panic and disarray in the city centre, between the two channels of the river. Their senior commanders there held what onlookers later described as 'a violent altercation', on horseback, in the middle of the street, which resulted in the whole force immediately marching out northwards to the 'Protestant Hills' on the road to Mallow, where Dalrymple hoped to establish a fortified camp. Consequently when, at 11 am, Grouchy ventured forward under a flag of truce, he met only apologetic burgesses bearing civic keys on a velvet cushion, and offering no further military resistance. Cork therefore fell smoothly into French hands and – still more fortunately for Hoche – so did its crucial port of Cobh, where the warehouses were found intact, and almost half of the shipping was successfully captured by the invaders. By 10 pm that same evening a fast pinnace had been despatched to Brest, to convey this decisive news to the Directory.

Dublin

During the first two weeks of the invasion, the British authorities in Dublin had been shaken to their very core. Not only had they been assured that peace with France was imminent; but they knew that the British regular army was serving in a multitude of exotic places that were all a very long way from Ireland. The new commander-in-chief, Lord Carhampton, had been in his post for scarcely two months, and his general mobilisation plans against invasion had not yet been put into place. The auxiliary home defence forces of Yeomanry, as distinct from the less localised Militia, had been incorporated only in October. Their organisation was highly idiosyncratic; few of its men had so far received uniforms, and no-one yet knew whether their efforts would be a help or a hindrance in the defence of the kingdom. As for the Dublin stock market, the run on the Bank of England before Christmas had already made it gloomy, and it collapsed completely when the loss of Cork was announced. There was a rush to the ports as wealthy men attempted to transfer their families and more portable valuables to safety in England.

Marching in the opposite direction, however, went Carhampton's untested legions. Thirty-one of his thirty-eight militia units, and many of the fencibles, had orders first to concentrate on the headquarters of the five military districts, and then to advance towards the south-western end of the island. Dalrymple, commanding the southern district, was told to hold Cork if he could, but to withdraw northwards if he could not – as was in fact the case. He was to be reinforced through Limerick from Smith's command in the west. Meanwhile Carhampton himself would gather his main army along the road from Dublin through Carlow to Clonmel and Ardfinnan, drawing troops from Crosbie's eastern and Ralph Dundas' central districts. Lake, starting from Blaris camp near Lisburn, would eventually follow on with the bulk of the Ulster garrison, to act as the strategic reserve.

Lord Carhampton arrived at Ardfinnan camp, just beyond Clonmel, in the afternoon of 9 January, only to learn that the position there was already outflanked. The French had ignored Dalrymple's tendered bait on the Mallow road out of Cork, and had instead marched resolutely through Fermoy to Cahir, just five miles north of Ardfinnan. The British commander-in-chief therefore beat a hasty overnight retreat back to Clonmel, where he established a defensive line on the river Suir supported by the hills behind it, with the old town acting as an advanced fortified bridgehead. With over 6,000 of his best men, including three regular cavalry regiments, he believed his position was secure enough, and was reminded that no less an assailant than Cromwell had received a bloody repulse from Clonmel's walls in 1650. He was further encouraged during the morning of the 10th when the French cavalry was repeatedly worsted on the outpost line, while their main infantry force seemed to arrive very cautiously and uncertainly. The impression of military disorganisation was deepened when a baying mob of several hundred ragged Irish pikemen – obviously very newly recruited – fanned out to the flanks, exhibiting no semblance of either drill or solemnity.

Carhampton's confidence was shaken, however, when snow started to fall in the late afternoon and then, just as light was fading, the entire Franco-Irish line began a rapid advance. One British cavalry regiment tried to charge, but found itself unexpectedly entangled in a hastily-assembled hedge of the despised pikes. The supporting gunners behind Clonmel were unsighted, while those in the town itself found time for only two or three salvoes before they were engulfed in wild hand-to-hand combat. The attackers poured over the makeshift barricades that had been planted in the many gaps in the walls, and fierce fighting took place at the old West Gate and in the narrow streets of the town. An unearthly mixture of French shouts and banshee Irish wails added a terrifying quality to the swirling whiteness of the dusk. Matters might still have gone against Hoche if only his opponent had been able to see what was happening; but in the murky confusion Carhampton fed reinforcements in from the east end of the town, when it was its western end that was collapsing. The French stormed over the Old Bridge and spread a panic throughout the left and rear of the British position. Many of the red-coated militiamen suddenly remembered that they, too, were Irish Catholics, and that as many of their officers seemed to be absentees from the militia, as their old landlords had been from the counties. Some whole regiments dissolved into the protecting night, leaving the orderly and steady part of the retreat to a solid core of Scottish fencibles, gun crews anxious to save their pieces, and officers who had lost their men. Two-thirds of the force would eventually be re-assembled at Kilkenny, over thirty miles to the north-east; but the fact remained that over 2,000 were killed, captured or – mostly – deserted. Hoche lost little more than a quarter of that number, evenly divided between French and Irish, and won a victory as striking, in its way, as that of Cork. He could also add a few more guns to General Debelle's improvised artillery park, and pass on many captured muskets to his Irish irregulars. It gave him particular satisfaction, furthermore, to send four captured colours back to Paris.

The further Hoche advanced, the more the local people began to believe not only that his army existed, but that it was capable of winning victories. They started to abandon their initial suspicions, and in many social circles it suddenly became acceptable to express at least a measure of disloyalty to George III. The Yeomanry lost its initial flush of enthusiasm and began to stay at home, leaving tasks undone that militia or fencibles would now have to make good. There was even an outbreak of armed revolt among the dissenting Protestants of Antrim, some 250 miles to the north, while Hoche received a rising flood of Irish volunteers. Of his 10,000 men who had entered Cork on 4 January, 2,000 had been left behind to organise the city, collect recruits and supplies, and set up the new government; yet his front-line strength had already grown back to 10,000 for the battle of Clonmel. By the time he had taken the surrender of Kilkenny castle, and flown his standard there during 13 and 14 January, the field army had expanded to 12,000 while the Cork garrison had itself doubled in size. It was as well that it had, since General Dalrymple now sought to redeem himself by recapturing the city, hoping that it would have been left unguarded. He made his attack on the 13th with the remains of his original force, strengthened by militia units from Galway; but by this time the news of Clonmel had arrived and the expectation of defeat was starting to spread throughout the British camp. His men made only a half-hearted effort, and became dispirited when the promise of an easy victory proved to have been misplaced.

Meanwhile Hoche was pressing forward his march through Athy towards Dublin, outflanking the British once again when they tried to block the road at Carlow. By this time Carhampton was bitterly aware that he had underestimated his opponent's speed no less than his numbers, while himself failing to amass a body strong enough to stand against the main French striking force. On 17 January he abandoned his troops at Carlow, since they were now in the French rear, and personally made haste back to Dublin, to supervise the new concentration of forces that was assembling there. Lake had arrived to reinforce the city's garrison with the bulk of his men from Ulster, although he was just now having to send back four militia regiments to help suppress the rising in Antrim. More than 10,000 troops were nevertheless available to man the walls of the capital when Hoche vainly summoned it to surrender on 19 January. He outnumbered the garrison by barely a third, and was markedly inferior in both guns and in naval communications. Nor was he able to repeat the *coup de main* of Clonmel when he attempted a hasty storming on the 21st. It was repulsed with what the London newspapers later reported as '1,000 casualties', and both sides were forced to resign themselves to a lengthy siege.

Thus did January pass into February, and then into early March, with British control reduced to a few islands – such as Dublin, Belfast, Londonderry and Limerick – surrounded by a hostile or indifferent green sea. There were adventures, to be sure, such as Crosbie's attempt to take Cork with the men defeated at Clonmel. He had the advantage of marines landed by the navy; but ultimately he fared no better than Dalrymple. Then there was a much-trumpeted arrival of 3,000 regular infantry from Portsmouth who had been diverted from Abercromby's expedition to the 'living death' of the West Indies, and who were delighted to find they had been so reprieved. However, it turned out that they were completely new to the military life and unaccustomed to its disciplines, so their bibulous celebration of their deliverance to Dublin rendered them incapable of bringing a speedy end to the siege there. They provided the final proof, if proof were needed, that Mr Pitt had at last exhausted his pool of manpower. Although Bridport's fleet still controlled the Irish Sea, there were all too few troops fit to send across it.

Cape St Vincent

Not even British control of the seas would remain undisputed for long, for the French navy had returned to the fray by the end of January. Despite active British patrols it was able to establish a persistent, if relatively small-scale, flow of reinforcements to Hoche, including the Yankee William Tate's notorious 'Black Legion' of jailbirds and deserters who had originally been intended to burn down first Bristol and then Liverpool. In view of the situation in Ireland their incendiary skills were now directed against

Wexford instead, although they were badly treated by the local population and surrendered lamely before they could do any damage. Nevertheless, some more serious French reinforcements were now becoming available to Hoche's army, especially after Bonaparte finally captured Mantua on 2 February. Most serious of all was the main Spanish war fleet, which now left the Mediterranean with a strength of no less than twenty-seven battleships – decisively more than the fifteen available to the British blockading squadron based on Lisbon. Vice Admiral Sir George Keith Elphinstone had just succeeded Jervis in that command, and as Calder, his fleet captain, counted out the enemy ships which successively came into view off Cape St Vincent on the hazy morning of 14 February, all thought of offering a battle fled from his mind. The British were very likely to lose it, and even if it were drawn, there might still be over a dozen enemy ships left free to continue to Brest and combine with the French. In the event Elphinstone let them all pass, and shadowed them at a respectful distance. Only Commodore Nelson in HMS *Captain* (74 guns) objected to this passive course. He declared that it would have been unthinkable under Jervis, and launched an unauthorised single-ship attack against the mighty *Santissima Trinidad* (136 guns), apparently hoping to provoke a more general action. But alas, the gesture was brushed scornfully aside by the Spanish giant. *Captain* was dismasted and forced to strike her colours, leaving nothing to prevent Admiral Cordova from taking his great Spanish armada to Brest. Once there, he was excellently poised by early March to make decisive interventions in St George's Channel and the Irish Sea, both by cutting British reinforcements to Dublin and by protecting French reinforcements to Hoche. Still more ominously for the City of London, he was now in a position to cut off all coastal trade anywhere along the western seaboard of England, Wales or Scotland. There was no longer any need to burn down Bristol or Liverpool, as Tate had wanted, since those cities could fulfil no economic function while their essential sea lanes were closed. Financial confidence was unable to survive such a telling blow. The Bank of England had already stopped payments in specie; now it was in danger of stopping every other type of payment as well.

Cape Trafalgar

The French Revolutionary War did not continue long beyond the fall of Mantua and the Spanish fleet's arrival in Brest. Austria signed preliminaries for peace at Leoben on 18 April, leading to the Treaty of Campo Formio on 18 October. Meanwhile the siege of Dublin was resolved relatively amicably by the Armistice of Kilmainham on 24 March, which would eventually come to be seen as the preliminary to the Treaty of Lille, as it would be signed on 3 September. In London all thoughts of reverting to warfare were dashed in April and May by the naval mutinies at Spithead and the Nore, which finally provoked the replacement of Pitt's deeply unpopular Tory administration by a coalition of Fox's Whigs with Portland's. Many of the peace terms which Lord Malmesbury had rejected were now perforce accepted, although a number of concessions were won in the sugar islands in return for recognition of Wolfe Tone's young Hibernian Republic as a genuinely independent state, still free to trade with Bristol and Liverpool – and to forward rents to absentee landlords living in England – but no longer subject to the rigours of British law or the British army. Surprisingly few voices were raised against this arrangement and many of the Anglo-Irish nobility (such as Richard and Arthur Wellesley, both of whom would serve their turn as *Taoiseach*) threw themselves wholeheartedly into making a success of the government of the Irish Republic.

Peace brought a blessed relief which lasted for a whole generation; not only in Britain, where the unbearable strains of war had been largely economic, but especially in France, where the damage had been measured much more in blood and political upheaval. Peace allowed French democracy to flourish as it was supposed to, free from the fear of military tyranny or the perverted social distortions which attended mass mobilisation. The spring elections brought a prudent and moderate government to power, and the pretensions of both the army and the extreme left were finally crushed when the attempted coup of Fructidor was defeated in September. General Hoche triumphed as the true upholder of liberty, while the would-be usurper, Bonaparte, fled into emigration, to be reviled as bitterly as Lafayette and Dumouriez had been when they had followed the same road. Meanwhile the armies and navies of Europe could at last be stood down, after five years of strenuous effort, and all but their most loyal and dependable officers could be retired. The frontiers were reopened, and international tourism experienced an enthusiastic revival.

Thus it came about that on 21 October 1805 the half-pay Commodore Nelson would by chance encounter the disgraced General Bonaparte in a thermal station near Cape Trafalgar in south-western Spain, and they would drink nostalgically together to all the victories and glories that might have been ... if only the wrong damned politicians had not been elected to office, and if only there had never been this confounded unnatural Europe-wide peace.

NOTES

1. The quotation comes from a letter from Richard Wellesley to William Pitt, 4 September 1796, quoted in Archibald Alison, *History of Europe from the Commencement of the French Revolution to the Restoration of the Bourbons* (Edinburgh and London), vol.III, p.350. It refers, of course, to Ireland as a whole.
2. Established on 16 October, including Modena, Bologna, Ferrara, Reggio, etc.
3. Michael John Carroll, 'Wolfe Tone and the French Invasion of 1796: A Brief History of Events' in his *A Bay of Destiny* (Bantry, 1996).

4. News of the French arrival had reached Cork from Crookhaven late on the 22nd, just before Mr White's messenger arrived from Bantry itself: Carroll, *op.cit.*

5. Unknown to the French, the British fleet never had the slightest chance of interfering with the Bantry operation. Quite apart from its confused intelligence picture (many believing the French were heading for Portugal rather than Ireland), it was held in Portsmouth until 3 January by contrary winds. This seriously discredited the policy of open blockade (*ie* with the main fleet waiting in its home port), as opposed to close blockade (*ie* with the main fleet waiting at sea, just over the horizon from the blockaded enemy port). Even if the winds had been kinder to Bridport, he would still have had to sail 400 miles to Bantry after receiving news that the French had sailed; whereas the French voyage from Brest to Bantry was just 275 miles. The problem was further compounded because the blockading squadron that was off Brest, under Colpoys, went back to Portsmouth for supplies as soon as it realised the French had escaped, and not to Cork or Torbay. That left only two ships of the line in the area of Bantry, and they were weather-bound in Crookhaven and Cobh respectively. See discussion in A.T. Mahan, *The Influence of Sea Power upon the French Revolution and Empire 1793–1812* (2 vols, Sampson Low Marston, London, 1892, and recent US reprint by Scholarly Press, n.d.), vol.I, pp.339–66; and C. Lloyd, *St Vincent and Camperdown*, pp.17–21.

6. Many topographical details of places mentioned in my narrative may be found in the indispensable *Illustrated Road Book of Ireland* (The Automobile Association, Dublin, new edn, 1970).

THE REALITY

The background scenario for my story portrays what I believe to be historical truth, both within Ireland and in more general strategy. I have tried to stick to historical topography and orders of battle, and all the characters mentioned by name were real people. However, the sad and premature death of Jervis, soon to become Earl of St Vincent, is the first 'alternate' fact in the foreground of the narrative. In reality his health would fail only after he had suppressed the mutinies of 1797, and even then he would live on until 1823. Also in reality he arrived in Lisbon only on 22 December 1796, but for the sake of dramatic unity I have brought that date forward by one week. The second 'alternate' fact is the unhistorical lifting of the fog off Ushant on 19 December, after which we rise to an altogether different plane of reality...

The real Captain Fustel allegedly received twice the agreed sum, in view of the massive strategic value of his 'small errors of navigation' which kept Hoche separated from his army. Without Hoche's presence in Bantry Bay, his troops never landed. Nevertheless, most modern historians accept that if they had landed, Cork would indeed have fallen quickly. Even the Irish pikemen would doubtless have played their part, since in reality they twice repulsed British dragoons in Leinster during May 1798 (Ferguson, *The Army and the Irish Rebellion of 1798*, p.94). Overall, of course, the real risings of 1798 were put down with ease, not least by cavalry, in stark contrast to the

dramatic success of my putative rebellion of 1797. Yet the historical point
to remember is that in reality the British defences of Ireland were massively
reinforced only after the Bantry expedition had failed, and as a direct result
of it. Equally, in 1798 Humbert landed only 1,000 French troops, or less
than ten per cent of what Hoche might have put ashore at Berehaven.

In reality Tate's force did not go to Wexford but landed (and surrendered) at Fishguard, in south-west Wales, on 24 February 1797. Nor did
Admiral Jervis at Cape St Vincent pay any heed to Spanish numbers, but
charged in regardless, to win a famous victory. Keith, by contrast, would
win a reputation for excessive prudence when he engaged in shadow-boxing
with Admiral Bruix in the Mediterranean in 1799. We may therefore doubt
that he would have engaged the enemy on 14 February, had he been in
command. Equally the real naval mutinies nearly did topple the Tory
government but, for want of an additional shock such as the loss of Ireland,
it managed to hang on. By the same token the moderates in the French
Directory nearly did weather the storm of Fructidor, but narrowly failed.

In recording these portentous events I am particularly grateful to Andy
Callan, Mike Cox, Julian Humphries, Jonathan North and Ned Wilmott
for their technical advice and information. I also found it useful to wargame
the operation with Richard Madder, and especially enlightening to consult
some of the present inhabitants of the Bantry area. I wish to thank Michael
J. Carroll of the Bantry bookstore, as well as his namesake in Cork; Rupert
Tansley of Bantry Community Arts; and Jim O'Sullivan of Castletown Bere
(formerly Berehaven).

BIBLIOGRAPHY

Alison, Archibald, *History of Europe from the Commencement of the French Revolution to the Restoration of the Bourbons* (12 vols, 9th edn, Edinburgh and London, 1856; recently reprinted in USA by AMS Press, 14 vols, n.d.); vol.III, ch.XXI and vol.IV, ch.XXII.

Blackstock, Alan, *An Ascendancy Army: The Irish Yeomanry 1796–1834* (Dublin, 1998), especially p.141.

Carroll, Michael John, 'Wolfe Tone and the French Invasion of 1796: A Brief History of Events' in his *A Bay of Destiny* (Bantry, Co. Cork, 1996).

Ferguson, Kenneth, 'The Army and the Irish Rebellion of 1798' in Alan J. Guy, ed., *The Road to Waterloo* (London, 1990), pp.88–100.

Flanagan, Thomas, *The Year of the French* (1979; New York, 1980); a novel of the 1798 rising.

Jones, Colin, *The Longman Companion to the French Revolution* (London, 1988; paperback edn, 1990).

Lavery, Brian, *Nelson's Navy: The Ships, Men and Organisation 1793–1815* (London, 1989; revised edn, 1990).

McAnally, Henry, *The Irish Militia 1793–1816: A Social and Military Study* (Dundalk, 1949).

Lloyd, Christopher, *St Vincent and Camperdown* (London, 1963).

BONAPARTE'S CAMPAIGN IN EGYPT

BY CHARLES S. GRANT

The Lure of the Orient

In 1798, as the prospect of an invasion of England became less and less a sound military option, French eyes turned elsewhere in search of ways both to damage England and to expand France's own dominions. There were two particular advocates of an invasion of Egypt. The first was Charles Maurice de Talleyrand-Périgord, foreign minister, consummate diplomat, politician and a great survivor. He subsequently served Napoleon throughout the period of Empire. The second advocate was a young, ambitious and successful general, Napoleon Bonaparte. This gauche young soldier, twenty-nine years of age – saviour and hero of the army of Italy, and protégé of the Directorate – was currently commander of the 'Army of England' massing along the Channel. Between them, Talleyrand and Bonaparte persuaded the Directory that Egypt, which had long been of interest to France, should become their objective. Bonaparte's particular interest in such a venture dated back to at least early 1797, when he wrote to the Directory: 'The day is not far distant when we should appreciate the necessity, in order really to destroy England, of seizing Egypt'.[1] The risk was low – after all, the British had no fleet in the Mediterranean – and the potential advantages were considerable. The principal objective would be to damage England through her trade route to India, but there was far more on offer. There were aspirations of colonial expansion, and, of course, the commerce, economic growth and produce that possession of Egypt would bring. Against the persuasive tongues of Talleyrand and Bonaparte, resistance from the Directory collapsed.

The Directory's instructions to Bonaparte were set out in a decree dated 23 Germinal, Year VI (12 April 1798):

> The Executive Directory,
> Considering that the beys who have seized the government of Egypt have formed most intimate ties with the English and have made themselves wholly dependent on them; that in consequence they have committed open hostilities and the most horrible cruelties towards Frenchmen, whom they daily molest, rob and murder.

35

Considering that it is its duty to pursue the enemies of the Republic wherever they may be found;

Considering, furthermore, that, the infamous treachery by which England has made itself master of the Cape of Good Hope having rendered access to India by the normal route very difficult for the ships of the Republic, it is necessary to open another route thither for the Republican forces, to combat the satellites of the English Government there and to stop that source of its corrupting wealth,

Decrees:

ARTICLE 1. The Commander-in-Chief of the Army of the East will lead the land and sea forces under his command to Egypt and will take possession of that country.

ARTICLE 2. He will drive the English from all their oriental possessions which he can reach, and notably he will destroy their settlements on the Red Sea.

ARTICLE 3. He will cause the isthmus of Suez to be cut through and he will take all necessary measures to ensure to the French Republic the free and exclusive possession of the Red Sea.

ARTICLE 4. He will improve the lot of the inhabitants of Egypt by all means in his power.

ARTICLE 5. So far as possible he will maintain good relations with the Caliph and his immediate subjects.

ARTICLE 6. The present decree will not be published.

The French conquest of Egypt was thus set under way, but, as the last Article made clear, secrecy was of paramount importance. Just how important would become apparent as subsequent events unfolded.

The French fleet

Bonaparte now applied himself to concentrating the necessary forces while maintaining the pretence of planning an invasion of England. The force that he assembled for the conquest of Egypt was based at several Mediterranean ports:

Toulon: Generals Kleber, Bon and Reynier – 14,000 infantry, 860 cavalry, 1,160 gunners.

Genoa: Generals d'Hilliers and Murat – 6,000 infantry, 850 cavalry, 250 gunners.

Civita Vecchia: General Desaix – 6,900 infantry, 1,080 cavalry, 250 gunners.

Ajaccio: General Vaubois – 3,900 infantry, 680 cavalry.

In addition Bonaparte had 180 guides à cheval, 300 guides à pied and 60 field and 40 siege guns. Only 1,200 horses were to be taken, with the balance to be made good in Egypt. In all, the army numbered some 54,000 men.

To carry this force 'the fleet assembled under the command of Admiral Brueys', and was composed of thirteen ships of the line, one, the *Orient*, carrying the Admiral and the General-in-Chief, being of 120 guns, two of 80, and ten of 74. There were, moreover, two Venetian ships of 65 guns each, six Venetian frigates and eight French, seventy-two corvettes, cutters, gun boats, and small craft of all kinds. The transports collected, as well at Toulon as at Genoa, Ajaccio, and Civita-Vecchia, amount to four hundred. Five hundred sail in all therefore were to crowd the waters of the Mediterranean.[2]

The chase

Bonaparte sailed from Toulon on 19 May 1798. Though his preparations had not gone unnoticed by the British, the destination of his army was still unknown. Admiral the Earl St Vincent sent the following instruction to Nelson on 2 May.

> Whereas I have received certain intelligence that considerable armament is making at Toulon, and a number of transports collecting at Marseilles and Genoa for an embarkation of troops, you are hereby authorised and required to proceed with such of the squadron under your orders as may be at Gibraltar up the Mediterranean, and endeavour to ascertain by every means in your power, either upon the coasts of Provence or Genoa, the object of the equipment, the destination of which is differently spoken of – such of the islands of Sicily and Corfu on the one hand, Portugal or Ireland on the other, and in the latter event, that is to join a squadron of Spanish ships said to be equipping at Cartagena: to which you will also have attention; and in case of you receiving any information which you may judge of importance to communicate to me, you are to despatch the "Bonne Citoyenne" or "Terpsichore" with it; and continue on this service, with the rest of the squadron, as long as you think necessary, and your stock of water will enable you to do, taking special care, should this armament be coming down the Mediterranean, not to suffer it to pass the Straights before you, so as to prevent you joining me in time to impede a union between it and the Spanish fleet in Cadiz Bay.
>
> St Vincent[3]

On 2 May, Nelson moved into the Mediterranean. He captured a privateer on the 17th and learnt from its crew that there was a fleet of fifteen ships in Toulon ready to sail. Fate now intervened with a heavy gale on 19 May which scattered Nelson's ships and caused much damage. So it was that the French departed Toulon unnoticed. After frantic repairs, Nelson's ships again put to sea on 27 May and arrived at Toulon on the 31st, to find the French gone. Nelson set off in pursuit, the destination of the French being still unknown to him. On 22 June he heard that they had captured and left Malta, heading east.

Ships passing in the night

Nelson was none the wiser regarding the location of the French at the end of June. Reporting to St Vincent from his flagship on 29 June, he wrote:

Upon their whole proceedings, together with such information as I have been able to collect, it appeared clear to me, that either they were destined to assist the rebel Pasha and to overthrow the present Government of Turkey, or to settle a Colony in Egypt, and to open a trade to India by way of the Red Sea; for, strange as it may appear at first sight, an enterprising Enemy, if they have the force or consent of the Pasha of Egypt, may with great ease get an army to the Red Sea. And if they have concerted a plan with Tippoo Sahib to have vessels at Suez, three weeks, at this season, is a common passage to the Malabar Coast, when our India possessions would be in great danger.[4]

Nelson had sailed straight for Alexandria and arrived on 28 June, but, finding no sign of the French, departed again on the 29th. In fact, because the French fleet was slower, he had overtaken them and got to Alexandria before they had: the French in fact arrived the day after his departure. It is extraordinary that the two fleets missed each other, passing as close as they must have done. The British fleet now continued its search for the enemy towards Turkey.

Having captured Malta en route and dropped off a garrison there, the French had approached the Egyptian coast on 27 June, when, after nightfall, Bonaparte ordered the frigate La Junon to sail ahead to Alexandria to take on board the French Consul and see what intelligence he could provide. The La Junon arrived off Alexandria at 1 pm on the 29th, just missing the British fleet, and anchored. The party despatched to fetch the Consul arrived back at about midnight, and his debriefing indicated the impracticality of attempting a landing at Alexandria itself, as this would be opposed. From the naval point of view the beach at Aboukir, about fifteen miles away, was the preferred option. However, the need for haste – prompted by fears that Nelson's fleet might arrive – led to Marabout, about eight miles to the west, being chosen instead, despite naval objections. The landing began at midday on 1 July. Bonaparte intended to land all five divisions. Menou's, Desaix's and Reynier's were on transport ships about three miles offshore, while Kleber's and Bon's were about twice as far away aboard warships.

The landing went on all through the night and seems to have been a fairly chaotic and haphazard affair. The sea was rough and many men suffered from terrible seasickness. Bonaparte moved from his flagship to a Maltese galley at about 4 pm and finally landed from a small launch at one o'clock in the morning. By this stage there were about 5,000 men on the beach. The bulk of Kleber's, Bon's and Menou's divisions were ashore, but much of Desaix's division was still out at sea, and Reynier had only landed a few hundred men.

Bonaparte reviewed his troops at three in the morning and then gave orders for the march to Alexandria. He took with him Kleber's, Bon's and

Menou's divisions and left the remainder to guard the beachhead. The men had no food, water or rest and were now faced with the march to Alexandria, followed by an attack. The army had no horses, and no artillery had yet been landed. The march attracted increasing interest from groups of Bedouin, which eventually amounted to about 400 men. These rode between the gaps in the column of march with great shows of bravado but made no real attempt to mount an attack. The French reached Alexandria at eight o'clock in the morning and took up positions before the walls. General Menou's division was posted to the east, facing a triangular fort; Kleber was in the north at Pompeii's gate; and General Bon faced the Rossetta gate to the west.

The defensive state of Alexandria was appalling. The walls were decayed, while there was little powder and few guns. The city itself had shrunk within the old walls, occupying only a small part of its original ground area. The French were able to take the walls despite sporadic fire and bombardment from a hail of missiles and stones, and a bitter fight through the streets ensued before a deputation arrived at Pompeii's Pillar to surrender the town to Bonaparte at about midday. The leader of the city, Mohammed al Korain, held out in a tower until the night of 2 July. Respecting his resolve, Bonaparte appointed him commandant and charged him with procuring supplies for the French and restoring order.

Returning to the disembarkation, this was complete by 5 July, whereupon Bonaparte instructed Admiral Brueys – who was unable to bring the fleet into Alexandria because of silt in the harbour – to find a suitable anchorage nearby. The Admiral therefore moved the fleet to Aboukir Bay, where he was able to load fresh provisions and water. However, Brueys was conscious of the vulnerability of the fleet and sent several messages to Bonaparte asking for permission to depart from this exposed anchorage. The answer that came back each time was a firm 'no'; Bonaparte wanted to be sure he was secure in Egypt before sending away his sole means of evacuation.

An opportunity missed

Prior to the arrival of the main British fleet, on 21 July two frigates carried out a bold reconnaissance of the French fleet. *Seahorse* and *Terpsichore* sailed into Aboukir Bay and hove to no more than a mile from the French. The *Seahorse* used some signals she had gained from a captured French frigate (the *Sensible*) while the *Terpsichore* hoisted French colours over English to make it appear she was a prize. What they saw was that the French fleet lying off Aboukir was singularly ill-prepared to meet an enemy. The French position had all the potential to be a strong one – the fleet was in line, with its back to the coast, which should have rendered it impossible to turn, while to the north the forts of Aboukir itself and the island of Bequieres secured one end

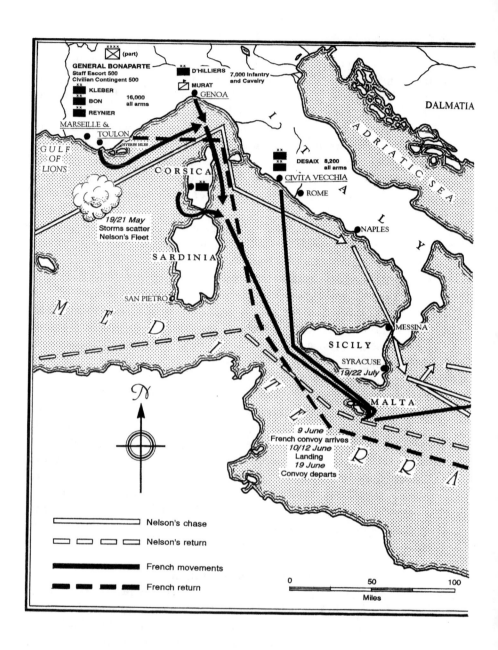

GENERAL BONAPARTE
Staff Escort 500
Civilian Contingent 500

KLEBER
BON   16,000
                   all arms
REYNIER

D'HILLIERS
MURAT

7,000 Infantry
and Cavalry

GENOA

MARSEILLE &
TOULON

HYERES ISLES

GULF
OF
LIONS

CORSICA

I T A L Y

DESAIX 8,200
         all arms

CIVITA VECCHIA

ROME

NAPLES

DALMATIA

ADRIATIC SEA

19/21 May
Storms scatter
Nelson's Fleet

SARDINIA

SAN PIETRO

M E D I T E R R A N E A

MESSINA

SICILY

SYRACUSE
19/22 July

MALTA

9 June
French convoy arrives
10/12 June
Landing
19 June
Convoy departs

N

Nelson's chase

Nelson's return

French movements

French return

0   50   100
Miles

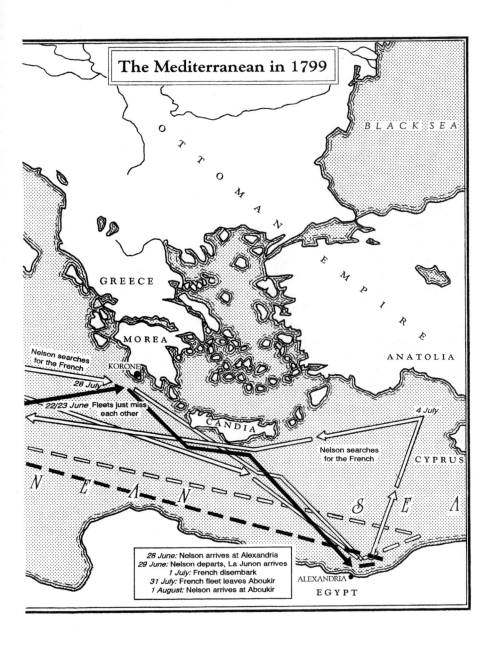

The Mediterranean in 1799

BLACK SEA

OTTOMAN EMPIRE

GREECE

MOREA

ANATOLIA

Nelson searches
for the French

KORONE

28 July

22/23 June Fleets just miss
each other

CANDIA

4 July

Nelson searches
for the French

CYPRUS

N   E   A   N

S   E   A

28 June: Nelson arrives at Alexandria
29 June: Nelson departs, La Junon arrives
1 July: French disembark
31 July: French fleet leaves Aboukir
1 August: Nelson arrives at Aboukir

ALEXANDRIA

EGYPT

of the line. However, the fleet was anchored too far offshore, and the normal naval practice of closing the ships up and stringing cables between them (to prevent their line being penetrated) had not been followed.

Having conducted their reconnaissance of the unsuspecting French, the *Seahorse* and *Terpsichore* slipped away to find the British fleet. Regrettably, at least for Nelson, they had no idea where that fleet might be, and after searching for some time they only arrived in Syracuse after Nelson had already left, ignorant of the intelligence they carried.

The battle of the Pyramids

Meanwhile, Bonaparte – ignorant in turn of the impending danger to his fleet – had taken Alexandria and moved south. After several skirmishes, including a battle at Shubra Khit, the French encountered Murad Bey at the battle of the Pyramids on 21 July. Here Bonaparte met the Mamelukes. These superb horsemen, attired in silks and mail, were formidably armed, each having a long carbine, two brace of pistols (one pair in his saddle-holsters, the other in his girdle), a stiletto, and a well-tempered sabre, with the keenest edge possible. In addition he carried an axe at his saddle-bow, and a slave followed with his javelin. In fact a Mameluke might have two or three slaves who followed him into battle. A Mameluke charge was a spectacular if ill-disciplined affair, with little cohesion but wonderful bravery. However, it was more appropriate to mediaeval combat than to the closing years of the eighteenth century, and was not designed to withstand – nor had previously been confronted by – massed musketry fire delivered by disciplined, close-order infantry prepared to stand their ground. In this respect the French infantry squares were indestructible.

Murad Bey's Mameluke forces, drawn up behind defensive works, rested their left flank on the pyramids near Gizeh and their right on the Nile. However, his reserve, under Ibrahim Bey, was positioned on the Nile's east bank, from where it was unable to provide any assistance. In addition to Mamelukes the Egyptian forces included large masses of ill-equipped and poorly-armed infantry or *fellahin*.

When the French advanced against Murad Bey the Mameluke cavalry dissipated their strength charging piecemeal against the French squares. Sometimes claimed to be Napoleon's only tactical innovation, these divisional squares consisted of three demi brigades, one in front and one to the rear – each six ranks deep – and the third making up the two sides. Advancing in this fashion, the French outflanked and destroyed the Mameluke cavalry. The town of Embabeh was then stormed and the *fellahin*, trapped therein, lost heart on seeing the Mamelukes defeated and fled in the face of French artillery fire. Many drowned in the Nile. French casualties amounted to just thirty men, while Mameluke losses were said to total 2,000; in addition 400 camels and fifty guns were captured. The battle shattered Mameluke power in lower Egypt, and Napoleon, entering Cairo three days later, now felt sufficiently secure in Egypt to send orders to Admiral Brueys allowing the fleet to depart.

The French fleet escapes

On 20 July, the day before the battle of the Pyramids, Nelson was still in the dark at Syracuse, from where he wrote to St Vincent:

> My lord, From my letter of the 12th you will be informed of my conduct to that time. I have now to acquaint you that having spoke to several vessels from the westward, and one from Corfu, I know, as far as their reports, that the French Fleet are neither to Westward of Sicily nor at Corfu. Yesterday I arrived here, where I can learn no more than vague conjecture that the French are gone eastward... [5]

From Alexandria the British fleet had searched in vain, travelling 400 miles to Turkey, then 300 miles to Crete, 700 miles west to Sicily and then east again. At last, as they passed Greece, they encountered a French brig, from which Nelson learnt that the French had been seen four weeks earlier off the coast of Candia, heading south-east. Information gathered in Syracuse, where the fleet took on water on 28 July, supported this intelligence. Nelson now knew that the French destination had, indeed, been Alexandria. He therefore set sail for Egypt, and arrived at Alexandria on 1 August.

Much had changed during the month Nelson had been away. He found the French flag flying and the bustle of military activity; the harbour was full of empty transport ships, but there was no sign of the fleet. The transports looked inviting, however, and he signalled to HMS *Majestic* (74 guns) and HMS *Leander* (50 guns) to edge closer and engage them, but they were met by an unexpected and damaging fire from the old fort, the French having dismounted some heavy naval cannon from their ships to enhance the harbour's defences. Nelson withdrew in disgust, leaving *Leander* and a damaged *Majestic* to watch the harbour while, heading east along the coast, he continued his search for the French fleet. Rounding the point of Aboukir Bay he found the fort there well manned and gunned, a couple of corvettes in the bay, considerable activity on the beach, but no sign of Bruey's fleet. Once more he headed east.

Nelson had again missed the French by a single day. On 30 July a dust-encrusted ADC – the young Eugene de Beauharnais, with a troop of dragoons for escort – had arrived in Aboukir Bay from Cairo. (Eugene was Bonaparte's stepson, being his wife Josephine's son by her first marriage. Just seventeen years of age when he served with Bonaparte in Egypt, he would be made a general in 1804, a Prince of the Empire the following year, and subsequently Viceroy of Italy.) The despatch he carried would have far-reaching consequences, for it was Bonaparte's new orders for Admiral

Brueys, permitting him to depart from Egyptian waters. Within an hour the French fleet was a scene of intense activity. Its foraging and water-collecting parties were hastily recalled, and before dawn on the morning of 31 July the French fleet had slipped anchor and moved out of the bay in the direction of Corfu. Sometime that night they passed within a dozen miles of the British fleet, heading in the opposite direction. Neither knew of the other's presence.

Nelson was now in a foul temper and, worse, he was afraid. The French fleet had achieved all it had set out to do and was in all probability on its way back to France. Nelson was particularly conscious of St Vincent's order to take special care, 'should this armament be coming down the Mediterranean, not to suffer it to pass the Straights before you, so as to prevent you joining me in time to impede a union between it and the Spanish fleet in Cadiz Bay.' There now seemed every likelihood that the French were to the west and, depending on whether they were aware of the location of the British, would be in a position to do just what St Vincent had forewarned Nelson about – that is, to block the Straits of Gibraltar. Now, Nelson realised, the hunter might become the quarry. The resultant flight of the British fleet back down the Mediterranean was, but for the absence of a pursuer, reminiscent of a rout. Nelson's relief was palpable when, twenty-six days after leaving the coast of Egypt, he sighted the Strait of Gibraltar without seeing any signs of the French fleet. In fact Admiral Brueys had no idea of the opportunity which fate had presented him. His sole interest had been to get safely back to Toulon, which he did, by coincidence, on the very day that Nelson came in sight of the open strait. The two fleets had missed each other one final time.

St Vincent was not forgiving or understanding of Nelson's failure to destroy the French and terminate the invasion of Egypt. The following extract from his dispatch to Lord Spencer, First Lord of the Admiralty, gives his view on Nelson's performance in the Mediterranean:

> My Dear Lord, Admiral Nelson and his fleet have now rejoined me and I have discussed the last few months at length with him. From his account, despatches and other intelligence I conclude that Admiral Nelson is deficient of two of the essential qualities of a great naval commander. He is unlucky and I fear lacks tenacity. No commander can afford to be unlucky and yet bad luck or misfortune have dogged his expedition. But one example is the mishap of the storm on 19 May which caused him to arrive too late to prevent the departure of the French fleet from Toulon. As to his tenacity, I judge that had he been more resolute he could have intercepted the French Fleet on at least three occasions. He failed and as a result the French now own the eastern Mediterranean, they have captured and garrisoned Malta, they have a fully supplied an undamaged army in Egypt threatening our interests in India and we are the laughing stock of Europe. I respectfully suggest the young admiral is not yet ready for independent command.

This was harsh judgement indeed on the man who had helped St Vincent – then Admiral Jervis – to win his victory and title just over a year earlier at Cape St Vincent.

The conquest of Egypt

Between July and December the French tightened their control on upper and lower Egypt, suppressing a revolt in Cairo and reorganising the country under French rule. Bonaparte had brought with him some of the best brains in France. On 20 August he published an order for a meeting the next day 'to draw up regulations for the organisation of the Institute of Cairo and to designate the persons who should compose it'. At this meeting was draughted the document published on 22 August, stating that:

> There shall be in Egypt an Institute for the sciences and arts, which shall be established in Cairo. This establishment shall have for it's principle objects:
> 1. The progress and propagation of the knowledge of Egypt.
> 2. The research, study, and publication of the natural, industrial and historic data of Egypt.
> To give advice on the different questions on which it shall be consulted by the government.

The Institute was divided into four sections: Mathematics, Physics, Political Economy, and Literature and Art. Its work provided the foundations for present-day understanding of ancient Egypt.

In November the French fleet, this time unharried by the British, reappeared with substantial reinforcements. However, even before these arrived Bonaparte had set in place a number of initiatives to improve and strengthen the army. The most exotic of these experiments was the Régiment de Dromedaires, which, following various experiments with camel-mounted troops – including medical evacuation and baggage transport – Bonaparte created in 1799.

A variety of foreign units were also raised. These included a unit of Indigenous Guides, also called 'Omar's Company'; the Legion Greque, which grew to brigade size to include infantry, cavalry and artillery; and the Legion Cophte, formed in September 1799. The last was supposedly recruited from Copts, the oppressed native Egyptian Christians, but few volunteers were obtained from this community and the unit was mostly made up of Egyptian Moslems, Turks and other natives recruited in the Delta and upper Egypt. Bonaparte also brought with him the Legion Maltaise, raised in Malta, in part to remove any threat which restless Maltese might have posed to the French occupation force. Finally, a company of Mamelukes was raised and subsequently became the Company of Syrian Janissaires à Cheval.

While Bonaparte set about organising the administration of lower

Egypt he gave General Desaix the task of pursing Murad Bey into the Upper Nile district and destroying him. Desaix, with Belliard as his second-in-command, had a force of 1,000 cavalry, 3,000 infantry, 100 guns, a fleet of riverboats and a camel train. His army set out at between two and three o'clock each morning, to avoid marching in the heat of the day, until he made contact with Murad at El-Luhan on 6 October. On the 7th Desaix brought up his supplies, and that night the French slept under arms, formed up in squares. On the 8th, at the battle at El-Lahun, Desaix's small force of 3,000 faced perhaps 6,000 Mamelukes. When their charge was defeated with a loss of some 400 dead and wounded the Mamelukes withdrew, with the French in pursuit. After this Murad changed his tactics. Resorting instead to harassment, he conducted a running fight with the French by striking at the marching column's rear and lines of communication. Progress in these circumstances, coupled with negotiating obstacles on the Nile, was slow. Reinforced by some 2,000 Janissaries, Murad confronted the French again on 22 January 1799, at Sabhud, sixteen miles south of Girga. Desaix had meanwhile been reinforced by additional cavalry, and this time the French caused very heavy casualties amongst Murad's Meccan infantry before the Egyptian army broke and fled.

Following the battle of Sabhud, Desaix pursued Murad through Abydos, Peneria, Thebes, and Hermonthis, all the way to Syene, where the pursuit continued across to the right bank of the Nile. The French arrived here on 2 February, two days after the Mamelukes had left. Desaix's force had covered 250 miles in ten days and was exhausted, and it was not until the 4th that Desaix moved off. Leaving Belliard at Aswan with the 21st demi brigade, he headed north along the right bank. Elsewhere, Davout met the enemy at Redesieh on 11 February, and, despite a sandstorm, defeated them. Desaix, meanwhile, carried on downstream to Asyut, arriving on 8 March and remaining there ten days. He then marched 180 miles back upriver to Qena, not far from Thebes. His marches during the period from 4 February to 27 March totalled 550 miles.

Back at Syene, Belliard was told by spies that Murad Bey was attempting to cut him off from Desaix by marching across the desert from Asyut. He therefore marched out of Syene during the night of 24/25 February, leaving his river flotilla behind in the region of Qena as he moved rapidly off in pursuit of Murad. Two thousand Meccan infantry, under Sherif Hassan, located the flotilla below Karnak on 3 March. Amongst its ships was *L'Italie*, which had some 200 marines, 300 wounded and the band of the 61st demi brigade on board. This was attacked with musket fire and replied with its cannons, but in endeavouring to get his vessel out of harm's way the captain grounded it, after which it was boarded and taken by the Meccans. Some barges were also captured. The French prisoners were slaughtered, and the band of the 61st was forced to play for its captors before suffering a similar fate.

On 4 March Belliard was informed that 6-7,000 Meccans had landed at Kosseir, but it was only two days later that he heard of the capture of *L'Italie* and the fate of its crew. He then crossed the Nile and moved down the right bank. On 8 March, with little more than 1,000 men, he encountered an enemy concentration of 3,000 Meccan infantry and 550 Mamelukes at Abnud. The ensuing battle lasted three days but saw the French once again victorious.

On 25 May Belliard left Qena on the Nile to march 150 miles across the desert to take Kosseir on the Red Sea. It was through Kosseir that the Meccan reinforcements were arriving, and the seizure of this small port was consequently of strategic significance if this flow of fresh troops was to be stemmed. Belliard took just 350 infantry (who, we are told, were mounted on camels), 400 camels carrying supplies, one gun, and an escort of sixty friendly Arab tribesmen. Seizing Kosseir on 29 May, he installed two-thirds of his force as a garrison before setting off back to Qena on 1 June, where he arrived three days later. By this time Desaix had established control of the Upper Nile by means of a series of garrisons and outposts scattered along both banks.

1799: the conquest of Syria

With the Upper Nile under control and the French presence well established in the Lower Nile, Bonaparte decided that the time was right to expand his conquests. There was growing intelligence of a Turkish threat to launch an attack into Egypt. Bonaparte decided to take the initiative and invaded Syria with approximately 13,000 men. General Bon, with 1,500 men and two cannons, was sent ahead to seize Suez, where he arrived on 7 December 1798. The invading force was to rendezvous at Katia (Cathich), General Legrange – from Reynier's division – being sent there in readiness on 23 December. The main army arrived in early February. On 6 February Reynier was ordered to set out to seize El Arish, his advance guard arriving there on the 9th. Conditions on the march were dreadful, as the following account bears witness:

> The desert not only had the monotonous and sad aspect of the preceding days, it was frightful and boundless. A horrible whirlwind agitated it, the roads were impracticable; one could not see more than four paces ahead; we marched knee deep in moving sand, and the tempest, which had become violent, raised clouds of dust in the midst of which we could not see each other. Our artillery could not advance, it was necessary to halt every instant and push the wheels, to help the teams blinded by the dust and stopped by the gusts of wind. At last, after a horrible day, we were obliged to sleep about a league from the point we should have arrived at,

worn out and crushed; but the wind had gone down, we could light fires
with the dried up shrubs and make our coffee.[6]

Nor did rain, when it eventually came, bring any relief:

> We left Colionnes for Gaza. To our great astonishment we noticed, when
> about half-way on our road, that the sky was getting covered with clouds
> and soon a torrent of rain soaked us through. It was the first time that we
> had seen rain since our arrival in these burning regions; but in compen-
> sation, what a shower! In an instant the ground was soaked, and whilst the
> infantry had mud up to their knees, the artillery, sinking up to the axle-
> trees, could only advance with the greatest difficulty. The soldiers pushed
> the wheels and the drivers lashed their teams without cessation.

Bonaparte, with Bon's division, arrived at El Arish on 17 February, while
Kleber had arrived the previous day. General Lannes, who had taken over
Vial's division, arrived a day later. After a stubborn resistance, El Arish
surrendered on 20 February.

When the march continued on the 21st, Kleber's division, which formed
the vanguard, lost its way, but managed to rejoin the army before it reached
Gaza. The latter was taken without resistance on 24 February, the French
army looting the town and remaining there for four days before resuming its
advance. On 1 March the French halted at Er Ramle, between Jaffa and
Bethlehem, where the Christians had stayed but the Moslems had fled.
Setting out again two days leter, they arrived before Jaffa the same day.

On 4 March preparations to take the city began. The garrison refused
terms, despite a breach having been made in the walls, and at 2 pm on 7
March the city was taken by storm. The storming of Jaffa witnessed some of
the worst excesses of the campaign, with dreadful slaughter and pillage. On
the 8th Bonaparte sent Eugene Beauharnais and Croisier into the city to see
if some sort of normality could be restored. They returned with several
thousand prisoners who had been assured that they would be spared, but for
some unknown reason – lack of sufficient food, the risk that they might
again take up arms, a desire to impress the garrison of Acre – Bonaparte had
them all killed.

It was at about this stage of the campaign that bubonic plague
appeared in the French ranks. The army nevertheless moved on to St
Jean d'Acre (or Acre), and on 17 March occupied the port of Haifa at the
southern end of the Bay of Acre. The French siege train arrived by sea
two days later and was unloaded the next day. With it came another
4,000 infantry who had recently arrived from France. En route they had
captured British Commodore Sir Sidney Smith and destroyed two of his
ships. (Sir Sidney had commanded a small fleet – five ships in all – which
had been tasked with making diplomatic overtures to Turkey. The capture of the Commodore and the loss of two ships had left the remaining

three with no choice but to abort their mission and try to regain the relative safety of Gibraltar.)

Acre had the characteristic walls of a fortified Crusader city, which, though in need of repair, were fundamentally sound. It stood out on a peninsula, two-thirds surrounded by sea, and the walls boasted several prominent towers. Its walls were about a thousand yards in circumference, and it housed a population of between 10,000 and 12,000. Its defence had not been prepared with any care, however, and the French naval presence effectively isolated the occupants.

The ensuing French siege lasted thirty-four days. A brave attempt by Turkish forces to relieve the city met with defeat at Mount Tabor on 16 April at the hands of General Kleber. Two days later a number of captured Turkish leaders were delivered to the gates of Acre under a white flag to make it clear to the garrison that there was no hope of relief and that if they surrendered now they would not suffer the same fate as the defenders of Jaffa. Common sense and self preservation prevailed and the city capitulated the next day, a breach having, coincidentally, been made in the walls the preceding afternoon. As a result of its capitulation the fall of Acre was not followed by the same awful atrocities as had accompanied the fall of Jaffa. Indeed, quite the opposite. The population were treated well and were included in the new local administration.

Any pretence of opposition now crumbled, and a deputation of Syrian chiefs and sheikhs arrived to make peace with the French. Five days after the fall of Acre, Bonaparte made a triumphal, almost biblical, entry into Damascus. The road was strewn with palms, the streets lined with people throwing flowers, and considerable treasures were offered (and accepted) by the young general. He now set about reforming the government of the country. He appointed a new administration, put new laws in place, encourage trade and ensured that the taxation system did not cripple the economy or provide an incentive for revolt.

Much had been learned from the similar and less successful experience in Cairo. Members of the Institute of Cairo were called forward by sea to establish a second Institute in Syria. Bonaparte travelled to Jerusalem to direct the work of the Institute there. Meanwhile contracts were tendered and agreed for the repair of the fortifications of major towns, and local regiments were recruited to assist in garrison and police duties. Plans were also prepared for building a number of marching forts, strategically placed along the land-route back to Cairo, and a number of mounted and dismounted Jannissary regiments were raised. These were organised and drilled on French lines and subsequently formed part of the French army sent to aid Indian native princes fighting against the British on the subcontinent.

It was during Bonaparte's stay in Damascus that he met Yasmini, the daughter of one of the local princes. This beautiful young girl travelled in his retinue whenever he explored the country, and he developed a considerable infatuation for her. However, when he left Damascus he nevertheless bade farewell to Yasmini, who seven months later gave birth to a son. Bonaparte never officially recognised the boy as his offspring, but he still granted Yasmini a very generous allowance. Known to many as Ali Bonaparte, the boy grew up to become a governor of the French colony of Syria.

Bonaparte returns to Egypt

After two months of frantic political, civil and military activity Bonaparte departed by sea from Acre, leaving General Kleber in Damascus as Governor of Syria, and arrived back in Alexandria in early June.

In July news reached Desaix that Murad Bey had made his way across the desert and had appeared with a force of about 300 Mamelukes at Faiyum, with the intention of heading north to rendezvous with a force of some 20,000 Turks which he knew were due to arrive at Aboukir. Desaix left Upper Egypt in pursuit while a second French force deployed out of Cairo. Bonaparte arrived to join the army marching from Cairo on 14 July in the hope of bringing Murad to battle, but the latter had already moved on. On the 15th, after receiving news from Alexandria of the Turkish landing at Aboukir, Bonaparte turned his force round and marched north. Arriving at El Rahminiya on the 20th, he rested his men for a day while he received reinforcements and then set out for Aboukir.

Aboukir

The Turkish army, commanded by Mustafa Pasha, Seraskier of Rumelia, had been landed from a fleet of five battleships, three frigates and fifty to sixty transports. Sources differ regarding its strength, the figures given varying from close to 20,000 to anywhere between 7,000 and 15,000.[7] They all agree, however, that it had no cavalry.

Immediately after the landing a redoubt east of Aboukir village, manned by 300 French troops, was stormed and the occupants killed. However, the local fort – defended by just thirty-five soldiers – held out for three days before surrendering. The Turkish army did not attempt to exploit these early successes, but instead set about preparing an entrenched position that was three lines deep, each line stretching across the entire width of the peninsula. Meanwhile, by 24 July Bonaparte had mustered a force of about 10,000 men close to Aboukir. Despite the fact that Desaix's division had not arrived he gave orders for an attack the next day.

The battle began in the early morning of the 25th:

> Murat with his cavalry brigade and an infantry brigade under Destaing, drawn from Alexandria, formed the advanced guard; behind him came Lannes on the right and Lanusse, commanding Rampon's troops, in the

second line. Menou, from Rosetta, with a small force, was on the farther side of the bay, and Marmont was left in Alexandria, much to his disgust. He was not the only discontented man, for Davout, who had just joined from Cairo, expected a good command but was only given two squadrons and 100 of the Dromedary Corps, with which he was to link the attacking force with Alexandria and to keep off the Arabs.[8]

The first Turkish line, based on two mounds, was attacked frontally by Destaing and Lannes and from the rear by Murat's cavalry. The Turkish defenders broke and were driven back, cut down or pushed into the sea. By now Murat's cavalry were on the right, Lannes' division was in the centre, Lanusse was on the left and Destaing in the rear. They now advanced against the second Turkish line.

> Murat again pressed forward, but his repeated charges were thrown back by the fire of the [Turkish] gunboats. Bessieres led the Guides up to the ditches of the works but could not cross, and the French were held in front of the serried foe until a check to them tempted the Turks from their strong position. In Lanusse's division Colonel Fugieres led the 18th Regiment. One of the finest regiments of the Armée d'Italie, which, with Suchet in its ranks, had swept in fine array onto the field of Rivoli. Bringing up his men against the works at the double, Fugieres found that they were getting too much strung out, and just as they were close to the ditch he made the head of the column mark time. Like a horse pulled up at a fence, the regiment failed to throw themselves on the redoubt and drew back. Out poured the Turks to cut off the heads of the wounded and so earn the rewards offered by their chiefs. Murat, with his fine eye for a field of battle, saw the chance and threw his cavalry in the rear of the Turks; the 18th rallied, and, with the rest of Lanusse's division, came on again, while Bonaparte sent Lannes forward. Then came a confused carnage of the Turkish mass, which unbroken had been so formidable.[9]

Murat's cavalry charge, which passed through the Turkish lines all the way to the fort, took place at about midday. As the Turkish position disintegrated the French fleet hove into view. It had been out at sea, but on nearing Alexandria it had sailed in the direction of the sound of gunfire. Outgunned, outnumbered and outsmarted, the Turkish vessels were no match for the French. With the exception of some transports which surrendered, the entire fleet was destroyed in less than an hour. Meanwhile, some 2,000 Turks had taken refuge in Aboukir fort while as many again were cut down or bayoneted. Perhaps 4,000 more were driven into the sea, where they either drowned or were shot from the beach. As the Turkish hulks blazed in the bay Napoleon's army rounded up the last demoralised remnants of the Turkish army. The battle was over and victory complete by one o'clock in the afternoon. Mustafa Pasha's army had been comprehensively destroyed. Murat himself captured Mustafa, sustaining a pistol shot to the jaw while disarming him and removing a couple of his fingers in the process. Bonaparte received his prisoner with courtesy.

The battle of Aboukir ended Turkish attempts to oust the French and destroyed Turkey's offensive capability. Within a month Bonaparte was back in Syria to conclude the treaty of Damascus between France and Turkey, by the terms of which the latter recognised France's colonies of Egypt and Syria. France in return promised to mount no further operations into Turkish territory. Turkey also promised military support for French operations in India.

A foothold for the future

France now had secure and stable governments in both Syria and Egypt. The Turkish army and navy had been so badly damaged at Aboukir that neither posed any significant threat, so that the treaty agreed at Damascus seemed likely to hold for the foreseeable future. France now had a platform for operations into India and a secure land trade route. Tippoo Sultan, France's principal Indian ally, had perished at the fall of Seringapatam in May 1799, which had brought French influence in Mysore to an end. However, the French had other contacts in the subcontinent, particularly with the Mahrattas. The Mahratta Confederacy in the north of India included several brigades organised on European lines, initially by a Frenchman, Benôit de Boigne. Further French advisors crossed into India and established contact with the Mahrattas in 1800. Military support followed, and eventually resulted in the establishment of large armies of well-equipped and French-trained soldiers.

In 1802 Baji Rao II, the Peshwa or hereditary ruler of the Mahrattas, was defeated by Holkar of Indore at the battle of Poona. The Peshwa had been an ally of the British, who sought his restoration. Holkar's refusal to comply led to the Second Mahratta War, in which the British launched simultaneous campaigns into the Deccan and Hindustan commanded respectively by Sir Arthur Wellesley and the commander-in-chief, General Gerard Lake. Wellesley fought a successful and memorable campaign in the Deccan. On 23 September 1803 he was victorious at the battle of Assaye, albeit with heavy losses. Another victory the following month enabled the Peshwa to be reinstated. Farther north in Hindustan, however, General Lake was not so fortunate. A Mahratta army led by Pierre Cuillier Perron, a French adventurer, had been reinforced by both French troops and French-trained Janissaries from Syria and Egypt, who had arrived by both sea and land and consolidated in Delhi in the spring of 1803. In the summer General Lake was defeated by Perron in two major battles and was driven south. The French-trained Janissaries performed particularly well in this campaign, their cavalry providing the army with a distinct edge over the small number of British and sepoy dragoons.

The end of 1803 saw the remains of the Mahratta Confederacy, very much under French influence, consolidated in Hindustan. Ensuing campaigns were inconclusive, as the war in Europe deprived the Indian subcontinent of substantial reinforcements for the next ten years and the division between British and French dependencies hardened. In 1807 French Hindustan was formally admitted to the French Empire.

Returning to the year 1800, France was now also dominant in the Mediterranean, holding Malta and threatening British interests in Sicily and Naples. The work of the Institute was progressing in many ways, and plans were drawn up to execute Article 3 of the Executive Directory's original mandate to Bonaparte, which was 'to cause the isthmus of Suez to be cut through'.

Napoleon's eyes now turned back to France, where political problems and military defeats had set the winds of change blowing. Reviewing his orders from the Directory, he was confident that he had achieved all he had been asked to do and more: France had strong and growing colonies in both Egypt and Syria; there were more than 60,000 French soldiers and a further 15,000 locally recruited troops spread between the two; Turkey was now an ally; and the road to India was in French hands. The young general resolved that it was time to go home.

He sailed from Alexandria on 22 August, leaving Kleber as governor in Damascus and General Andreossy as Governor in Cairo. Berthier, the Chief of Staff, accompanied him, along with Generals Desaix, Lannes, Marmont, and Murat. Bringing Desaix had been a particularly difficult decision: his enormous success in the Upper Nile – gaining him the nickname 'the just sultan' – had played a significant part in the subjugation of Egypt, and his talents were likely to be missed. However, France itself was in difficulty and, on balance, Desaix could serve his mother country best by fighting on Europe's battlefields. (It is on such decisions that history turns – in the following year Desaix would be at Marengo to snatch victory for Bonaparte from the jaws of defeat, and perish in so doing.) Bonaparte also took his four ADCs (Eugene Beauharnais, Duroc, Lavalette and Merlin) and Bessieres with a detachment of Guides: no fewer than five future Marshals of France.

The journey back was broken only by a short stop in Malta to visit the French governor before Bonaparte arrived in France to be fêted and honoured from Toulon to Paris. Ambitious though he undoubtedly was, he can hardly have suspected at the time that he had founded two permanent colonies and established the conditions that would result in a third, which would all one day be part of an Empire that he would rule.

NOTES

1. *Correspondence*, vol.III, no.2103, p 230.
2. Thiers, *History of the French Revolution* (London, 1845).

3. J.S. Tucker, *Memoirs of Earl St Vincent* (London, 1844).
4. *Despatches and Letters of Lord Nelson* (London, 1846).
5. *Ibid*.
6. Captain G.L.B. Killick, trans., *The French Army in Egypt (Memoirs of Lt Vertray)* (Kennett & Co).
7. Mustafa, the Turkish commander, apparently wrote to the Turkish government on the eve of battle that he had only 7,000 men fit for combat. Bonaparte, reporting the battle to the Directory on 28 July, says that 9,000 Turks were killed. His second report on 2 August raised the figure to 18,000. Other sources which give the Turkish strength include Sir Sidney Smith (7,000), Smith's secretary (8,000 to 9,000) and Kleber (9,000).
8. Phipps, *The Armies of the First French Republic* (Oxford, 1926–39).
9. *Ibid*.

THE REALITY

Almost all that has been recounted up to 1 August is factually correct. However, no order was sent to permit the French fleet to leave Aboukir Bay and Nelson found them there on the 1st. Though it was late in the day, he seized the initiative and attacked. In the battle of the Nile which followed that afternoon and evening, the French fleet was almost annihilated. It had been badly positioned, just as previously described, and Nelson was able to get behind their line and roll it up. The loss of the fleet isolated Napoleon from France and reinforcement. British naval supremacy in the eastern Mediterranean subsequently enabled Sir Sidney Smith to play a vital role in denying Acre to Bonaparte. The Admiral provided advice and support to the defenders, both from the sea and with extra guns and gunners in the fort. The lack of French naval supremacy also meant that while the Turkish army was indeed defeated at Aboukir, their fleet was not destroyed.

Bonaparte did not leave Egypt with a stable French government and platform for operations into India. (Indeed, the Second Mahratta War of 1803–5 finished off any lingering French influence in India and consolidated Britain's hold on the subcontinent.) Instead he slipped away, leaving Kleber and then Menou to command the demoralised French forces. Desaix did not accompany Bonaparte to France, but left later, being delayed for a while by the British fleet before getting back in time to rescue Bonaparte at Marengo. In 1801 British and Turkish forces reconquered Egypt and expelled the French.

JUNOT'S VICTORY IN PORTUGAL, 1808

BY PHILIP HAYTHORNTHWAITE

'The most trivial circumstances', Napoleon once remarked, 'lead to the greatest events'.[1] It is an interesting speculation that if the frigate HMS *Brazen* had not made quite such good time to Maceira Bay in August 1808, and if the convoy carrying British reinforcements had arrived instead, it might have been that the British commander at the battle of Vimeiro would have been Sir Arthur Wellesley; and history might have been changed.

The British expedition to Portugal in 1808 was not the first to that country, and as before it arose from Britain's hostility towards France and her allies. The first revolts in Spain, in reaction to Napoleon's occupation, convinced the British government that aid should be made available to that country: as the Foreign Secretary, George Canning, declared in the House of Commons on 15 July 1808, any opponent of France 'becomes *ipso facto* the ally of Great Britain', and that 'no interest can be so purely British as Spanish success'.[2] In pursuit of this aim, a small British force from Sicily and Gibraltar, commanded by Sir Brent Spencer, had already been sent to the region, although the assistance he offered to the Spanish at Cadiz had been declined. To consolidate British involvement in the Iberian Peninsula, a larger force was assembled to assist Spain, command of which was entrusted to Sir Arthur Wellesley. In addition to his undoubted military talents – he had enjoyed great success in India and had recently held a command in the expedition to Denmark – Wellesley had influential family connections and had the trust of the ministry, of which he had been a part (as Irish Secretary). The combination of his abilities and his high connections made him a very credible choice for command of the expedition.

Portugal in 1808

In early June 1808 Portugal had risen in rebellion against the French occupation, and a 'supreme *junta*' had been established at Oporto. Such was the extent of the rebellion that the commander of the French army of occupation, General Andoche Junot, had considered abandoning the country and retiring to join the French forces in Spain; but instead he elected to concentrate his forces around the capital, Lisbon. Consequently, the decision was made by the British government to direct their first effort against the French in Portugal, an operation which would also have the effect of distracting some of the French forces from their attempts to crush the burgeoning rebellion in Spain. Wellesley was instructed to use his own judgement as to whether to initiate operations using his own force and that of Spencer, or to await further reinforcement. His command consisted of some 8,500 infantry, a mere handful of cavalry, and two artillery companies with fifteen guns (two-thirds light 6-pounders and the rest 9-pounders). Added to these was Spencer's force, some 4,500 infantry and six light 6-pounders. Much was lacking: there was inadequate transport, and for want of draught horses Spencer's guns could not be used.[3]

The British land

Wellesley decided to disembark his force at Mondego Bay, where he was joined by Spencer's command (1–5 August), and to advance upon Lisbon by the coast road, so as to enable him to receive supplies and reinforcements by sea. These reinforcements he was promised in a despatch he received while making plans for the disembarkation at Mondego Bay: first, some 4,000 men under brigadiers Wroth Acland and Robert Anstruther, and following them a further 10,000 under Sir John Moore. Much less welcome must have been the news that they would be accompanied by no less than three general officers who were senior to Wellesley and who would deprive him of overall command.

With one of these, Sir John Moore, Wellesley could have collaborated easily due to their mutual respect. Recently returned from an abortive attempt to co-operate with Sweden in the Baltic region, Moore had a high reputation in the army, had a much more charismatic personality than Wellesley, and was idolised by those with whom he had been associated in his attempts to create a force of expert light infantry. However, he was not a 'friend' of the ministry but was regarded as an opponent politically, and had no record of victory as had Wellesley, even though the latter's Indian successes tended to be held in somewhat less regard than actions won in Europe. Indeed, elements in the government seem to have doubted the wisdom of appointing Moore at all, but, having decided that he should go to the Peninsula, then placed over his head (and thus over Wellesley too) the current commander at Gibraltar, Sir Hew Dalrymple. It is likely that Dalrymple's appointment was intended to be only temporary, to enable Wellesley to distinguish himself sufficiently to allow him to be appointed to the chief command, with Dalrymple returning to Gibraltar; and, perhaps to prevent the possibility of Moore taking command should any misfortune befall Dalrymple, the latter was allocated Sir Harry Burrard as his second-in-command. These decisions must have come as severe blows to both Wellesley and Moore, and with lesser men might have led to their resignations; but to their credit, both elected instead to do their duty. Indeed while still aboard HMS *Donegal* in Mondego Bay, Wellesley wrote to Lord Castlereagh (Secretary for War) that 'whether I am to command the army or not, or am to quit it, I shall do my best to insure its success; and you may depend upon it that I shall not hurry the operations, or commence them one moment sooner than they ought to be commenced, in order that I may acquire the credit of the success'.[4]

Once ashore, Wellesley organised his little force into six brigades (three comprising three battalions each, the others only two), and distributed his artillery among them. As he began his march on Lisbon, it was hoped that he might collaborate with the Portuguese army of General Bernadin Freire, but that general was unwilling to follow Wellesley's plan of march and thus reinforced him with only a small Portuguese detachment.

Junot's preparations

Andoche Junot, the French commander in Portugal, was a somewhat mercurial character and an old companion of Napoleon, and had made a notable forced march to reach Portugal. His entire strength was about 25,000 men, but the need to retain some garrisons considerably reduced his available resources for field operations. Nevertheless, upon learning of the landing at Mondego Bay he determined to assemble the maximum number of troops and to reduce his garrison commitment to a bare minimum, believing (with some justification) that the best way to minimise Portuguese resistance would be to defeat the invaders. He was even prepared to denude the garrison of Lisbon, in the belief that the presence in the Tagus estuary of Admiral Siniavin's Russian fleet might help discourage any Portuguese attempt at revolt, even though Siniavin was among the many Russian officers deeply unhappy about their alliance with France. In the event, Siniavin was determined to do only the bare minimum that might be expected from an ally.

While Junot gathered his forces, he despatched General Henri-François Delaborde with some 4,500 men to march towards the invaders, to observe and if possible disrupt their progress. As he advanced, Wellesley made contact with Delaborde on 16 August near Obidos, the French advance guard retiring after some skirmishing. On the following day Wellesley discovered Delaborde's force drawn up on the hill of Roliça, and advanced to turn his flanks; but the French withdrew to a similar position about a mile away, and Wellesley followed. Again he intended to turn the flanks, but his centre pushed forward rather too impetuously, and once engaged had to be supported. Severe fighting ensued and one of Wellesley's battalions, the 29th Foot, was led forward somewhat unwisely by its commander, Lieutenant-Colonel George Lake (son of General Gerard Lake), and was very badly mauled, losing about a quarter of its strength and Lake, who was killed. Delaborde's men held their position against repeated assaults, but once a lodgement had been made upon the crest of the hill, and the British flanking movement made its appearance, Delaborde judged it prudent to withdraw. His retreat began in an orderly manner, but his units became crowded together in a pass at the rear of his position, and were handled severely by their pursuers. Despite the disparity in numbers of the two forces, those actually engaged were about equal in numbers – only about a third of Wellesley's troops had been in action – and while Delaborde had lost about 600 men and three of his five guns, Wellesley's loss was only 474, 190 of whom had fallen in the ranks of the 29th. Roliça might only have been a small action, but it assumed greater importance as an example of Wellesley's ability in light of what was to happen over the next few days.

Wellesley's first reinforcement – the brigades of Acland and Anstruther – had sailed from Harwich and Ramsgate respectively, but the winds had held them up longer than had been anticipated. Nevertheless, Wellesley was anxious to receive this augmentation, and knowing that the fort of Peniche (the headland south-west of Roliça) was still in French hands, he decided to by-pass this post and take up a position at the next bay to the south, that of the river Maceira, where the reinforcements could be landed. On 19 August he was arranging for his troops to encamp on the high ground inland from the mouth of the Maceira when he was told that instead of the expected convoy, a single vessel had arrived in the bay: HMS *Brazen*, carrying Sir Harry Burrard, his superior. Whatever chagrin Wellesley may have felt, he reported dutifully to Burrard and was informed that instead of continuing the march on Lisbon, the whole force should gather about the town of Maceira to cover the arrival of reinforcements. These, Burrard stated, would consist not only of the brigades of Acland and Anstruther (wherever on the high seas they might be), but also Moore's command, which had actually arrived off Mondego Bay just as Burrard was arriving at Maceira. Moore's force, however, was becalmed – the same fate which had overtaken Acland and Anstruther – and it was not for some days that Moore was able to begin disembarkation. This was cancelled by a message from Burrard – carried by the *Brazen*, from which Burrard had disembarked – that he should re-embark and proceed to Maceira Bay. When Moore arrived there himself (aboard *Brazen*) on 24 August, for a reconnaissance and to receive his orders, he found that the campaign had been decided.

As remarked at the beginning of this chapter, but for the vagaries of the sea and weather, it might have been that Acland and Anstruther arrived in Maceira Bay before Burrard, and had the opportunity to disembark before Junot delivered his attack; which attack would in that case have been met by Wellesley in command rather than Burrard. Had this been the case, no matter how competently Junot had handled his advance, it is perhaps likely that Wellesley's victory at Roliça would have been repeated at Vimeiro; but instead, it was upon the circumstances of the winds and tides that the outcome was decided.

Fifty-three years of age, a Guardsman and favourite of the Duke of York,

Sir Harry Burrard was an honourable if somewhat unenterprising man. He had recently held a command at home, but had led a division in the expedition to Denmark in 1807 and had campaign experience extending back to the American War. Perhaps of greater significance, however, was his participation in the disastrous expedition to Ostend in 1798, in the raid intended to destroy the Bruges Canal, in which he had been second-in-command to Sir Eyre Coote. This enterprise had succeeded in its objective, but the seas proved too rough to permit the British force to be evacuated as planned; they were attacked, and after Coote was wounded it had fallen to Burrard to surrender the entire expedition to save it from annihilation. The sight of Maceira Bay must have reminded Burrard most forcibly of his plight of a decade before, for the landing-ground at Maceira was anything but easy; indeed, when the tide was incoming it was quite impossible to land, and even at other times it was a hazardous undertaking. Between two rocky headlands was the only landing-point, some 300 yards of sandy beach 'which the huge breakers had converted into a sheet of raging foam ... the raging breakers, raising their heads houses high when they were still some considerable distance from the land, rolled in from the Atlantic and Bay of Biscay, and, hemmed in on either side by the two headlands, pressed forward in lofty walls of water, that swept in a roaring storm of foam over the beach.'[5] It would have been unnatural if the memory of Ostend had not affected Burrard's perception of the task ahead, and his consequent desire to protect his embarkation point at Maceira Bay led to a fatal division of his forces when Junot attacked; but though criticised, Burrard's great caution – some even thought it timidity – is easy to understand and even to sympathise with.

Vimeiro

Just over a mile inland from the beach was the village of Maceira, and beyond it, overlooking the river Maceira and the shore, a range of high ground. To the south of the river was what Sir John Fortescue called 'the western ridge',[6] to the north 'the eastern ridge', with the river turning south in a gorge between the two. Near this gap, between the spurs of high ground, was the village of Vimeiro, with a small hill to the south of it – hardly the 'rugged isolated height' described by William Napier;[7] Jonathan Leach described it as 'a hill of no considerable height'.[8] It was upon the high ground that Wellesley had intended to position his brigades, less as a matter of defence (for he was expecting to advance) than as a convenient position for encamping. Burrard, however, while appreciating that the high ground also formed a defensive position for protecting the landing-ground at Maceira Bay, was so conscious of the need to cover the latter that he determined to position part of the army in the area around Maceira village. From there, this detachment could be used as a reserve to reinforce the other positions and, more importantly, could protect the beach itself should French troops attempt to penetrate the British position by outflanking the western ridge. Even though this was surely unlikely, Burrard could not overcome his caution, knowing from bitter experience that any attempt to disembark reinforcements, or even evacuate the army, would be quite impossible if the troops on the beach were attacked and thus had the enemy to contend with as well as the elements.

With Acland and Anstruther still becalmed at sea, Burrard had at his disposal only the six brigades of Wellesley's original force, the organisation of which had remained unchanged after Roliça, save for the transfer of the 50th Foot from Catlin Craufurd's brigade to Henry Fane's Light Brigade. The latter included Burrard's only truly expert light troops, four companies of the 95th Rifles and the German riflemen of the 5th Battalion, 60th Royal American Regiment; it was posted to hold Vimeiro hill. The two weakest of Burrard's brigades – those of Barnard Bowes and Miles Nightingall, together numbering only four battalions – were posted as the reserve; on the right, along the western ridge, was the brigade of Rowland Hill, while those of Craufurd and Ronald Ferguson were on the eastern ridge. The Portuguese contingent, under the Irish officer Nicholas Trant, encamped further to the north. The army's baggage, which Wellesley had proposed to gather around Vimeiro village so as to be ready to advance without delay, was withdrawn by Burrard to the area around Maceira. The troops were in these positions when, early on 21 August, clouds of dust announced the approach of Junot's army.

Burdened by a large convoy of supplies, Junot had made slow progress in his march from Lisbon, but had gathered in various detachments as he progressed, notably the division of General Louis-Henri Loison, which had been ordered from its position in front of Badajoz in support of Delaborde, but had not arrived before the defeat of Roliça. When Junot and Loison joined Delaborde, their combined force was about 17,000 strong, out-numbering Burrard's army, with more artillery, and with in excess of 2,000 cavalry, infinitely superior in that arm of service. It is unlikely that Burrard and Wellesley were aware that so great a force had been assembled against them, their intelligence being limited severely by their paucity in cavalry. Some members of the Lisbon Police Guard had deserted from the capital and joined the Anglo-Portuguese cavalry (Trant's small cavalry contingent had been brigaded with Burrard's), and they may well have carried news of the inaction of Siniavin's fleet, which may have led the British commanders to believe that Junot would have had to have left a much larger part of his army in Lisbon than he actually had. Furthermore, since at Roliça some members of Delaborde's 4th Swiss Regiment had deserted and gone over to the British, Burrard may have been inclined to believe that such disaffection might be widespread throughout Junot's army, which was, of course, not the case. Nevertheless, Wellesley did express his disquiet at the positioning of the reserve, which remained around Maceira even when the direction of the dust-clouds revealed that a French attack along the coast was evidently not being contemplated.

Junot's options were either to advance to strike the British positions at several points, or to concentrate his attack on one position; in either case he could expect difficulty in having to assault an enemy on high ground. The former might have seemed the preferable option, but instead Junot elected to make a hefty demonstration against the strong position of the western ridge, and upon Vimeiro, while concentrating his attack instead upon Burrard's left flank.

Having at his disposal something of a surfeit of general officers, Burrard ordered Wellesley to take command of the right – Hill and Fane – and assigned Brent Spencer (hitherto Wellesley's deputy) to the left. It soon became obvious from the clouds of dust (virtually the only indicator the British had of Junot's movements due to their limited reconnaissance facility) that their French opponent was intent on dividing his forces, though in what proportion it was difficult to ascertain. In the event, Junot detached some 4,000 of his infantry (under Delaborde) to demonstrate against the British right, while the remainder, led by Loison, he sent against the left.

Battle is joined

Although only intended as a demonstration to occupy part of Burrard's army, Delaborde's attack – which began before the remainder of Junot's army was ready to make its assault – was pressed with considerable spirit down the road which ran alongside the river Maceira, between the western ridge and Vimeiro hill, which was also attacked. Wellesley had adopted what was at that time something of a novel tactic, of sheltering his infantry on the reverse slopes, so that most of Hill's brigade was invisible to the French, only the battalion light companies being deployed and in view. Similarly, Fane had thrown out most of his riflemen in heavy skirmish order, keeping only the 50th in reserve, and they halted the *tirailleurs* who preceded Delaborde's right brigade. The sudden appearance of Hill's troops from behind the crest of the hill, and those of Fane's not already in action, caused Delaborde's attack to falter, and then retire in disorder as the British fired and advanced with the bayonet. This advance was only limited, however, as Wellesley called them back to their original positions. Despite their losses and disorganisation, Delaborde's command rallied quickly, which greatly impressed British eyewitnesses: as William Napier remarked, 'the rapidity with which the French soldiers rallied, and recovered their order after such a severe check, was admirable.'[9] Thereafter, Delaborde made no further serious attack, but maintained a heavy skirmishing fire to keep the British occupied.

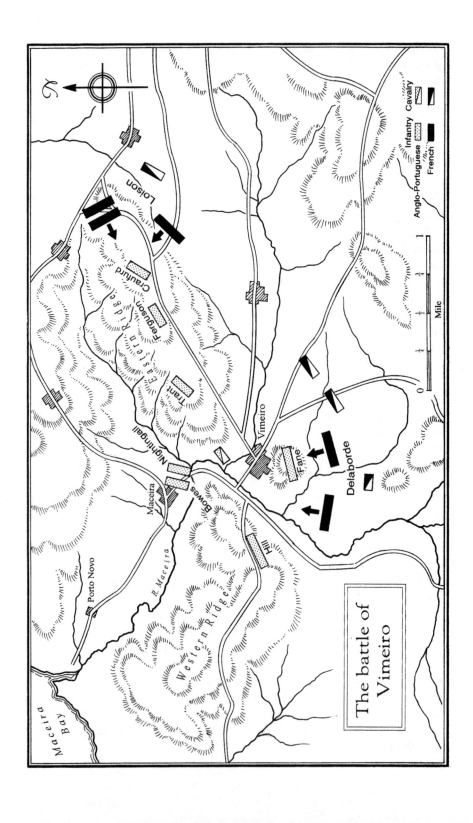

The battle of Vimeiro

Maceira Bay

Porto Novo

R. Maceira

Western Ridge

Maceira

Bowes

Nightingall

Trant

Eastern Ridge

Ferguson

Craufurd

Loison

Vimeiro

Fane

Delaborde

Anglo-Portuguese
French

Infantry   Cavalry

0   ¼   ½   ¾   1

Mile

The French attack upon Burrard's left had a very different outcome. Loison's division massed to advance along the eastern ridge, as Spencer moved his brigades further left to oppose them. The French were again preceded by a very heavy screen of skirmishers, against which Spencer threw forward his battalion light companies, the only trained light infantry immediately to hand (the 71st, recently converted to light infantry, was at the rear of Ferguson's brigade and so was not among the first in action). It was at this point that the British army's shortage of light infantry was felt most keenly (the light troops trained by Moore at Shorncliffe, including the 43rd and 52nd, were still at sea with Anstruther).

Brent Spencer was not, perhaps, the brightest of individuals (Wellesley described him as 'exceedingly puzzle-headed'[10]), though under fire was coolness personified; but at this moment his judgement appears to have been at fault. The British skirmishers which had been thrown forward to oppose the hordes of French *tirailleurs* were both heavily outnumbered and not as expert as their opponents, and consequently were handled roughly and pushed back. Seeing this – and perhaps intent on buying time until the whole of his wing of the army could come up – Spencer ordered out a number of battalion companies to join the skirmishing; which troops, unfortunately, had even less idea of the requirements of that service than had the outnumbered light companies. Their plight was described graphically by an observer:

> Getting bewildered among the corn-fields and olives, the young hands scarce knew which way to turn, the old ones, too, were puzzled, and when a blaze of musketry opened on them, from they knew not where, after firing at random a few shots in the air, they were literally mowed down, falling like ninepins amid the standing corn; the remnant were soon flung back ... leaving the scene of action mottled with their slain. [It was, he recalled] the most unequal contest that could well be imagined, and mortifying that so many of those fine young fellows should have been thus sacrificed.[11]

These skirmishers were hustled back in short order, and with some of the battalion companies having been deployed, in retreating the whole mass disordered Craufurd's two battalions and Ferguson's three; and these, faced with overwhelming force as Loison's attack drove on, fell back in great confusion. Observing the retreat of the British, Trant's Portuguese contingent also retired in disorder.

When it had become obvious that Junot was making his main attack upon the British left, Burrard must have realised his error in retaining his reserve around Maceira, and to his credit immediately sent orders to the commanders of those brigades to move forward in support of Spencer. By the time they were able to act, however, Loison's assault was driving along the ridge, and the reserve was faced with the task of clambering uphill over difficult terrain towards an enemy emboldened by their recent success. Nightingall's brigade made a spirited attempt – led by the 29th, which was probably especially eager to avenge the death of its colonel at Roliça – but in such circumstances such a manoeuvre had little chance of success, and it was abandoned without having had the slightest possibility of recovering the guns overrun by Loison's attack.

Faced with the entire collapse of his left wing, Burrard made his way to the right to join Wellesley, and leaving orders with the reliable Hill and Fane, they both rode to the centre of the position to attempt to bring some order to the situation, and to re-form the army around the unbroken brigade of Bowes and the now somewhat mauled brigade of Nightingall. Considerable elements from the left wing were still resisting, but were unable to halt Loison's advance, which began to descend from the eastern ridge. Here, the French received a check from Burrard's small force of cavalry, barely 200 of the 20th Light Dragoons and about the same number of Portuguese. These were led against Loison's leading elements by Lieutenant-Colonel Charles Taylor of the 20th; although their charge came to grief (Taylor was killed and his regiment all but destroyed as an effective unit), its effort had been sufficient to oblige Junot to pause and reorganise. This delay was even more valuable for Burrard and Wellesley, for its allowed the latter to improvise a defensive line between Maceira and the high ground. Consequently when Junot renewed his attack with Loison's division the position held, but only just, and only thanks to the reinforcement of Hill's brigade, marched over from the right. Three separate assaults were beaten off by the British around Maceira – the first two at least were pressed with great spirit – but some havoc was wrought among the British supply-convoy, part of which could not be removed before the fighting approached it, so that much ammunition was lost when some wagons blew up. Fane, in the meantime, had continued to hold off Delaborde.

As if by common consent, the fighting subsided for the day, both sides having suffered considerable losses and both being in need of reorganisation. There was no doubt, however, which side had gained the day. Burrard was still clinging to the position covering his beachhead, but his army had been mauled dreadfully, his cavalry destroyed, and most of his artillery and much of his supplies lost. Junot, however, despite having sustained heavy losses, especially in the attacks on Maceira, held all the high ground and thus dominated his enemy's position (to prevent being outflanked, Fane had retired through Vimeiro village to join Burrard around Maceira). Junot, however, was conscious of the need to consolidate his victory; he was appraised of the fact that British reinforcements were on the way, and some of the many prisoners taken when the British left flank had collapsed had confirmed that at least two brigades were overdue, and thus might be expected almost hourly. For the British, the arrival of such reinforcements was awaited with even greater anxiety.

Despite the severe handling they had received, morale among the British troops was surprisingly good, boosted at the end of the day by the successful defence of Maceira. Among the officers, however, there was apparently widespread discontent with the way Burrard had handled the battle, so that while all ranks tended to trust Wellesley for his recent conduct, little confidence can have resided in the abilities of the commanding general. After an anxious night (spent resting and distributing those supplies which were available), hearts must have lifted at first light with the sight of a new ship in Maceira Bay; but sunk again when it was realised that it was not bringing reinforcements, but instead something of which the army had no pressing need: another general.

Early on the morning of the 22nd this general – Sir Hew Dalrymple – landed and took command of the troops, probably much to Burrard's relief. Despite his age (he was born in 1750) Dalrymple was not altogether an unlikely choice as commander, in that during his service as governor of Gibraltar he had established close relations with the Spanish 'patriot' party, and was an intelligent man; but he was not what might be described as a 'fighting general'. Moore's assessment was probably fairly accurate: 'a man certainly not without sense, but who had never before served in the field as a general officer, who had allowed a war of sixteen years to pass without pushing for any service except in England and Guernsey, and who seemed to be completely at a loss in the situation in which he was placed.'[12] Furthermore, Dalrymple appeared intent on ignoring the opinions of his most capable subordinate, Sir Arthur Wellesley, who recorded that 'in the first interview I had with Sir Hew Dalrymple, after his arrival in Portugal, on the morning of the 22d of August, I, who am supposed to have been his adviser ... had reason to believe that I did not possess his confidence; nay, more, that he was prejudiced against the opinions which I should give him.'[13]

Dalrymple's situation was grave, but Wellesley believed it was not hopeless. He thought it possible that the army, even in its unfavourable position, could resist another attack that day, and could cover the disembarkation of reinforcements, *provided* that these were not long delayed (though Wellesley did admit that they would have to quit these positions before long, or else 'we shall be poisoned here by the stench of the dead and wounded; or we shall starve.'[14] Neither Dalrymple nor Burrard were so sanguine about the army's ability to resist, although the alternative – an embarkation when transports arrived – would be virtually impossible should Junot attack during the operation. It was at this moment that the appearance of a French officer, with aides and a trumpeter, was reported by Fane's picquets (some of the riflemen had to be restrained from taking a shot at such an easy target!).

This came about as the result of deliberations between Junot and his senior commanders. Although the French had clearly prevailed in the battle of the 21st, their enemy was not quite beaten into submission; and while Junot was confident that a renewed attack would achieve success, his losses had been considerable, and a second battle might leave him fatally weakened either for an encounter with the British reinforcements or to face a massed revolt by the Portuguese. Although he realised that he would have to attack again upon the appearance of British reinforcements off the coast, he perceived a chance, before they arrived, to achieve his objective without sustaining further casualties. Thus, shortly before noon on the 22nd, he sent his cavalry commander, General François-Etienne Kellermann (a hero of Marengo and the son of Marshal Kellermann), as an emissary to the British. Kellermann asked the commander of Fane's picquets to be escorted to Sir Harry Burrard – he had no knowledge of Dalrymple's arrival – and was received by the British commanders in Maceira. Wellesley appears to have presumed that his mission was merely to arrange a temporary cease-fire to permit the disposal of the dead and collection of the wounded (many lay still untreated on the field), but from Kellermann's initial remark concerning ways of 'settling this affair without further bloodshed' it was obvious that more profound negotiations were the object. Given the respective circumstances of the armies, it was clear that these could not be favourable to the British, but when both Dalrymple and Burrard appeared very anxious to explore a negotiated escape from their predicament, Wellesley seems to have been filled with foreboding and muttered to his own staff, 'with a cold and contemptuous bitterness' that 'You may think about dinner, for there is nothing more for soldiers to do this day.'[15] Despite Wellesley's opinions, however, it is not difficult to understand, and even justify, the willingness of the British commanders to extricate themselves from a hazardous situation, for the prospect of holding a bridgehead, let alone landing reinforcements in the face of the enemy, must surely have given rise to trepidation in even the stoutest heart.

The Convention

Having arranged a temporary armistice for the duration of the parley, the representatives of both sides met in the small house in Maceira which was serving as the British headquarters. Junot's negotiation was conducted mainly by Kellermann (who understood English, although the discussion was carried out in French), and it was something of a triumph for the French commander. He was careful not to propose any terms so stringent that they would have to be rejected – outright surrender, for example – but initially set out conditions more strict than he was actually prepared to accept, so as to give the British the illusion that they were achieving something substantial. The outcome achieved Junot's overall aim of removing the British presence from Portugal, at least temporarily.

By the terms of the Convention of Maceira, which was concluded late that night, the British troops commanded by Dalrymple would be evacuated from Maceira Bay as soon as transport ships were available, taking with them their arms and personal baggage, with the artillery captured the previous day being retained by the French. The British prisoners taken, chiefly during Loison's attack, were to be freed (thus cleverly relieving Junot of the problems of having to feed and guard the considerable number who had fallen into his hands), and any British wounded unfit to travel with the army would in due course be taken to Lisbon, and sent home in merchant ships once they had recovered. Those Portuguese still with Dalrymple's force were permitted to rejoin Freire's army if they wished, or were to be allowed to return home unmolested. Supplies which could not be carried by the troops were to be surrendered, although a considerable proportion had already been destroyed in the fighting around Maceira.

Finally, and most decisively, the armistice was extended for a period of one month, during which it was agreed that no offensive action would be taken by the forces under Dalrymple's control. This effectively precluded the use of the expected reinforcements. Moore's force, together with the brigades of Anstruther and Acland, numbered about 15,000 men, a larger army than that which had just been defeated by Junot at Vimeiro; but as they were covered by the terms of the Convention they could not be landed, and obviously it would not be possible for them to remain aboard ship for a month until the armistice expired. The fact that Dalrymple seems not to have argued forcibly against this term suggests that he believed it would have been too hazardous to attempt to disembark these troops with Junot's army in the field ready to oppose any such manoeuvre. The whole expedition had no real choice but to return home.

While obviously not happy with the outcome, Dalrymple probably believed that his actions had saved the British forces from the likelihood of a catastrophic defeat; but scarcely a member of those forces would have agreed with him, and when Moore arrived on the 24th, expecting to be ordered to disembark his own contingent when it had followed him to Maceira Bay, he found 'everything in the greatest confusion, and a very general discontent'.[16]

The discontent was universal, and directed towards the army's commanders, for all appeared to have concurred with Wellesley that they might have stood at least an even chance of resisting another attack. Ironically, when Moore arrived he found the other convoys, transporting the brigades of Acland and Anstruther, in the bay, where they were now preparing to evacuate as much of Dalrymple's army as could be crowded onto the ships.

The defeat of the expedition was greeted in Britain with dismay. The reaction to the first receipt of the news included the expected angry exchanges in parliament, but criticism increased when the opinion of the army, expressed at first in private communications, became public knowledge: that it did not regard itself as having been defeated as much as let down by its commanders. One expression of this was the fact that the brigade commanders and Brent Spencer wrote to Wellesley that: 'Anxious to manifest the high esteem and respect we bear towards you, and the satisfaction we must ever feel in having had the good fortune to serve under your command, we have this day directed a piece of plate, value 1,000 guineas, to be prepared and presented to you', inscribed with their names and details of the subscription, 'in testimony of the high regard and esteem they feel for him as a man, and the unbounded confidence they place in him as an Officer.'[17] Although a private gesture, inevitably it became known publicly, and served further to emphasise the widespread criticism of the unfortunate Dalrymple and Burrard, and the fact that the officers concerned had, by implication, no such confidence in them.

Public criticism of the outcome of the expedition was widespread, extending even to William Wordsworth's somewhat hastily-composed and undistinguished poem *On the Convention of Maceira*:

> Maceira! Maceira! Thy name shall be accurs'd,
> Where Albion's arms should have laurels gathered,
> All turn'd to ashes, and her repute sadly burst...'

That section of the press which supported the government directed its attention towards Dalrymple and Burrard, but not with such extreme criticism that it reflected badly upon the ministry which had appointed them; while the anti-government newspapers questioned the entire undertaking to aid Spain. William Cobbett, that most trenchant critic of the ministry, in expectation that the war in the Iberian Peninsula would be renewed by Britain, declared that the whole affair would prove to be 'nothing but a drain upon this country, without the smallest chance of any ultimate benefit ... the sooner we abandon the undertaking the better ... [We may] cause some expense and some mortality to France; but we, at the same time, weaken ourselves in a degree tenfold to what we weaken her.'[18] Not surprisingly, the ministry and its supporters tended to concentrate upon the merits of Wellesley, 'the victor of Roliça' (thereby giving that success perhaps greater fame than it merited), but others were less generous. Typical comments referred to support for Wellesley among the friends of the government, and to his family influence; Cobbett, for example, in a speech at Winchester, linked his return from Portugal with the fact that the Wellesley family received some £23,766 annually from the public finances, equivalent, he said, to the poor rate on sixty parishes. The newspaper *The News*, in similar style, remarked that even if Wellesley were acquitted of responsibility for the failure of the expedition, 'who that witnessed the sinister efforts of his friends, will not suspect that he has owed his acquittal less to the eviction of that innocence than to the influence of those efforts?', especially when compared with the lack of support for the other generals, 'unbefriended individuals'.[19]

These individuals, in fact, escaped with only mild and almost unofficial censure. The government had no wish for a repeat of the Whitelocke court-martial (in consequence of that general's handling of the disastrous South American expedition), which had only recently concluded, and although an enquiry into Maceira was ordered, it was of rapid duration and was somewhat under-stated. However, neither Burrard nor Dalrymple held active commands again, both being tarnished by the criticism they received, exemplified by Byron's line: 'For chiefs like ours in vain may laurels bloom'. Misfortune seems to have followed poor Burrard, for shortly after the conclusion of the Portuguese enquiry he lost his second son, a midshipman in the Royal Navy, when a boat from the royal yacht *Royal Sovereign* was upset in Weymouth harbour. Some five years later, however, Dalrymple petitioned for some recompense for the hurt he had suffered on being criticised over his conduct in Portugal, and was rewarded with a baronetcy.

The aftermath

No such difficulties beset Junot and the French, though they still had problems of their own. The victory at Vimeiro, and more especially the results of the Convention of Maceira, won for Junot not only deserved plaudits but that most coveted distinction, the baton of a Marshal of France. (Perhaps not surprisingly Kellermann, who had always thought himself insufficiently rewarded for his decisive charge at Marengo, privately expressed some unhappiness that his negotiating skills had not been rewarded adequately, at least in his own estimation.) The expulsion of the British from Portugal had helped redress the balance of the French position in the Iberian Peninsula following the disaster of Dupont's surrender at Bailen (19 July 1808), but in itself was not necessarily a decisive blow. The battle at Vimeiro had mauled Junot's army perhaps more severely than he admitted, and while he could maintain his hold on Lisbon and central Portugal, he would require reinforcement before the rebellion in the north and south could be suppressed. Nevertheless, the removal of the British presence at this crucial time would allow Napoleon to direct his efforts against the Spanish armies without the distraction of attempting to cope with a foreign expeditionary force aiding the indigenous armies. Napoleon was thus presented with a real opportunity to conclude the war in the Iberian Peninsula without the prospect of years of attrition which might have worn down the resources of his

Empire and cast a baleful influence upon his campaigns in other parts of Europe.

The real problem arising from the battle of Vimeiro was that which faced the British government following the return of their defeated expedition. The fact that the expedition itself did not think it had been defeated served only to exert additional pressure upon the ministry to make a rapid decision about how they should proceed. None of the choices facing them were appealing. To abandon the Iberian Peninsula, as much of the opposition was urging, and to await another opportunity to oppose Napoleon on land somewhere else, would fly in the face of the accepted policy of offering assistance to all those engaged against the French, and would overturn the assurances of support which had been given to the Spanish and Portuguese leaders. Forces were available to resume the war in the Peninsula – not only those which had returned from Portugal without landing, but others in addition – but if the decision to renew the conflict were made, the location was in doubt. Direct assistance to the Spanish via Cadiz was a possibility, but the unenthusiastic reception to the suggestion that Spencer might have remained there (prior to his joining Wellesley) counted against the idea. A landing in northern Spain might be feasible – perhaps at Ferrol (where the abortive expedition of 1800 had landed), Corunna or Vigo; or alternatively a return to Portugal. The latter would have to be undertaken without delay, ideally before French reinforcements might enable Junot to crush the Portuguese forces, even though the season would be advancing: Wellesley had noted that as winter approached, not only would the roads become more difficult and the army need tents, but the supporting fleet could only operate (and thus resupply the army) off Oporto or Lisbon.

A further question facing the government was the matter of who to appoint to command any new expedition. Moore had made it clear that he had – very generously – waived any claim of seniority over Wellesley, following the latter's achievements in the early stages of the late campaign, and he was also known to believe that Portugal was indefensible should the French triumph in Spain. Wellesley, therefore, might be expected to be the ministry's choice for supreme command should a renewed foray to the Peninsula be sanctioned. But the task he would face would be daunting, and very much more difficult than if Junot had been defeated at Vimeiro, and if it had been the French, not the British, who had been expelled. Furthermore, the longer any new British expedition was delayed, the more damage the French would inflict upon the Spanish and Portuguese forces. The possibility of a second and much worse British defeat could not be discounted, which surely the British government could not afford to sustain; and even if the French could be driven from Portugal, it would require such an effort as to reduce very severely the chances of being able to provide immediate aid to whatever Spanish forces still remained in the field against Napoleon. Even to hold Portugal under such circumstances held out the prospect of years of costly warfare.

These, then, were the choices facing the British government, all fraught with difficulty. The course they elected to pursue is a matter of record, but it is an inescapable conclusion that matters would have been very different indeed had not Junot prevailed at the battle of Vimeiro.

NOTES

1. E.A.D.M.J. Las Cases, *Memoirs of the Life, Exile and Conversations of the Emperor Napoleon*, (London, 1836), vol.II, p.40.
2. For an extract from that speech, see Sir Charles Oman, *History of the Peninsular War* (Oxford, 1902), vol.I, p.222.
3. For an assessment of the artillery at the outset of the campaign, see Major J.H. Leslie, *The Services of the Royal Regiment of Artillery in the Peninsular War* (London, 1908), pp.5–13.
4. *Dispatches of Field-Marshal the Duke of Wellington*, ed. J. Gurwood (London, 1834–8), vol.IV, p.55.
5. A.L.F. Schaumann, *On the Road with Wellington*, trans. A.M. Ludovici (London, 1924), p.1.
6. Sir John Fortescue, *A History of the British Army* (London, 1910), vol.VI, p.220.
7. Sir William Napier, *History of the War in the Peninsula* (London, 1832), vol.I, p.204.
8. J. Leach, *Rough Sketches of the Life of an Old Soldier* (London, 1831), p.50.
9. Napier, *op.cit.* vol.I, p.258.
10. For his confidential assessment of Spencer, see Oman, *op.cit.* vol.IV, p.552.
11. John Patterson, in *Colburn's United Service Magazine* 1844 vol.III, pp.279–80.
12. *The Diary of Sir John Moore*, ed. Sir J.F. Maurice (London, 1904), vol.II, p.259.
13. Wellington's *Dispatches*, vol.IV, p.203.
14. *Ibid* p.115.
15. M. Sherer, *Recollections of the Peninsula* (London, 1825), pp.42–3.
16. *Diary of Sir John Moore*, vol.II, p.257.
17. Wellington's *Dispatches*, vol.IV, p.137.
18. Cobbett's *Weekly Political Register*, vol.XX, no.19, column 581 (this publication was unpaginated but had numbered columns).
19. *The News*, 6 November 1808.

THE REALITY

This account was compiled on the premise that Burrard, rather than reinforcements, arrived before the battle of Vimeiro; and that Junot gathered all available forces and concentrated his attack upon the British left, as, indeed, William Napier advocated. For an account of the events of August 1808, see the histories of Sir William Napier and Sir Charles Oman, as given in the footnotes; and for the outcome of the campaign, M. Glover, *Britannia Sickens: Sir Arthur Wellesley and the Convention of Cintra* (London, 1970). All the quotations footnoted above are genuine and all refer to the precise period of the Vimeiro campaign (with the exception of Cobbett's comment in note 18, which actually dates from November 1811), although not all of them are used precisely in their original context.

BIBLIOGRAPHY

Fortescue, Sir John, *A History of the British Army* (London, 1910).

Gurwood, J., ed., *Dispatches of Field-Marshal the Duke of Wellington* (London, 1834–8).

Leach, J., *Rough Sketches of the Life of an Old Soldier* (London, 1831).

Leslie, J.H., *The Services of the Royal Regiment of Artillery in the Peninsular War* (London, 1908).

Napier, Sir William, *History of the War in the Peninsula* (London, 1832).

Oman, Sir Charles, *A History of the Peninsular War* (Oxford, 1902–1930, reprinted, London, 1995–7).

Schaumann, A.L.F., *On the Road with Wellington*, trans. A.M. Ludovici (London, 1924, reprinted 1999).

DECISION IN BAVARIA: THE AUSTRIAN INVASION OF 1809

BY JOHN H. GILL

The Habsburg monarchy was in a grim state in early 1808. Fifteen years of defeat and humiliation at the hands of the French had seen a dramatic collapse of its position in the European balance of power. Not only was it expelled from Italy and Germany, but with the Holy Roman Empire destroyed, Prussia crushed, and Russia allied to France, the old moorings of Vienna's security had been destroyed. Austria was isolated in Europe, nearly bankrupt, and threatened from every quarter: by the French in Italy, Germany and Silesia, and by the Russians on the borders of Galicia. With its army only beginning to recover from the cataclysmic war of 1805, and with no prospects of an alliance, the old monarchy seemed to face France alone, barely able to influence its own destiny.

In this atmosphere of vulnerability and anxiety, Napoleon's unexpected intervention in Iberia in the spring of 1808 came as a terrible shock. For many in Vienna, the sudden eviction and imprisonment of Spain's Bourbon dynasty darkly foreshadowed the potential fate of Austria's Habsburgs. However, for Count Johann Phillip Stadion, the old monarchy's determined foreign minister, France's entanglement across the Pyrenees also seemed to offer a fleeting opportunity for Austria to redress the reverses of the preceding two decades and to restore its position within Europe. Convinced that Napoleon planned to crush Austria as soon as the Spanish affair was settled, Stadion created an atmosphere of desperation, urgency and imminent danger in the Habsburg capital, and, as the French predicament in Iberia became apparent, he began to promote a pre-emptive war to ward off the anticipated threat. Driven by Stadion and an active pro-war faction, the Habsburg monarchy consequently adopted a policy of confrontation with Napoleon and, by the autumn of 1808, Stadion had placed Austria – almost irrevocably – on a course towards an offensive strike against Napoleon the following spring.

The Austrian Army

The army Austria assembled to launch this offensive was arguably the finest force fielded by the Habsburg monarchy during the entire Napoleonic epoch. Eight years of sporadic reform had improved its ability to cope with the challenges of militant France and the evolving nature of land warfare.

73

The most noticeable change was the introduction of the corps system to the army's organisation. Previously arrayed for battle in ad hoc wings, lines, and columns, the field forces of 1809 were for the first time divided into nine regular corps of roughly equal strength, supplemented by two Reserve Corps containing the army's heavy cavalry and grenadiers. In the tactical realm, new drill regulations provided the basis for improvements in the infantry's ability to move, skirmish and confront cavalry on the battlefield. Furthermore, the high command took steps to bolster morale and make military service more appealing, by reducing periods of service, limiting corporal punishment and strengthening the bond between the soldier, his regiment and his emperor.

These reforms, however, did not arise from a comprehensive plan, and much of their potential benefit was lost through inconsistent application. The advantages of the corps system, for example, eluded most of the Austrian generals, who were uncomfortable with the independence and initiative it demanded of them. Moreover, in the hasty mobilisation for war during the early months of 1809, there was no time to familiarise commanders and their staff with the new organisation through training and manoeuvres. The operational movement of corps and divisions, a traditional Austrian weakness, remained slow and cumbersome, a problem compounded by the 'endless scribbling' required by Habsburg command and administrative procedures. Tactical improvements also fell short of expectations. Innovations such as skirmishing – an art which placed a premium on tactical adaptability at the lowest levels – were stifled by the oppressive formality of the Austrian drill books. A Prussian volunteer bitterly observed: 'In the Austrian Army there is no body of troops exclusively dedicated to fighting in open order.'[1]

The army commander and the principal author of these reforms was the Archduke Charles. Younger brother of Kaiser Franz, the thirty-eight-year-old Charles was a soldier of considerable bravery, skill and experience. He had participated in his first campaign in 1792 and had commanded major formations from 1796 to 1805, gaining a number of successes against the French, albeit against their rather less distinguished generals. He was also a military theoretician of some note and he endeavoured to raise the educational level of the Austrian officer corps by publishing his own works and sponsoring a professional journal. In these theoretical works, as in his battlefield performance, however, Charles seldom ventured beyond the comfortable confines of eighteenth-century military thinking. Indeed, his approach to warfare was characterised by vacillation, self-doubt and pervasive caution. His courage, experience, intelligence and devotion to the dynasty notwithstanding, he lacked what Clausewitz called 'the sacred fire' and was more concerned with avoiding defeat than straining every sinew to win. The army and its leader, then, though much improved in comparison to previous campaigns, still suffered from serious flaws, flaws which would severely hamper Austrian operations in the coming campaign.

Recognising his army's faults, Charles initially counselled against renewing the struggle with Napoleon. Stadion, on the other hand, was adamant. The minister argued persuasively that Austria had only the briefest of moments in which to act; it must strike, and strike early, before Napoleon broke Spain and turned his fearful attention towards the Danube. 'We must anticipate the danger and, without waiting for the eruption of Napoleon's plans, choose the most advantageous moment to bring our tense political relations with France to a quick and permanent decision,' he exhorted the monarchy's leaders.[2] Though the Kaiser hesitated from the autumn of 1808 until January 1809, Stadion's unrelenting pressure gradually eroded his resistance. The decision in favour of war was finally taken at a conference on 8 February 1809. Charles, deep in one of his pessimistic moods, was resigned rather than enthusiastic, declaring gloomily that 'I did not vote for war. Let those who made the decision assume the responsibility.'[3] His grim pessimism, however, did not slow the couriers who were soon spurring through the monarchy with orders for the army to mobilise in preparation for a new struggle with France.

Mayer's plan

The man responsible for Austria's plan of operations was General-Major Anton Mayer von Heldensfeld, Charles' Quartermaster General. Full of his own importance and nearly insolent toward Charles at times, Mayer was a difficult subordinate and colleague; but he was also a thorough, energetic and intelligent soldier with considerable combat experience. As sketched for Mayer, the army's initial goal was to defeat Marshal Nicholas Davout's Army of the Rhine in central Germany. French and allied German Confederation of the Rhine (Rheinbund) troops in southern Germany were also to be attacked, and all operations were to be undertaken with an eye toward supporting rebellion in those German states assessed to be particularly restive and inclined toward Austria. If all went well, initial operations would conclude with Davout soundly defeated and the Austrian army ensconced in a central position along the Neckar and the lower Rhine rivers before Napoleon could organise and transport significant reinforcements out of France.

Mayer kept the chief object of the Austrian offensive, Davout's army, firmly in focus and crafted his plan to place as many Habsburg troops as possible in a central position in the principal theatre of operations. He therefore massed five of Austria's nine regular corps (I to V Corps) and both of its Reserve Corps (127,000 men) in Bohemia, prepared to advance west towards Nuremberg. Two more regular corps (49,800 men) were to assemble south of the Danube, on the Inn (VI Corps) and at Salzburg (VIII Corps) respectively. It was hoped that Prussia would ally itself with Austria and contribute an additional 40,000 troops to the initial offensive.[4]

Mayer also planned operations on the monarchy's other borders. To the east, he detailed VII Corps to Cracow for an offensive strike into Poland, to knock the Grand Duchy of Warsaw's army out of the conflict and to put pressure on Prussia to join the Habsburg cause. To the south, IX Corps at Klagenfurt and Laibach would watch the frontier with Italy and contribute to the conquest of the southern portions of the Tyrol.

The French reaction

In distant Spain, Napoleon was following Austrian military developments with careful attention. In January 1809, as Vienna's intentions became apparent, he ordered the mobilisation of his Rheinbund allies and sped back to Paris to oversee preparations which he hoped would deter Austria from war. Before long, a tidal wave of orders was flooding out to his commanders, ministers and ambassadors, directing démarches to the Tsar, the call-up of conscripts, the marches of individual regiments and everything in between.

With most of his veterans in Spain, this intense activity was necessary if Napoleon was to meet the expected Austrian offensive with at least equal numbers. His shortage of troops was compounded by the wide dispersion of the forces immediately available. He hastened to concentrate them, but the middle of March still found French and Rheinbund battalions scattered from Hannover to Strasbourg. Of the five corps destined for southern Germany, only the French II, Bavarian VII and Württemberg VIII Corps (approximately 55,500 men in all) were fairly well assembled south of the Danube. Marshal Andre Massena's veteran IV Corps (33,700 men) was strung out on the roads leading from Strasbourg to Ulm, while Davout's enormous III Corps (61,300 men) – the core of the army – had only just begun to collect itself around Bamberg. Napoleon, however, was not overly concerned. Although he exerted himself to reinforce and concentrate his troops in Germany, he believed he would have enough time to prepare. As his Chief of Staff, Marshal Alexander Berthier, wrote to Davout on 27 March: 'His Majesty is still of the opinion that the Austrians cannot be ready before the end of April.' But Napoleon had misjudged his foe. The Austrians invaded Bavaria the very next day.

The Austrian decision to attack on 28 March 1809 only came after intense and acrimonious internal debate. When Mayer had first formulated his operations plan, he made important assumptions regarding enemy and friendly dispositions. In the first place, he expected to find the principal French forces, the target of the Austrian offensive, in Thuringia and northern Bavaria. Further, Stadion assured him that Prussia would join the Austrian cause, committing at least 40,000 men to the struggle in central

Germany. Given these considerations, the central position in Bohemia seemed to offer Austria the greatest strategic flexibility.

By mid-March, however, both of these assumptions had evaporated. An accumulating body of intelligence pointed to a French concentration south of or near the Danube (this was made up of Massena, Oudinot and the two Rheinbund corps), while a note from the Prussian foreign minister delicately explained that the King of Prussia 'regards a rupture between Austria and France as a misfortune for Europe in general and particularly for Germany.'[5] The Prussians would not march.

Citing these new circumstances, some of Mayer's rivals in the Austrian high command argued for a drastic change in plan: the bulk of the army should shift south of the Danube and advance across the Inn. Mayer was incensed by what he saw as an inordinately cautious – indeed, pusillanimous – plan. He acknowledged that an advance up the Danube valley offered better roads, allowed a closer connection to IX Corps on the Italian border and placed the army in the best position to block a French counter-thrust toward Vienna. In repeated conferences, however, he argued forcefully that Austria's best chance for success lay in catching the French army while it was still dispersed. An offensive from Bohemia, while more hazardous, would put the Habsburg army in a position to destroy Davout's scattered command north of the Danube before French forces south of the river could come to its assistance. Using Charles' own words – that a 'campaign must be opened quickly and with all strength at the decisive point' – Mayer won the day.[6] Furthermore, he capitalised on this success to drive home a second point: that the advance would have to begin soon, to hit the French before they were completely assembled, even if that meant moving before the Austrian army was itself fully prepared. Alarmed, the cautious corps commanders objected that 'most branches of the army are not yet ready for combat.'[7] They pointed out that some 54,000 men, including most of the army's light troops, were still on the march to join their regiments. In addition logistical arrangements were incomplete (magazines were not fully stocked, and horses and equipment for the considerable supply train were still being collected), some of the artillery had not yet arrived, and ammunition was not at authorised levels. But Mayer prevailed, and, on 20 March the Habsburg host departed its cantonments in central Bohemia and crowded onto the roads to the Bavarian border.

The Austrians attack

The active French intelligence apparatus noticed the Austrian move almost immediately. On 21 March, Colonel André Charles Méda of the 1st Chasseurs reported that 'The corps encamped in the districts around Pilsen, Saaz, Prague and Klattau are advancing toward the frontier.'[8] Davout forwarded this and other news to Berthier at Paris and ordered increased vigilance along his outpost line: 'Exercise the closest surveillance and keep the horses saddled at night.' The Bavarians along the Inn River noted similar developments. A report from Marshal François Lefebvre, commander of the Bavarian VII Corps, dated 27 March observed that 'There are large magazines of forage and considerable herds of cattle at Wels, and 20 bakeries there are working day and night ... Many troops are headed for Salzburg'. That very night, the alert Colonel Méda hastened a messenger to Davout: 'Your Grace, I have the honour to dispatch to you a sergeant as courier bearing the declaration of war ... I will gather in my outposts and warn the entire line.' Breathless couriers were soon splashing through the rain and sleet towards Paris, carrying this message and similar ones from Lefebvre to their Emperor. Napoleon, receiving these dispatches at 9 pm on 30 March, calmly remarked, 'They have crossed the Inn, it is war', and set to dictating orders. Eight hours later, he and his staff were on the road to Germany.

As Napoleon was learning of the unexpected Austrian invasion, the Archduke's army was slowly rolling into Bavaria. Under Charles' direct command, the bulk of the army pushed due west through the difficult passes of the Bohemian mountains in four large columns. On the northern-most route, I Corps was to advance from Plan to Pegnitz, covering the army's right flank. The next column – II and III Corps from Haid – would pass through the Amberg area before heading for Lauf. Leaving their assembly areas around Bischofteinitz and Prestitz, IV Corps, with the two Reserve Corps, would also march via Amberg, but would then turn slightly south-west toward Neumarkt in der Oberpfalz. The most demanding and critical mission fell to V Corps along the southern line of advance. This lone corps was to advance from Neugedein to Regensburg via Cham, leave outposts along the Danube toward Straubing and a garrison in Regensburg, and then swing north-west to Neumarkt, shielding the army's left flank as it marched. The opening phase would conclude when all four columns con-verged at Nuremberg, where Charles hoped to catch and defeat Davout's isolated corps.

While Charles led his 127,000 men toward Nuremberg, the 49,800 men of VI and VIII Corps were to clear the area between the Danube and the Tyrol and deceive the French as to Austrian intentions and dispositions. Charles hoped that these two corps, under command of VI Corps' commander, Feldmarschall-Leutnant Johann Hiller, would occupy Franco-Bavarian troops south of the great river and prevent them from interfering in the destruction of Davout.

The first few days of the invasion went smoothly for Charles. Nudging back French and Bavarian light cavalry screens, the Austrians were within striking distance of Amberg and Regensburg by the time Napoleon left Paris on the 31st. However, serious problems were already beginning to manifest themselves. Though the war was only four days old, the army's logistical

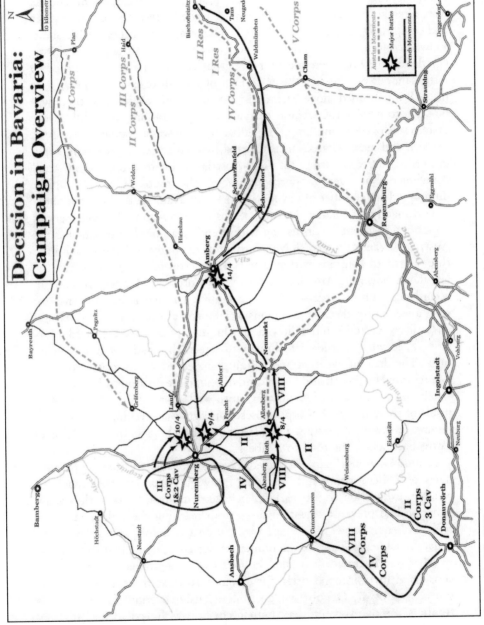

Decision in Bavaria: Campaign Overview

© John H. Gill, 2000

arrangements were near collapse and a profusion of supply vehicles was clogging the narrow roads through the Bohemian mountains, delaying the march of the rearward combat units. Steady rain, snow and sleet compounded problems on the main routes of march, and the corps commanders were already complaining that their men needed a rest-day to repair shoes and equipment. As one officer recalled, 'The weather was abominable and it snowed continually.'[9] There was a noticeable decline in the army's spirits. Charles acceded to the request for a rest-day on the 31st and attempted to restore morale by directing the gratis issue of a half-litre of wine per man, but his well-intentioned move backfired when it was discovered that there was no wine to issue – the wagons carrying the wine rations were still on the eastern side of the mountains.[10] Equally troubling was a dramatic increase in the sick and incapacitated men reported by each corps (approaching seven per cent of effective strength). The Austrian habit of dropping off small detachments at every opportunity along the route of march further diminished the number of bayonets and sabres available to the main body.

Fortunately for Charles, Davout's corps was too scattered to offer serious opposition. Although skirmishing with French rearguards intensified as the Austrian advance slogged slowly westwards, the night of 7 April found the three northern columns within twenty kilometres of Nuremberg. On the left flank, however, Archduke Ludwig's V Corps was lagging behind. In accordance with his orders, the young Ludwig had garrisoned Regensburg with a weak brigade (two battalions of infantry, a squadron of cavalry and an artillery battery) and followed the highway north-west toward Nuremberg, leaving another detachment to screen the road towards Regensburg. The dreadful weather and nagging anxiety about his open left flank had retarded his march and his column did not close up around Berngau (six kilometres south-west of Neumarkt) until well after dark on 7 April. As a result of these delays, V Corps' closest supports that evening were twenty kilometres away, consisting of IV Corps at Feucht and the two Reserve Corps back along the road to Amberg.

A mud-spattered courier reached Charles at Lauf late that night with news of Hiller's command. As with Ludwig, Hiller reported that bad weather, exhaustion, logistical deficiencies and uncertainty about the enemy situation had prevented his two corps from reaching their planned objectives. Hiller, however, chose not to mention the failure of his cavalry to collect reliable intelligence, the numerous detachments he had left behind, or what one historian has called Hiller's own 'operational anxiety'.[11] He considered his command utterly inadequate to clear the enemy from the south bank of the Danube while simultaneously covering the monarchy's frontiers. As one staff officer commented, he was forced to 'feel his way ahead in enemy territory as if in a fog'.[12] Needless to say, Hiller's advance was cautious and exceedingly slow.

Napoleon had stepped down from his carriage onto the cobbled pavement of Donauwörth shortly before dawn on 4 April. A strategy was already forming in his mind. Had the Austrian attack been delayed, he had intended to use Regensburg as a pivot for his operations and cut the enemy army off from its base of support in Bohemia. Although the unexpectedly early invasion had put Regensburg out of reach, this notion of separating Charles from Bohemia continued to influence Napoleon's analysis of the situation. Clues to his thinking appear in the orders he issued en route to the Danube valley. Initial reports from Davout and Lefebvre strongly suggested that the overwhelming mass of the enemy army was pressing toward Nuremberg and that Charles had placed only a token force south of the Danube. In Strasbourg on 2 April, therefore, the Emperor had directed II, IV, and VIII Corps to assemble at Donauwörth and told Général de Division Beaumont to move his division of provisional dragoon regiments from Strasbourg to Augsburg immediately. As a result, Napoleon was pleased to find the Württembergers already in place north of the Danube and soon learned that Massena's IV Corps and Général de Division Nicholas Charles Oudinot's II Corps would arrive later that day.

These three corps and their associated cavalry gave Napoleon a mass of 55,000 men to throw against Charles' left flank while Davout held the Austrians in the front. Lefebvre's VII Corps, though outnumbered, would have to contain Hiller's force, but could fall back on the fortress of Augsburg or escape north of the Danube in the unlikely event that the Austrians became energetic. Beaumont's provisional dragoons, raw as they were, would add a French presence south of the Danube. Furthermore, Napoleon hastily sent officers flying to every corner of the Rheinbund to sweep up every available soldier. His brother Jerome's X Corps would remain in northern Germany to keep the population from becoming restive, but a Westphalian division at Metz, a French division in Hannover, the Saxon IX Corps at Dresden and a collection of smaller German contingents, all-in-all some 31,000 men, were soon on the march for Bavaria.

Meanwhile, Napoleon wrote to Davout, informing him of the general plan and directing him to hold one of the big III Corps divisions out of the immediate fight if possible. Having set the army in motion, he rode out to inspect fortifications, meet with his corps commanders and receive the enthusiastic cheers of Massena's battalions as they crossed the turbulent Danube. 'In one month we will be in Vienna,' he told them.[13] At 2 am the next morning (5 April) these men and their emperor headed north by forced marches for Nuremberg.

Battle at Allersberg

Saturday 8 April dawned 'dreary, raw and rainy', in the words of one veteran. For the Austrians of Archduke Ludwig's V Corps it meant an unpleasant day's march through cold drizzle to Allersberg before turning north-west towards Nuremberg and, they hoped, more or less comfortable lodgings in a village or town. However, as the lead elements of the corps – troopers of the Kienmayer Hussar Regiment – were passing through Allersberg they noticed French light cavalry on the hills to the south. Supported by a battery of horse-artillery, the hussars quickly formed up and chased off the prying Frenchmen.

Cresting the nearest hill, the Austrian horsemen then spotted French infantry columns hastening up the road from Hilpoltstein. This was the lead brigade of Oudinot's corps, which had left Donauwörth by the Weissenburg road on 5 April. Austrian infantry were soon brought up to confront them and a hot, if rather undirected, action slowly unfolded along the wooded hillsides. As more French infantry arrived, Oudinot fed them into battle on his right, extending the skirmish line to the east. Ludwig and his advisors did likewise. With some 5,000 men and two batteries detached between Neumarkt and Regensburg, V Corps only had 18,000 men available for this fight and it was all the Austrians could do to contain the eager if inexperienced Frenchmen. The battle would likely have ended in a draw had Général de Division Dominique Vandamme's Württemberg corps not appeared unexpectedly on Ludwig's right flank at around 3 pm. The Austrian commander had fed most of his men into the struggle with Oudinot by this time, and his weak right quickly began to crumble under the sudden onslaught of the Württembergers. As the V Corps chief of staff desperately tried to shift several battalions to cope with this new danger, the Württemberg Light Infantry Brigade burst through a gap in the Austrian centre and threatened to cut the corps in two. The Austrian retreat rapidly degenerated into a panicked rout as units lost all sense of cohesion in the broken, wooded terrain. Only the fall of night and poor co-ordination between Oudinot and Vandamme saved V Corps from complete destruction. As it was, Austrian losses exceeded 5,000 as against French and Württemberger casualties amounting to no more than 1,200. Its morale shattered by the sudden surprise of the Württemberg attack and the disorderly retreat that followed, V Corps withdrew toward Neumarkt in great confusion.

The repercussions of the battle of Allersberg were felt throughout both armies. For the French and their German allies, it was confirmation of Napoleon's military superiority, a prelude to greater triumphs. There was a palpable sense of the initiative shifting. The Habsburg troops, on the other hand, were deeply shaken by the defeat of V Corps and the knowledge that Napoleon had now personally taken the field against them. They were by no means crushed or broken, but from 8 April on the tide of events increasingly ran in favour of the French.

Napoleon had reached the Allersberg battlefield at dusk on the 8th.

Riding among the jubilant Württembergers, he had congratulated them and their commander before sending them off into the damp night in pursuit of Ludwig's corps. His plan for 9 April was for Vandamme to complete the destruction of V Corps while Oudinot and the 3rd Heavy Cavalry Division joined Massena and the 2nd Heavy Cavalry Division to strike the left flank of Charles' main force at Nuremberg.

The decisive confrontation

The Austrian I and II Corps had spent 8 April in desultory skirmishing with Davout near Nuremberg, as Charles endeavoured to concentrate his army for a decisive blow. During the day, however, as evidence of a significant battle at Allersberg mounted, he sent first III Corps and then the two Reserve Corps toward Neumarkt to support Ludwig. As the full extent of the V Corps debacle became clear late in the evening, the archduke ordered IV Corps to probe southwards at first light in the hope of re-establishing contact with his overly extended left flank.

Charles' dispositions had two immediate consequences for the fighting that raged around Nuremberg on 9–10 April. First, by sending III Corps and the Reserve Corps to assist Ludwig's battered command the Austrian commander dispersed his troops in the face of the enemy and made it impossible for either of these corps to contribute effectively in the coming battle. Second, his orders to IV Corps meant that it would fight a meeting engagement when it collided with the advancing French on the 9th. The Austrians could perform very well indeed in a set-piece combat on clear terrain, but they were at a serious disadvantage when pitted against the mobile French in battles that demanded open order tactics and a high degree of battlefield flexibility.

Feldmarschall-Leutnant Franz Rosenberg's 13,000 men thus found themselves in considerable difficulty when they and Oudinot's 17,000 blundered into one another in the early afternoon of 9 April. They held their own, however, until Massena's leading divisions arrived on their right flank. Forced back, the corps suffered heavily under punishing attacks by Oudinot's division of cuirassiers. Thanks to self-sacrificing charges by the Vincent Chevauxlegers and Stipsicz Hussars, Rosenberg was able to disengage his battered battalions as darkness fell and withdraw to the north, where I and II Corps could provide support.

After a chill night punctuated by sharp exchanges of musketry, Napoleon sent the French II and IV Corps forward against the new Austrian position. Charles had his three available corps deployed just east of Nuremberg in an open 'L' formation, with I Corps on the right (north), II Corps at the apex, and Rosenberg's weakened IV Corps on the exposed left. Although the French attack developed slowly, the steadily increasing pressure forced Charles to repeatedly draw units from his right to shore up Rosenberg's flagging troops. Napoleon, with Davout's large corps of veterans almost unengaged, watched the battle ripen. By early afternoon, however, elements of the Austrian I Reserve Corps, hastily recalled by Charles, were beginning to appear on the road from Altdorf and Oudinot had to call off his push against Rosenberg to face this new threat. Although the Habsburg position was not as compromised as he had hoped, Napoleon therefore decided he could wait no longer and unleashed Davout's two left flank divisions. Rolling forward under the leaden April skies, the 21,000 superb soldiers of Général Charles Morand's and Général Louis Friant's divisions crashed into the thinned lines of General der Kavallerie Heinrich Graf Bellegarde's I Corps. The Austrians held for a time, but their situation was hopeless. They buckled and broke. Davout then hurled his 3rd Division and the 3,000 'iron horsemen' of the 2nd Heavy Cavalry Division at II Corps. It was too much, and the Austrian position collapsed. As dusk turned to night, the road to Amberg was choked with a disorganised, panicked mob of Austrian fugitives streaming east.

Luckily for Charles, the Austrian III Corps under Feldmarschall-Leutnant Friedrich Franz Fürst Hohenzollern-Hechingen was marching up from Lauterhofen. In a series of sharp rearguard clashes over the next three days, Hohenzollern's men courageously covered the withdrawal of the shattered army (I, II, IV Corps) along the road from Lauf to Amberg. Simultaneously, V Corps and the Reserve Corps withdrew along the Neumarkt-Amberg road pursued by Oudinot, Vandamme and the 3rd Heavy Cavalry Division. For Charles, all thought of a drive to the Rhine was now gone. To save his army, he decided to make a stand at Amberg, ground he knew from a victory he had gained there in 1796. Deep in the grip of despondency, he wrote to the Kaiser telling him that 'with half the army in dissolution, I have no choice but to march back to Bohemia', and urged a quick peace to preserve the monarchy.[14]

The stubborn III Corps rearguard actions gave Charles time to restore some order in the rest of the army and establish a position north and west of Amberg. He hoped to check the pursuing French in a defensive battle so that his cumbersome baggage columns could withdraw back through the difficult defiles into Bohemia. With its supply trains secure, the army could then conduct a fighting withdrawal over the mountains and recover its strength behind their protective shield. Unfortunately for Charles, his plans began to unravel almost as soon as they were issued. As Hohenzollern's men, exhausted by unrelenting rearguard duty, neared the Amberg position on the afternoon of 13 April, General-Major Ludwig Thierry's brigade went astray. Massena's advance guard caught the Austrians unawares and, when the Baden and Hessian light horse crushed a retreating square, Thierry's defence disintegrated. The French captured Thierry and more than a thousand of his men in the wild chase that followed, and then swept up much of General-Major Nicholas von Kayser's brigade as well. Their momentum carried them to Karmensölden, five kilometres west of Amberg, where the Austrian II Corps brought the now disorganised pursuit to a halt.

In the meantime the rest of Napoleon's army had reached the battlefield. Nightfall found the French host arrayed in a semicircle north and west of Amberg: Oudinot at Ullersberg, Vandamme's Württembergers south of Ammerthal, Massena around and behind Siebeneichen, and Davout's corps in the arc of woods north and north-east of Trasslberg. Composing his orders that evening, Napoleon wrote: 'I am determined to eradicate Prince Charles' army today or at the latest tomorrow.'[15]

On the Austrian side of the field, the hilly terrain and the need to cover the roads through Amberg had forced Charles to adopt an unsatisfactory defensive position. He posted Bellegarde's I Corps on the right to guard the northern approaches east of the Vils; II Corps formed his centre between the Vils and the Ammerbach; V Corps held an extended stretch of open slopes on the left; and the two Reserve Corps were marshalled in the low ground south of Amberg. During the night, he sent the over-strained III and IV Corps back to secure the crossings over the Naab River for the forthcoming retreat.

Napoleon planned to open the battle by launching II Corps against the Austrian left, to threaten Charles' line of retreat and draw off his reserves before committing VIII, IV and III Corps in sequence from right to left. Shaking the rime off their coats and snatching a meagre meal and a shot of brandy, Oudinot's young conscripts went forward at mid-morning. A bitter contest for Lengenloh and Gailoh was soon in progress. The French seized part of the latter village, but could not take it all despite courageous exertions, and by noon it was clear that Oudinot's attack had stalled without seriously diminishing Charles' reserves. Anxious to nail the Austrian army in place and destroy it, Napoleon sent staff officers hurrying to his remaining three corps with orders for them to advance at once. Shortly before 1 pm, therefore, five French infantry divisions, supported by the 2nd Heavy Cavalry Division, advanced against the Austrian centre. Simultaneously, Davout's 4th Division and a light cavalry brigade swung wide to the east to pressure the Austrian right in the Krumb valley. Moreover, in order to provide a powerful reserve Napoleon concentrated the 1st Divisions of Davout's and Massena's corps and the 1st Heavy Cavalry Division in the Vils valley, around Trasslberg and Schweighof.

The French gained Shüflohe and Ammersricht in their initial onslaught, but the attack lost momentum as it came up to the main I and II Corps positions. However, as these advances degenerated into extended firefights other French forces were beginning to lend their weight to the attack. With Shüflohe cleared, Massena was able to deploy his 4th Division, and these

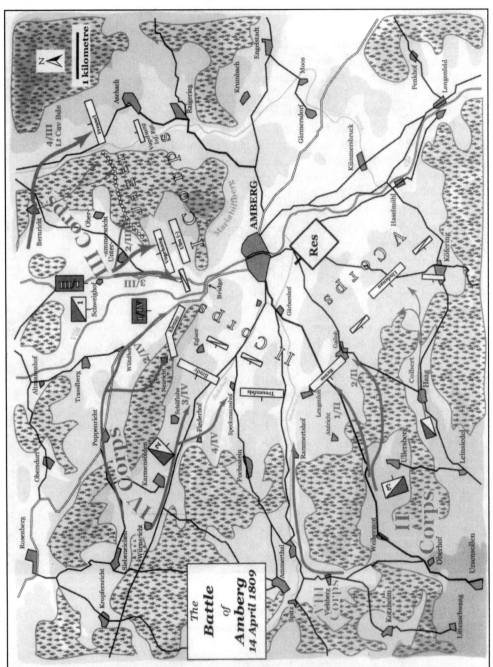

The
Battle
of
Amberg
14 April 1809

© John H. Gill, 2000

men were soon masters of Speckmannshof. The capture of this hamlet and the belated advance of the Württembergers up the Ammerbach valley forced back the left wing of II Corps and put nearly unbearable pressure on the seam between it and V Corps. Ludwig withdrew his right and Lengenloh fell to Vandamme's men. Meanwhile, Davout's 4th Division had thrown back Feldmarschall-Leutnant Graf Fresnel's weak division and was engaged with the Vogelsang Infantry Regiment in a brutal hand-to-hand struggle for possession of Aschach.

Napoleon now judged the time right to commit his *masse de décision*. Inspired by Massena, the 26th Légère and 18th Ligne of Général de Division Claude Legrand's 1st Division advanced from their reserve position southeast of Wützlhof. The last remnants of Austrian resistance on the west bank of the Vils dissipated almost instantly, and the two French regiments surged forward to drive a deep wedge between the Austrian I and II Corps. Though disordered by their rapid charge and their passage of the narrow defile between the river and the hills, the cheering French infantry was pushing towards Amberg itself when Charles rode up at the head of five grenadier battalions. Momentarily seizing a standard, he pointed at the approaching blue line and sent his men forward in a desperate counter-charge. The sudden attack by the grenadiers scattered the disordered French and sent them reeling back across the Vils bridge in great confusion. Massena himself was almost captured in the tumult.

Luckily for the French, two nearby commanders responded quickly and decisively on their own initiative. First, Colonel Louis Chouard – whose 2nd Cuirassiers had ridden forward to support the infantry – led his regiment in a violent charge that overthrew the grenadiers and hurled them back across the bridge. The 9th Cuirassiers and, shortly thereafter, the entire 1st Heavy Cavalry Division followed, rolling forward in a thunderous mass on both sides of the Vils. The other officer was General Legrand, the 1st Division commander. On observing the Austrian attack, he galloped to the Baden Brigade and led it forward at a trot. This combined infantry and cavalry assault was as irresistible as it was spontaneous, and the grenadiers tumbled back into Amberg with the French horsemen and Baden foot-soldiers hard on their heels.[16]

With the Badeners racing through the streets of the town and French heavy cavalry swarming around its outskirts, the centre of Charles' position was pierced. The rest of his line was in equally dire condition. On the left, II Corps was finally threatening to give way under increasing pressure from Massena and Vandamme. On his right, Davout's 4th Division had taken Aschach and French voltigeurs were probing out of the woods near Krumbach. The archduke ordered a general retreat and turned to General der Kavallerie Johannes Fürst Liechtenstein, commander of the reserves, to cover it. Throwing his dragoons and cuirassiers at the advancing French around Amberg, Liechtenstein gained time to establish his remaining grenadiers on a low rise south of Gärmersdorf. Here they formed a dam which held off pursuit long enough for the remains of the army to escape. By the time Davout's 1st and 4th Divisions were in a position to undertake a concentrated attack on Liechtenstein's position, night was falling and the demoralised Habsburg columns were headed for the bridges over the Naab.

Victory and defeat

The Naab, however, afforded the beaten Austrians but little shelter. His own spirit broken and his army incapable of offering serious resistance, Charles retreated to Bohemia, losing his baggage columns, his bridge train and thousands of prisoners in the process. Trapped in the mountain defiles, entire units dissolved, to be swept up by the French and their German allies. The news from the other theatres of war was equally disturbing. South of the Danube, Hiller was retreating to the Inn as rapidly as he could, impelled by vague reports of the calamities suffered by the main army. Further south, IX Corps found itself faced with imminent attack by overwhelming French and Italian forces from Italy and Dalmatia. Finally, VII Corps in Poland was at an operational dead end, occupying Warsaw but unable to accomplish its mission of eliminating the Polish Army.

Napoleon, on the other hand, was on the verge of another victorious war. By 17 April, he had concentrated his exhausted but exultant army at Waldmünchen on the very frontiers of Bohemia, and had sent his light cavalry probing as far as Bischofteinitz. In the course of the preceding two weeks, he had regained the initiative and inflicted a devastating defeat on the principal Habsburg army. He was now poised to invade the monarchy, complete the destruction of its army and occupy its capital. On 22 April, in Budweis, he received the first Austrian peace proposal. On 1 May, he dictated his own terms in Vienna.

NOTES

1. Georg Freiherr von Valentini, *Versuch einer Geschichte des Feldzugs von 1809 an der Donau*, 2nd edn (Berlin, 1818), pp.282–3.
2. Quote paraphrased from a Stadion memorandum of 12 October 1808, cited in Hellmuth Rössler, *Oesterreichs Kampf um Deutschlands Befreiung* (Hamburg, 1940), vol.I, p.393.
3. Charles to Mayer, according to the latter's recollections (Mayer, 'Journal für das Jahr 1809', Austrian State Archives, Nachlass Mayer von Heldensfeld, B/857, no.111).
4. All strength figures refer to infantry and cavalry only (*ie* they do not include artillery, engineers, etc).
5. Prussian foreign minister to the Austrian ambassador, 13 March 1809, cited in Adolf Beer, *Zehn Jahre österreichischer Politik* (Leipzig, 1877), p.361.

6. Paraphrased from *Gründsätze der höheren Kriegskunst für die Generäle der österrei-chischen Armee*, in Charles' *Ausgewählte Schriften* (Wien, 1893), vol.I, p.7.

7. From the main army's Operations Journal, quoted in Christian Freiherr Binder von Kriegelstein, *Der Krieg Napoleons gegen Oesterreich 1809* (Berlin, 1906), vol.I, p.98.

8. Colonel Méda's report, quoted in Delphin Charles Oré, *1er Régiment de Chasseurs* (Chateudun, 1903), p.119.

9. Pierre-Martin Pirquet, *Journal de Campagne* (Liege, 1970), p.82.

10. The wine story is true, as is the resort to a rest-day (the Austrians rested on 13 April after crossing the border on the 10th).

11. Binder von Kriegelstein used the phrase 'strategic anxiety' to describe Austrian worries about the safety of the monarchy (Binder, *op.cit.* vol.I, pp.95–7).

12. Recollections of Lieutenant von Hess, quoted in *Krieg 1809* (Wien, 1907), vol.I, p.218.

13. Quote from a speech Napoleon gave to the Württemberg troops on 20 April 1809.

14. Paraphrased from an actual letter Charles wrote to the Kaiser on 23 April 1809.

15. Quote from a note Napoleon sent to Davout on 22 April 1809.

16. This sequence is based on an incident during the battle of Znaim, 11 July 1809.

THE REALITY

A number of important changes were necessary to make this scenario viable. In the first place, the timing of the Austrian offensive was advanced by nearly two weeks from 10 April to 28 March 1809. This was based on the actual availability of Habsburg forces that spring. As the army could not have moved out of its dispersed assembly areas any earlier than 20 March and would have taken at least a week to get into position near the frontier, 28 March was the earliest reasonable date it could have entered Bavaria. Secondly, one of the factors that delayed the opening of the actual invasion was the last minute decision to change the line of operations from Bohemia to the Danube valley. Our fictional scenario thus left the base of operations unchanged to speed the crossing of the border and to pose a greater and more direct threat to Davout's rather isolated corps. Thirdly, this scenario grants the Austrian main army about 20,000 additional troops in the form of VIII Corps attacking out of Salzburg. This was the deployment called for in Mayer's original operations plan. It was changed early in the actual Austrian planning to increase the forces under Archduke John on the Italian front, but retaining it for this version allowed a greater concentration of force in Bohemia and made the possibility of a subsidiary offensive across the Inn more realistic.

Of course, all of these points assume a greater degree of aggressiveness and decision in the command culture of the Austrian Army than was actually the case. In reality, the conservative outlook of the Habsburg military leadership effectively precluded an invasion as early as 28 March, or the use of Bohemia as base of operations instead of the more secure Danube valley, or the assignment of only one regular corps to the Italian border to strengthen the main effort in Germany. Mayer was therefore left in this fictional account to provide a powerful command presence that might have given the army the impetus it needed to act more decisively. In fact, Mayer was cashiered in February in a tangle of malicious intrigues and replaced by General-Major Johann von Prochaska – 'one of the most mediocre officers of the army' as Archduke John described him in his *Feldzugserzählungen 1809*, ed. Alois Veltzé (Wien, 1909), p.28.

Finally, it is worth noting two considerations on the French side that might have made an early Austrian attack even more disastrous for the Habsburg Empire than the actual 10 April date. Firstly, much of the danger run by the French army that April arose from Napoleon's absence from the theatre of war and his representation by his Chief of Staff, Marshal Berthier, for the first week of hostilities. Had the Austrians attacked earlier, Napoleon would have learned of the invasion before Berthier had departed Paris and the two would logically have travelled together to the front, eliminating one of the major causes of confusion in the French command structure. Secondly, in the actual campaign Napoleon turned towards Vienna rather than crossing the river in pursuit after defeating Charles in a series of battles south of the Danube near Regensburg. He thus allowed Charles to escape into Bohemia and had to face a reinvigorated foe a month later at the battle of Aspern-Essling. Had the Austrians attacked out of Bohemia, however, it is highly likely Napoleon would have truly 'erased' them as they tried to flee through the mountain passes. With Charles and the main Austrian army neutralised or destroyed, the war would likely have ended much earlier, without the need for another major battle.

BIBLIOGRAPHY

Beer, Adolf, *Zehn Jahre österreichischer Politik* (Leipzig, 1877).
Charles, Archduke of Austria, *Ausgewählte Schriften* (Wien, 1893).
John, Archduke of Austria, *Feldzugserzählungen 1809*, ed. Alois Veltzé, (Wien, 1909).
— *Krieg 1809* (Wien, 1907).
Kriegelstein, Christian Freiherr Binder von, *Der Krieg Napoleons gegen Oesterreich 1809* (Berlin, 1906).
Oré, Delphin Charles, *1er Régiment de Chasseurs* (Châteudun, 1903).
Pirquet, Pierre-Martin, *Journal de Campagne* (Liege, 1970).
Rössler, Hellmuth, *Oesterreichs Kampf um Deutschlands Befreiung* (Hamburg, 1940).
Valentini, Georg Freiherr von, *Versuch einer Geschichte des Feldzugs von 1809 an der Donau*, 2nd edn (Berlin, 1818).

THE RUSSIANS AT BORODINO

BY DIGBY SMITH

Two Cossacks urged their rough little ponies down into the lower Kolotscha stream at the ford opposite the now-deserted hamlet of Novoie Selo, and rode cautiously across. It was 7.30 on a fine morning – the 7th of September – but very few of the 220,000 men of the Russian and French armies facing each other about a mile to the south of the ford had time to appreciate either the gently rolling countryside or the weather; their minds were on much more serious things. The massive artillery duel between the French *Grande Armée* and the Russians, which had started before six o'clock, hammered on, as, south of the Kolotscha, the 'Bagration Fleches' and their Russian garrisons were pounded into ruins in preparation for the impending assault.

The Cossacks rode forward over the crest of the little valley, taking advantage of the cover of the trees and bushes scattered over the plain to their front. About 100 yards behind them followed a group of sixty or so other Cossacks, grouped around a slight, middle-aged figure on a grey of obviously better breeding than most of the other horses. He wore the dark blue, silver-trimmed costume and black Astrakhan colpack of the Ataman of the Don Cossacks, his throat and left breast hung with orders and decorations. This was General of Cavalry Matvei Ivanovich Platov who, with his small escort, had left his own lines to establish what the enemy was up to on the northern flank of the battlefield.

Already the village of Borodino on the new Moscow-Smolensk road had been ripped from Russian hands by Prince Eugene's IV Corps, but his attempted exploitation of this local success, in an effort to attack the 'Grand Battery' on the slight hill south of the village, had been bloodily repulsed. The bridge over the Kolotscha had been destroyed and the situation had been static here for over an hour.

What was the enemy doing? Platov intended to find out.

After a ride of about ten minutes he had at least part of the answer. Apart from the garrison in Borodino itself (the 8e Légère and the 1er Croatian infantry regiments of Delzons' 13th Division) the open plain north of the stream and road was empty of troop formations. Having reached Bessubovo, Platov could see the great mass of French and allied artillery and baggage vehicles stretched westward along and around the road and the village of Valueva; but no troops, no flank guard.

This was an incredible opportunity! But this chance, this gift from God,

had to be seized – and quickly – before it slipped away. Platov must tell
Kutuzov at once and return with an adequate force to strike at this rich
target. With a little luck the Russians might well be able to frustrate
Napoleon's entire plan. Platov turned to his ADC, Colonel the Prince of
Hessen-Philippstal, and told him to report the situation to Kutuzov as
quickly as possible and request permission for Platov to raid the enemy train
with all of his 5,000 Cossacks.[1]

The absence of enemy troops north of the Kolotscha resulted from the
fact that Prince Eugene, in a renewed effort to carry out Napoleon's orders
to take the Grand Battery, had moved his entire command – consisting of
IV Corps, part of I Corps, Grouchy's III Cavalry Corps and two brigades of
Bavarian cavalry – back from Borodino and south over the Kolotscha so as
to approach his target over terrain unencumbered by such obstacles as the
stream. His failure to leave adequate forces to cover his northern flank was
to cost him very dear indeed.

Russian plans

As the Prince of Hessen-Philippstal splashed back through the ford at
Novoie Selo, he met Colonel von Toll of Kutuzov's staff. When the dis-
covery and Platov's suggested attack were outlined to him, von Toll agreed
entirely with the plan and joined Hessen-Philippstal in presenting it to
Kutuzov. Moreover, he suggested that not only the Cossacks but also
Uvarov's I Cavalry Corps should participate in the action.

Shortly after this, an ADC of General Tuchkov, commander of III Corps
– which was defending the sector just south of the Bagration Fleches –
rushed up to Kutuzov's headquarters to request reinforcements urgently,
Tuchkov's command being threatened by Napoleon's main thrust in that
sector. After a brief discussion, Kutuzov sent Bachmetiev's 23rd Division of
Ostermann-Tolstoy's IV Corps; nothing more could be spared so early in
the day. By 9 am the 23rd was heading south toward the point of danger.

At 9.30 am, von Toll and Hessen-Philippstal reached Kutuzov's forward
headquarters on the hill at Gorki, where they found him surrounded by a
crowd of ADCs, senior officers, guards, servants and a handful of black-
robed priests with icons and incense burners. Colonel von Toll quickly
explained the opportunity which had presented itself on their northern flank
and the plans to exploit it. Kutuzov listened with an air of apparent
boredom, scanning the battlefield to the south-west as he did so. 'Well
gentlemen,' he said when von Toll had finished, 'what should we do?' Major
General Eugen, Duke of Württemberg, commander of the 4th Infantry
Division of Baggowut's II Infantry Corps, was quick to answer. 'Sire, this is
indeed a golden opportunity, but if we are to exploit it fully, we must not
send cavalry alone; a force of *all* arms must be sent. At least one corps of
infantry should go as well.'[2] His suggestion being rapidly agreed to by the

other commanders present, Kutuzov nodded. 'Very well, take the Cossacks, Uvarov's cavalry – and Karl Fedorovich [Baggowut]: would you be so kind as to support him? Such a stroke might well relieve the pressure against our centre.'

Whilst these Russian deliberations continued, Prince Eugene's IV Corps (less Delzons' 13th Division), together with Grouchy's III Cavalry Corps, was moving forwards south of them to assault the Grand Battery. The French advanced skirmishers gradually pushed back the 5th, 6th, 41st and 42nd Russian Jägers deployed in the scrub and bushes along the Semenovska stream about 1,000 metres in front of the Battery, and began to fire at the gun crews in the Battery itself. Eugene's artillery had crossed the Kolotscha by means of three simple bridges, built to facilitate lateral movement behind the French front at Alexinki, and this was now brought forward to bombard the Grand Battery. The area between and around the opposing batteries rapidly filled with thick smoke, which offered some cover to the advancing French infantry. Flanking fire was also poured into the target from a battery left north of the Kolotscha, west of the Voina stream. This first assault was by Broussier's 14th Division and went in against Rajevsky's VII Corps in and around the simple earthwork at 10 am. It failed in the face of heavy canister fire and the French recoiled to the western side of the Semenovska stream to reorganise.

The charge

At 10.30, the trumpets and drums announced that the regiments of the Russian spoiling force were moving off to thrust into the vacuum left north of the Kolotscha by Eugene. A horde of over 5,000 Cossacks, loosely grouped into their *Pulks*, led the way; then came I Cavalry Corps – twenty-eight squadrons, or 2,500 horsemen – with twelve guns. Behind the cavalry marched II Corps, comprising 10,300 men (twenty-four battalions) and twenty-four guns.[3]

At 10.45 a second French assault, by Morand's 1st Division and Montbrun's II Cavalry Corps, was launched against the Grand Battery.[4] The infantry went in using the *ordre mixte*, with the 30e Ligne, under General Bonamy, in the lead and the 13e Légère following behind. At close range the 30e poured a volley into the Poltava Regiment of Paskevich's 26th Division, who were to the side of the battery, and then rushed in with the bayonet. Their assault came at an opportune moment, for it seems that the Russian guns had just fired their last canister rounds and were temporarily out of action.[5] After a bitter struggle and violent hand-to-hand combat, the 30e succeeded in taking the Grand Battery. Though wounded in the leg a few days earlier, General Raevsky, the Battery commander, was nevertheless able to escape capture.

General Bonamy was master of the Battery only briefly, as no additional

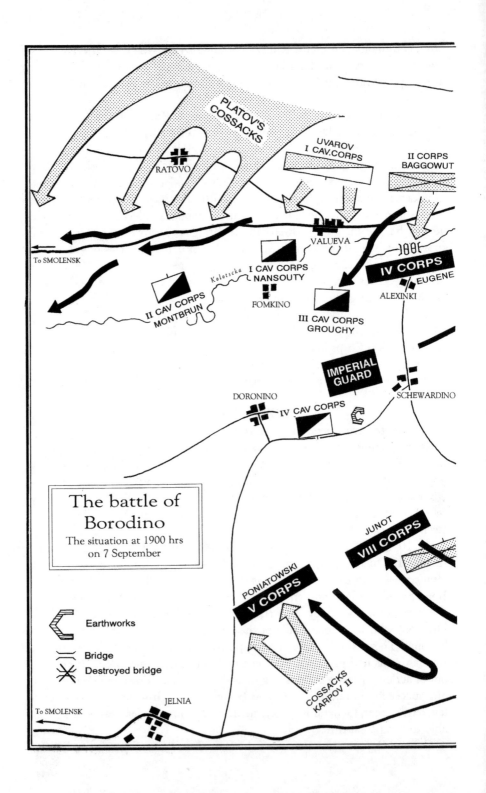

PLATOV'S COSSACKS

RATOVO

UVAROV
I CAV.CORPS

II CORPS
BAGGOWUT

VALUEVA

To SMOLENSK

Kolotscha

I CAV CORPS
NANSOUTY

IV CORPS

EUGENE

II CAV CORPS
MONTBRUN

FOMKINO

III CAV CORPS
GROUCHY

ALEXINKI

IMPERIAL
GUARD

SCHEWARDINO

DORONINO

IV CAV CORPS

The battle of Borodino
The situation at 1900 hrs
on 7 September

JUNOT

VIII CORPS

PONIATOWSKI

V CORPS

Earthworks

Bridge

Destroyed bridge

COSSACKS
KARPOV II

JELNIA

To SMOLENSK

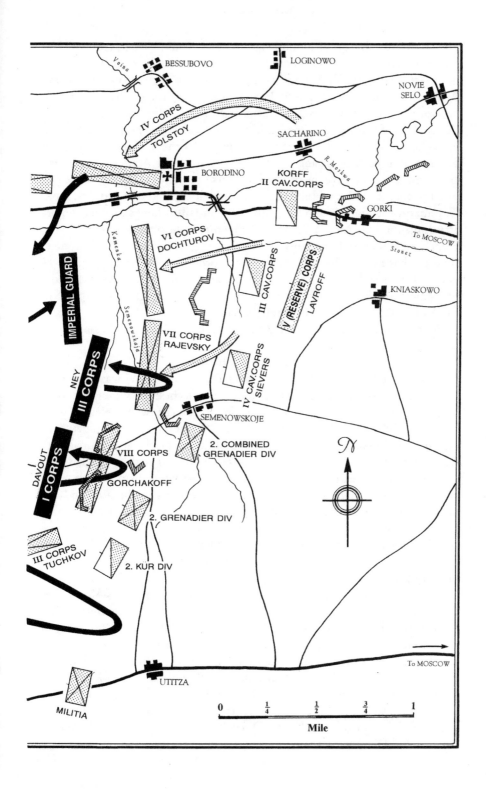

French troops came up to support him. As luck would have it, Kutuzov had just given General Ermolov the task of taking two (some reports say three) horse-artillery batteries and other units south to assist Bagration's 2nd Army as it reeled under massive French assaults on the Fleches (Bagration himself was wounded during the bitter fighting). As Ermolov passed along the bottom of the slight valley behind the Grand Battery, he looked up to his right and saw French uniforms swarming over the hill crest and Russian gunners and infantry fleeing down the reverse slope. Acting instinctively and on his own initiative, he ordered the horse-batteries to unlimber and fire into the enemy, and, grabbing the units nearest to hand (the 3rd Battalion, Ufa Infantry Regiment, and the 18th, 19th and 40th Jägers), led a counter-attack up the hill. After a desperate, fifteen-minute struggle, he drove the French out. General Bonamy, wounded several times with bayonets, shouted that he was the King of Naples in order to save his life, and it was not until he was brought before Kutuzov and correctly identified that the premature Russian jubilation died away. Strangely enough, this 'capture of the King' was to be repeated later the same day.

Eugene, meanwhile, had pulled back to regroup for a third assault.

The battle continues

Meanwhile, to the south, the battle for the Bagration Fleches was raging on.

We do not know if there were two or three fleches; eyewitness accounts vary, and no records were kept at the time of exactly what defences were hurriedly thrown up in September 1812. At the end of the nineteenth century, the Russians reconstructed two full fleches on the approximate site (each pierced to take a full battery of twelve guns) with a third, much smaller, V-shaped earthwork to the rear of and between them, with its apex pointing south. There are no strong natural features in the area and the approaches to the Fleches from the French lines are flat and open. The works themselves were built in a great hurry by the Moscow militia, and there was neither time nor tools to construct the gabions needed to give their loose earth walls the rigidity and strength required to stand up to the impact of artillery projectiles.

The garrison of the Fleches consisted of General Borozdin's VIII Corps (Neverovsky's 27th Division and Prince Karl von Mecklenburg's 2nd Grenadier Division) of General of Infantry Prince Bagration's 2nd Army of the West. In direct support, around the demolished village of Seme-novskaya, were Woronzov's 2nd Combined Grenadier Division, Duka's 2nd Kürassier Division and eighty-four guns. A screen of Jägers, made up of the 49th and 50th Regiments, was deployed in front of the works.[6]

Marshal Davout's I Corps made the first assault, Compans' 5th Division aiming for the southern fleche and Desaix's 4th going for the northern one. Friant's 2nd Division came up in support. The other two divisions of I Corps

Christmas Eve at Berehaven, 1796. During a brief lull in the gale, the newly-landed General Hoche (seated) receives a gloomy report on his logistic situation, while General Humbert (right) urges a bold advance without guns or baggage.

Below: The French capture the old West Gate at Clonmel, late in the afternoon of 10 January 1797. The contemporary artist has shown how few of the British defenders stood to fight, but he has forgotten the thick blizzard which engulfed the battlefield.

Left: Theobald Wolfe Tone, the founder and revered first president of the Hibernian Republic, which gained full international recognition by the Treaty of Lille, 3 September 1797. Wolfe Tone spectacularly realised his life-long dream that all Irishmen would at last be united in peace and harmony.

Below: General Bonaparte: conqueror of Egypt, Palestine and Syria.

Above left: Horatio Nelson was deficient in two of the essential qualities of a great naval commander – luck and tenacity – and failed to prevent French domination of the Mediterranean.

Above right: Sidney Smith, captured by the French fleet on his way to Acre.

Below: General Bonaparte receives the surrender of Acre.

Jean-Andoche Junot, duc d'Abrantes (1771–1813), French commander in Portugal in 1808 and the victor of Vimeiro.

Arthur Wellesley (1769–1852), the British commander victorious at Roliça but who occupied only a subordinate position in the defeat at Vimeiro.

Above: Vimeiro: British troops attempt, without success, to stem Loison's attack.

Below left: French infantry, 1809. Hard-marching veterans, such as these light infantrymen of Davout's III Corps, provided Napoleon with an important tactical edge in the opening phase of the 1809 campaign.

Below right: General-Major Anton Freiherr Mayer von Heldensfeld. As the Austrian Quartermaster General, Mayer developed the army's operational plans and energetically defended them against numerous skeptics.

Left: Matvei Ivanovich Platov, Count and Ataman of the Don Cossacks and catalyst behind the launching of the flanking raid at Borodino. This raid defeated Napoleon's plans to conquer Russia in 1812.

Below: General-Adjutant F. P. Uvarov, commander of the I Russian Cavalry Corps, leading his troops in the legendary flanking raid which tipped the scales at the battle of Borodino.

Opposite page, top: The church in Borodino village. It survived the battle relatively intact.

Opposite page, bottom: The Russian monument to the flanking raid at Borodino.

Right: General Bronikowski, governor of Minsk in November 1812. His energy and skill ensured a successful defence of the city and guaranteed Napoleon plentiful supplies throughout the winter of 1812.

Below: General Dombrowski came to the relief of Minsk at a crucial moment. He was rewarded by Napoleon and later commanded the Polish armed forces after the re-establishment of that kingdom in March 1813.

Admiral Chichagov, accompanied by his brilliant entourage, directs his troops as they surround Minsk. The Russian assaults were beaten off and the discouraged admiral and his army would soon blunder northwards towards Napoleon's depleted, but still aggressive, *Grande Armée*.

Alexander I flees the field of Kulm. Here the emperor of Russia can be seen making his way to Prague, accompanied by the multinational remnants of a once-great Allied army. Kulm marked the end of Allied hopes in the 1813 campaign.

The combat at Louvain on 17 June 1815. The Brandenburg Hussars charge the French 23rd Line and nearly succeed in breaking its square. Only a timely intervention by the 12th Chasseurs à Cheval saves the French infantry.

The rearguard action at Ligny on 16 June 1815. Rex's Landwehr stage a local counter-attack from the church at Ligny in support of the advance of the 19th Infantry Regiment.

Prussian troops on the battlefield of Waterloo. These re-enactors are celebrating the 180th anniversary of the great two-day battle and have just finished laying flowers at the Wellington Memorial Chapel.

The steep valley of the Lasne, which lay behind the Prussian army at Waterloo.

A French Chasseur à cheval trumpeter rallying French troops at Quatre Bras after Waterloo.

British light cavalry failed to intervene decisively in the pursuit of the French after Waterloo, and paid the price accordingly.

Napoleon receives the acclamations of the people of Paris after returning from his successful 1815 campaign. The temporary, but ornate, 'victory pavillion' seen in the centre of this picture was replaced shortly afterwards by the towering Eagle Monument, cast in the metal of hundreds of Allied guns, which can still be seen in the Tuileries Gardens today.

had been detached to Eugene's command in the north. I Cavalry Corps (General Nansouty) was behind Davout, and Marshal Ney's III Corps was to his rear, northern flank. At about 6.30 am Napoleon had ordered the first assault on the Fleches to begin.

The initial French bombardment was totally ineffective as the guns had been sited out of range of their targets, but when the error was discovered they were moved forward and the action began in earnest. The Jägers were overwhelmed by the French skirmishers and forced back through the Fleches, the French artillery moving forward with their infantry to give them maximum support. It is estimated that thirty light French field guns – 3- and 6-pounders – which accompanied the infantry at a scale of two per battalion, were brought to within 500 paces of the Fleches to pour canister into them, while a total of over 300 French and Russian guns took part in this epic contest. The din was incredible, and roiling clouds of smoke and dust reduced visibility to ten yards at times. The French drums beat the monotonous *pas de charge* and their infantry, dwindling continuously under the shot, shell and canister of the Russian artillery in and to both sides of the Fleches, pressed grimly forward. According to the Russian artillery officer Loewenstern, 'the execution wrought by our batteries was frightful and the enemy columns faded away perceptibly despite the reinforcements which arrived continually. The more effort the enemy put into the assault, the more their casualties piled up.'

At seven o'clock Compans' 5th Division stormed into the southern Fleche. A rapid counter-attack threw them out again, but in a second attempt the French retook the work. Despite mounting casualties among their commanders – Marshal Davout and Generals Compans, Duplain, Rapp and Desaix were all wounded – the French took both Fleches. However, these earthworks had been built open at the rear (the eastern side), and consequently provided no cover to protect the French from the Russian guns beyond them. The inevitable Russian counter attack which ensued included the 12th Division of Major General Vasilchikov, sent south from Rajevsky's VII Corps, and Duka's Kürassiers. This wrested control of the ruined earthworks from the French yet again, the latter being pushed back to the edge of the woods that lay between the lines.

Marshal Ney now threw Beurmann's 14th Light Cavalry Brigade into the fight as his III Corps came down from the north to help Davout. The first salvo of Russian artillery which ripped into this brigade caused the lead regiment (the 4e Chasseurs à Cheval) to break and flee, taking the second regiment with it. The third regiment (the Württemberg Prinz-Heinrich-Chevauxlégèrs) opened up to let the fugitives through and then charged the nearest Russian infantry square, albeit to no avail: the Russians stood like rocks in the swirling tide. Ledru's 10th Division now arrived at the northern Fleche and entered it. Buermann's much-reduced brigade reorganised itself and charged again, only to be hit in the right flank by Duka's Kürassiers. With five regiments on fresh, well-fed mounts, the Russians bowled their foes over and chased them off the field, capturing a Württemberg horse-artillery battery in the process. Only the arrival of Nansouty's I Cavalry Corps and the 25th Württemberg Infantry Division stabilised the critical situation. This 'Division' was a mere skeleton of its former self and had been reorganised into three battalions just before the battle; despite this, their impetus and élan was sufficient to retake the southern Fleche. The King of Naples, leading Nansouty's I Cavalry Corps, was so impressed by their conduct that he rode into the captured work to congratulate them.

It was now eleven o'clock. To the south of the Fleches, Napoleon's VIII (Westphalian) Corps was advancing to the south-east to support their Polish comrades of V Corps, which was still struggling through the thick, swampy woods toward their target, the Russian left wing at Utitza. Back at the Fleches, Latour-Maubourg's IV Cavalry Corps was thrown into the mael-strom of blood and steel; Konovnitsin's 3rd Russian Infantry Division came up from the south and Borozdin's 1st Kürassier Division charged in from the east. The concentration of men and weapons from both armies in so limited a space was incredible, and the artillery of both sides poured shot and canister into the melee with absolute disregard for the safety of their own comrades.[7]

It was at this point that an event occurred at the Fleches that tipped the scales in favour of the Russians. The Württembergers of the 25th 'Division', with Joachim Murat in the southern work, were by now so reduced in numbers that the next charge by Duka's Kürassiers broke their small square.[8] Murat, inside the square and clad as usual in some fantastically theatrical costume, was unable to urge his tired horse over the wall of the Fleche and was taken prisoner. As he and the Württembergers were taken to the rear, Russian infantry and artillery reoccupied the captured work and began to pour fire into the confused mass of the four enemy corps thrashing about on all sides. Murat's capture had been seen by several of his ADCs and the news spread quickly among I Cavalry Corps. After all their efforts so far, to lose their flamboyant leader *and* one of the Fleches simultaneously was just too much. Pressure from the Russians was as intense as ever, while the French horses were exhausted and no match for those of the enemy. Slowly, sullenly, they gave back before their exultant foes, who threw themselves into the fight with renewed vigour.

One reason for this development was the lack of French pressure against the Grand Battery. Instead of concerted efforts against both targets, Prince Eugene's command was no longer threatening the Battery. In the space between the Fleches and the Kolotscha where IV and III Cavalry Corps had previously been there was now only a thin screen of Bavarian cavalry, steadily being worn down by Russian artillery fire. How had this occurred? What had gone wrong?

Disaster on the flank

To answer these questions we must return to the open plain north of
Borodino. Here, heavy Russian forces had suddenly burst into view north of
Borodino at about 10.50 am and advanced rapidly to the west, causing
chaos in the army train towards Valueva. The 84e, 92e and 106e de Ligne
had advanced between Borodino and Bessubovo in an attempt to stop the
enemy. In the face of such strong cavalry they had been forced to form
square on the open plain, and Russian artillery, brought up to fire on them
at close range, had ripped these dense formations to shreds with shot and
canister. The 84e, caught in isolation and backed up against the flooded
Voina stream by Bessubovo, had broken under repeated cavalry charges and
been annihilated. The 92e and 106e fell back under similar heavy pressure,
lacking artillery and cavalry support. General Delzon was killed in the
wreckage of the 106e's square as his division was, for all practical purposes,
destroyed.

The garrison in Borodino, consisting of the 1er Croats and the remnants
of the 8e Légère, soon found themselves under fire from three sides. They
were forced to abandon the village and to fight their way back to their own
lines by crossing the Kolotscha to join the remnants of the Bavarian
cavalry.[9]

It was 11.30 when Prince Eugene received his first news of this crisis and
he at once broke into a sweat. He had made a serious tactical error for which
his imperial stepfather would not forgive him! He immediately ordered the
third assault on the Grand Battery to be abandoned and then turned his
Corps around to retrace its steps, in the hope of stemming the Russian
advance before too much damage was done. However, he did not dare to
leave his position in front of the Battery entirely denuded of troops, even
though he needed to take every unit that he could. The Bavarian cavalry
division would therefore have to screen the hole left by the withdrawal of his
main body. This was a very unconventional use of cavalry – to *hold* ground
in the middle of a battlefield – and their very high casualty rate in the hours
which followed shows what a high price they had to pay for the prince's
novel solution to his dilemma.

The transfer of his force back to the north of the stream was not so easy,
however. At their first sight of swarms of the feared Cossacks closing in on
them, the train personnel in the park on the new Moscow-Smolensk road
rode for their lives. Some, close to the three small bridges which had been
built over the Kolotscha at Alexinki, headed south for the safety of the
Imperial Guard. If they found other vehicles blocking their way, they frequently cut the traces of their own teams, abandoned their guns and
wagons, and rode off as fast as they could. A huge and jumbled mass of such
vehicles soon formed at Valueva. At Alexinki guns and limbers, caissons and
carts, jammed the bridges and fell off the open sides, so that movement in

either direction became impossible. Thus it was that although Prince Eugene's infantry and cavalry repassed the stream with little trouble, his artillery was held up south of it for over an hour, and was unable to participate in the battle to the north due to the fact that the northern bank dominated the southern and rendered the French gunners blind.

By this time Napoleon was aware that something was amiss. He rode north from the Schewardino redoubt to see for himself. When he arrived at Alexinki, the roar of explosions from amidst the massive sea of abandoned artillery wagons told him that the Cossacks were systematically destroying his precious reserve ammunition. He gave rapid orders for II Cavalry Corps to be pulled back from its position in reserve before the Fleches, and to cross the Kolotscha at Fomkino, cut through the swarm of refugees west of Valueva and strike into the Cossacks. Claparede's Vistula Legion was to be forwarded from the Reserve to support Eugene. The assaults on the Fleches were to continue with greater intensity, but V (Polish) Corps was told to abandon its drive in the south against Utitza and to pull back to Schewardino village, behind I and III Corps at the Fleches. The Westphalians were also to come north again in support of I Corps.

In the lull which followed the withdrawal of Eugene's and Grouchy's men from before the Grand Battery, the Russians reorganised, reinforced and resupplied its garrison. Noting the absence of any infantry before them, they advanced Dochturov's VI Corps to the Semenowskaya stream and brought five batteries (sixty guns) forward from the 300-gun Army Artillery Reserve. The thin – and thinning – screen of Bavarian cavalry could stand this assault no longer and, seeking cover from the galling fire, fell back to the west. Clouds of Russian Jägers trotted forward over the Semenovska stream to consolidate their hold on the area.

This tipped the scales in Russia's favour. Although Kutuzov was too cautious to press further forward with large formations, Napoleon's offensive had been thrown completely out of gear. In the north his forces – without artillery for over an hour – were badly mauled, and the loss of so much ammunition and over seventy guns in the chaos there crippled his counter-stroke. Murat's capture had dealt a heavy blow to the morale of his much-depleted cavalry, whose mounts were in no shape to match the enemy's well-nourished horses. On the Russian side, the absence of pressure against the Grand Battery enabled them to push down on to the Fleches from the north, but they were nevertheless running out of units to throw into the fight. Much of their artillery had been damaged, ammunition stocks were running low, and the 2nd Army had been knocked to pieces in the fighting around the Fleches.

Following the withdrawal of the Poles and Westphalians from the area of Utitza in the south, the Russians had redeployed their forces accordingly. Leaving only the Moscow and Smolensk militia, the Cossacks and one battery of horse-artillery in and around the village, Tuchkov I's III Corps was moved north through the woods to act against the southern flank of the central French salient still holding on in front of the Fleches. Now taken under fire from three sides, the losses of the French I, III and VIII Corps mounted horrifically.

The grim business of mutual destruction went on until nightfall; but at the end of the day, the Russians still held all their original positions and had retaken Borodino. The *Grande Armée* was a spent force, still too dangerous to leave in peace, but no longer in any condition to continue its advance on Moscow.

Stalemate

French and Russian losses were roughly equal, at about 35,000 killed, wounded and missing on each side, but Napoleon had also lost seventy-five guns and most of his reserve ammunition and artillery train. His cavalry had been reduced to a mere ghost of its former self. Even the Imperial Guard had been engaged. It had saved the day by taking up the remnants of the three corps falling back before Tuchkov's thrust and stopping the Russian advance, but had suffered quite heavy losses in the process. Napoleon's sacred reserve was no longer intact.

On 8 September the Russians licked their wounds and assessed their remaining strength. Although Kutuzov announced a victory to the Tsar, his armies – particularly Bagration's 2nd – were too badly damaged to advance and his ammunition needed replenishment from the rear, which would take at least three days. However, the Russian soldiers were well supplied with food and drink and their wounded were evacuated to covered accommodation in Moschaisk and other villages, whereas the unfortunates of the *Grande Armée* bled, starved and died in their hundreds on the battlefield.

At the sombre council of war that evening at Schewardino, Napoleon was beside himself with rage. Pacing rapidly to and fro, his staccato questions soon established the battered and reduced state of his army and the reason for the near-fatal success of Uvarov's raid in the north. Prince Eugene became the whipping boy for the entire disaster. In front of all his commanders, staff and orderlies, the crimson-faced Emperor screamed uncontrolled abuse at his stepson. As the prince wilted under the withering blast of imperial displeasure, the rest of the assembled worthies stared in horror, frozen into immobility, each dying of embarrassment at the spectacle. 'This is the last battle you will lose me, sir!' spat the Emperor. 'In all these years you have learned nothing! You no longer have a command. Get out of my sight!'[10]

As Eugene left the assembly, Napoleon's mood changed completely. He became calm and fully controlled again, as if nothing had happened. He was quick and decisive, taking frequent pinches of snuff as he listened to the reports. The list of casualties suffered amongst his senior commanders was long and depressing. Montbrun, Caulaincourt, Compere, Huard, Lanabere, Morion, Plauzonne, Romeuf, von Breunning, Damas, von Lepel and Chastel had all been killed. Marshal Davout and Generals Rapp, Nansouty, Grouchy, Morand, Friant, Desaix, Compans, Beliard, Tharreau, St Germain, Bruyere, Pajol, Defrance, Scheeler, Bonamy, Lahoussaye, Almeras, Sokolnicki, Bourdesoulle, Bessieres, von Borstell, le Rebeval, Chlopicki, Chouard, Domanguet, Dufour, Gengoult, Legras, Hammarstein, von Wickenberg, Krasinski, Queunot Mourier, Suberwiecz, Teste, Thury, Triaire, D'Henin, Cattaneo and Burthe had been wounded. After hearing the reports of the corps commanders, Napoleon thought for a moment, staring silently at the campfires glittering away to the east. 'Well then,' he said quietly, 'we will winter in Smolensk and finish this business next year. We move off tomorrow at five o'clock.'

The crowd of subdued officers drifted quickly and silently away as Berthier and his clerks began to scribble the orders for the next day. The bulletin dictated that night for consumption in Paris and the capitals of the Empire's satellites was suitably formulated and optimistic.

Also optimistic, but bearing a radically different slant, were the despatches sent from Kutuzov's headquarters to the Tsar in Moscow and from Alexander's jubilant court to the other theatres of war and to allied, neutral and even theoretically hostile courts. These told of a decisive check to Napoleon's planned advance on Moscow, his crippling losses, the continual drainage of strength as he withdrew westwards and the certainty of his destruction in the vastness of Russia in the coming winter. Travelling by relay couriers, this news reached St Petersburg by 24 September, Wittgenstein at Polotsk by the 21st, Tormassow's 3rd Army and Admiral Chichagov's Army of the Danube in the south on the 27th and Steinheil's Russian corps in Riga on 1 October. Copies were then sent to Britain by Royal Navy avisos.

Retreat

The *Grande Armée*, meanwhile, was trekking sullenly westwards, back toward Smolensk. The weather was mild and – initially at least – losses due to enemy action absolutely minimal. After four days however, this changed. From then on the ubiquitous Cossacks circled around their crippled foe like vultures, cutting-off foraging parties and deserters, destroying crops and supplies and intercepting couriers. In addition partisan groups under leaders such as Davidov also began to harry the hated invaders. No unit of less than battalion strength could risk being caught alone; to forage effectively it was necessary to despatch whole brigades, complete with artillery.

Napoleon's vanguard reached Smolensk on 29 September, and two days later the pursuing Cossacks were smartly repulsed in a clash just outside the crumbling city walls. Within the town great magazines of food, fodder, clothing, medical supplies, harness, ammunition and equipment had already been gathered, and the tired, ragged and hungry French troops were soon fed, reclothed, rearmed and re-equipped from these. The positive effect on morale was almost miraculous. Smolensk was put into a state of defence and strong forces were sent out to establish firm lines of communication with Warsaw, Lithuania and Prussia. A stream of orders was despatched to Paris, galvanising the government there into action to raise more conscripts and to disseminate propaganda on the success of the Russian adventure so far. Positive spin was to be ladled on to the bare facts to make them palatable to as wide an audience as possible.

The effects of the Tsar's messages to the outlying scenes of action were as follows. In each case, copies were delivered to the enemy under flag of truce. Salutes of artillery were fired and church-bells rung; *Te Deums* were held within hearing of the enemy lines. While Russian morale and determination soared, that of the French and their allies plummeted. Their veteran commanders remembered Napoleon's abandonment of his army in Egypt in 1799 and interpreted his 'whitewash' bulletin from Borodino with fair insight and accuracy.[11]

Wittgenstein's corps at Polotsk, with its reinforcements of regular troops and militia, seized the moment and from 24 September onwards mounted a series of aggressive actions against II and VI Corps. The ragged and starving Bavarians in the latter lacked the will to resist, and the two weak corps had to abandon the town and fall back. Wittgenstein 'steered' them south-west toward Wilna, and by 14 October they were at Dunelowitschi, thus isolating Napoleon in Smolensk and cutting his communications.

In the south, at Luboml, the Russian assault on 29 September by Tormsov's 3rd Army and Chichagov's Army of the Danube (newly arrived from Bulgaria) hit the now-outnumbered Austrians and their Saxon allies hard. Aware of the changed balance of power now obtaining, Schwarzenberg pulled back to Chelm. On 9 October, after receiving secret instructions from Vienna, Schwarzenberg informed the Saxons and Russians that the Austrians would adopt a purely defensive stance with immediate effect and withdrew south into Galicia. The Saxon corps was thus forced to pull back westwards, deeper into the Grand Duchy of Warsaw, to the town of Lublin.

Things in Latvia also swung rapidly against Napoleon. In mid-October, General Yorck, commanding the Prussian division there, concluded the 'Convention of Schlock' with General Diebitsch – a Prussian in Russian service – by the terms of which Prussia also became neutral. Marshal Macdonald, left with only with the 7th Division (half of which was itself German), had no alternative but to fall back south from Riga to Tilsit on the River Niemen, which he reached on 30 October.

In France the anti-war party grew more confident with every passing day.

They had their spies and informers both in France and around Europe, and it was apparent from these that domestic opinion was sick of the 'Tax of Blood' (as conscription had been nicknamed) and the ruin of France's commerce, bankrupted by the British naval blockade of their colonial connections and by Napoleon's retaliatory Continental System. Feelings culminated in the Malet Conspiracy of 22 October, when the anti-war party seized power and declared Napoleon deposed. Opposition to the putsch was weak and short-lived. The French were tired of glory and trophies which did not help to fill empty bellies or empty coffers. They were genuinely war weary and ready to follow any new leadership which promised the return of peace and flourishing, profitable trade. Napoleon was off the national stage and his magic could no longer hypnotise them. News of further French defeats in Spain also sapped the national will to hold down an increasingly rebellious Europe.

Meanwhile, far away in Smolensk, Napoleon was well aware that things were going very badly wrong. His flow of information from France – already spasmodic – ceased altogether on 25 October when Chichagov's main body cut his lines of communication by capturing the fortress and magazines of Minsk in a surprise night attack. The embryo, pro-Napoleonic Lithuanian government collapsed and the state meekly returned to the Russian fold.

Napoleon is captured

The following night (26 October) the Emperor left Smolensk secretly in a modest carriage with an escort of only two squadrons of Polish Lancers of the Guard, and rattled off westwards to put his empire to rights. Marshal Ney was left in command of the dwindling rump of the *Grande Armée*, which was increasingly isolated and unable to forage to replenish its dwindling stocks of food and fodder.

Just two days later, on 28 October, Napoleon's escort was ambushed and scattered by David Davidov's mixed command of regular hussars, Cossacks, militia and horse-artillery. Davidov had seen Napoleon once before, during his meeting with the Tsar on the Niemen in 1807, and as soon as he saw the Emperor standing by his coach in the flickering torchlight he knew the immense value of his prisoner. The game was up. Napoleon was rushed back to Kutuzov's headquarters at Witebsk where he was received almost with reverence.[12] From here couriers sped back to the Tsar's headquarters, requesting advice regarding both what to do with their illustrious guest and how to handle the 'public relations' aspects of this miraculous development. Meanwhile, four members of Napoleon's escort had escaped to Warsaw, from where news of the catastrophe leaked out in various directions and spread like wildfire across Europe.

Napoleon was sent back to Moscow under a strong escort – as much for his own protection from the enraged peasants as to prevent his escape or rescue. Once there, he was hurried into the towering, red brick walls of the Kremlin. The initial reaction of the Tsar and his court was to look upon their captive as an incredibly valuable bargaining chip with which they could extort great concessions from France. Appropriate overtures were therefore forwarded to Paris by diplomatic channels, but by the time they arrived the new French government was relatively firmly in the saddle. Offers of peace were already being sent to all of France's enemies and negotiations had been opened with the Bourbons, in exile in England, with a view to their restoration to the throne.

At a stroke, the value of the Tsar's 'bargaining chip' had dropped through the floor. No-one in the French government wanted him back or was willing to exchange great tracts of territory for his freedom. At best, it seemed, a quiet corner of Siberia beckoned the ex-emperor.

Surrender and peace

In mid-November, under pressure from the new French government, Marshal Ney and the dwindling remnants of his army (desertion had been rife for weeks) capitulated in Smolensk. The non-French contingents left for home at once with their arms, cannon and colours; the French core left last, with their personal weapons and colours but with only a token artillery component of twenty-four guns. They had a few squadrons of cavalry and practically no baggage train, as they had eaten most of the skeletal horses that had survived thus far.

Their re-entry into France was a very low-key affair at the end of a humbling trek through triumphant and vengeful German states, where they had to be given a large escort to ensure their safe passage. A further novelty for these demoralised survivors was that they had to pay heavily in advance for any food or drink that was provided (a considerable change from the halcyon days of 1806) and most of what was provided was stale at best or even rotten. Once back in their garrisons, they found that the army was to be drastically reduced in order to save money towards paying off crippling war reparations, and that a total reorganisation was to write off their proud regimental numbers which – in the not too distant past – had caused the populations of a dozen European capitals to tremble in fear.

At the subsequent Congress of Frankfurt early in 1813, the European monarchs eventually decided that Napoleon (still enjoying the Tsar's hospitality in the Kremlin) would best be taken care of in England, in the midst of his most implacable foes. Accordingly, he was granted a large estate centred on Warwick Castle – an appropriate site, just about as far away from a coastline as it is possible to get in the British Isles. Once there, Napoleon set to work at once, organising his miniature court and receiving streams of humble pilgrims from France, the United States of America and many other countries. He longed to see the New World but, as this was quite impossible, he settled down to make the best of central England. This formidable task was eased by the import of much wine and brandy and a staff of skilful and imaginative chefs. The ex-emperor never accustomed himself to the weather, but the discreet presence of Marie, Countess Waleska, and occasional visits from his son, the Duke of Reichstadt, lifted his spirits. He was always busy, usually with three or four projects simultaneously, and much enjoyed sparring verbally with his 'jailer', the unfortunate Sir Hudson Lowe, who usually came off worst in these contests: command of the French language had never been his strong point and his carefully-rehearsed arguments (based on evening out his last defeat at Napoleon's hands) were inevitably wrecked within moments of the next interview beginning.[13]

In the years that followed, Napoleon wrote his memoirs and became quite a close correspondent with the Duke of Wellington, who sometimes visited him. They never became close, but their respect was mutual and genuine. Napoleon had an irrepressible tendency to lecture and the Duke was too polite to interrupt him unless he became boring, which was seldom. His advice to the Duke helped to ensure that his terms as Prime Minister (1828–30 and 1833–46) were two of the most constructive, best organised and most beneficial periods of British history.

After Napoleon's death on 5 May 1821 he was buried with full military honours in Warwick Castle. His body remained there until 1840, when it was transferred to its present site, in Les Invalides in Paris.

A discordant footnote to these events should be mentioned. The slightly-unbalanced Bonapartist, Pierre d'Offshrueure, published numerous pamphlets over a period of years, claiming that Napoleon had been assiduously poisoned by the Duke of Wellington, who had supplied him with snuff laced with arsenic. These accusations were based on the tenuous 'evidence' of a series of receipts missing from the records of poisons sold to the Duke by his pharmacist. Subsequent forensic tests have shown that Napoleon's corpse did indeed contain fatal levels of arsenic, but the finger of suspicion seems not to point to the Duke but to a member of Napoleon's staff in exile with him in Warwick who was a major beneficiary in his will.

NOTES

1. Generalmajor M.I. Bogdanowitch, *History of the Campaign of 1812* (Leipzig, 1836), vol.I, p.350.
2. Eugen Herzog von Württemberg, *Erinnerungen aus dem Feldzuge des Jahres 1812 in Russland* (Breslau, 1846), vol.I, p.204.
3. Bogdanowitch, *op.cit.* vol.I, p.378.
4. General Carl von Clausewitz, *Hinterlassene Werke* (Berlin, 1832–7), vol.VII, p.107.
5. Report by General Ermelov to Kutuzov, 20 September/2 October.
6. Bogdanowitch, *op.cit.* vol.II, p.73.

7. Generalleutnant Freiherr Roth von Schreckenstein, *Die Kavallerie in der Schlacht an der Moskva am 7 September 1812* (Muenster, 1855), p.251.
8. O. Gerhardt, *Die Wuerttemberger in Russland 1812* (Stuttgart, 1937), p.199.
9. Clausewitz, *op.cit.* vol.VII, p.280.
10. Caulaincourt, *With Napoleon in Russia* (New York, 1937), p.476.
11. 29th Bulletin.
12. Davidov, *In the Service of the Tsar against Napoleon* (London, 1999). p.94.
13. Napoleon, *Memoires* (London, 1818), vol.XIII, p.113.

THE REALITY

The majority of the fictional version of this truly epic battle actually happened as related. The initial dispositions, the heavy opening bombardments, the loss of the village of Borodino, the great struggle for the fleches and the Grand Battery all took place, as did Platov's reconnaissance and a raid deep into the inadequately guarded French flank. Eugene's command *was* pulled back from Borodino, south over the Kolotscha and *did* assault – and, for about 15 minutes, take – the Grand Battery. Kutuzov agreed to Platov's Cossacks being supported (as suggested by von Toll), but he refused the Duke of Württemberg's suggestion that infantry should accompany them. Thus the raiding force consisted of the twenty-eight squadrons and twelve light guns of Uvarov's I Cavalry Corps (2,500 men) and some 5,500 Cossacks. The latter were a definite threat to scattered, isolated and demoralised men and to the non-combatant drivers of the great mass of vehicles along the new Moscow road, but were not suitable for action against formed, regular cavalry or against infantry in square. They might look threatening at a distance, but for tactical, battlefield purposes they carried no weight, not being trained for shock action. Another factor which made the raid even more toothless was that it lacked a well thought-out objective: the entire undertaking was simply an ad hoc 'bright idea' which *might* pay off.

As soon as the Russian force was seen coming west towards Bessubovo, the French 92e and 106e regiments of Delzons' 13th Division formed square north of Borodino village, as did the 84e, which was isolated just south of Bessubovo with its back against the little lake formed by a mill pond on the Voina stream. General Ornano's 12th Light Cavalry Brigade, consisting of the 9e and 19e Chasseurs à Cheval, were to the east of Bessubovo.

Frantic messages were sent to Prince Eugene, who was at this point organising the third assault on the Grand Battery. As soon as he heard the bad news, he abandoned the attack and pulled his IV Corps and the attached 1st and 3rd Divisions of I Corps back west of the Semenovska stream, recrossed the Kolotscha, and formed up west of Borodino to confront Uvarov's cavalry. This withdrawal did indeed leave a large gap in the French line opposite the Grand Battery, and this was filled by Montbrun's II, Grouchy's III and Latour-Maubourg's IV Cavalry Corps, which suffered terrible losses in the two hours for which they had to 'hold the fort'.

So, what actually happened in the raid?

The Russians split their force. Platov's Cossacks went west to menace the train while Uvarov's regular cavalry engaged the 13th Division's infantry squares. The Prussian Colonel Carl von Clausewitz was Uvarov's Chief of Staff and suggested that the squares be softened up with artillery fire – an eminently sensible idea – but Uvarov rejected this as a waste of time. He wanted to strike quickly and then run before French reinforcements came up. The inevitable result was that three charges by the Life Guard Hussars were beaten off with loss before the steady 84e withdrew over the mill dam to safety. They had to abandon their two regimental cannon, but this was a small sacrifice. Charges against the 92e and 106e were equally unsuccessful, and, as Eugene's force began to deploy in strength, the Russians were forced to call it a day.

It had not been entirely wasted, however; Napoleon called off the already abandoned third assault on the Grand Battery and rode from his head-quarters at Schewardino redoubt to the Moscow road to see the extent of the problem for himself. He also moved Roguet's division of the Young Guard north to the Kolotscha and had the Vistula Legion brought east to the Kamenka stream.

The Russian raid had thrown Napoleon's plan for the battle into disarray for two hours; that they failed to exploit this opportunity better in no way detracts from the validity of their decision to mount the attack. No-one in Kutuzov's headquarters at that time could appreciate that anything had been achieved at all, and when Uvarov reported the outcome Kutuzov replied: 'I know, may God forgive you.' When the Russian cavalry with-drew from Borodino, Prince Eugene was ordered to renew his assault on the Grand Battery.

By 3 pm (when Eugene's next attack started) the great struggle for the Bagration Fleches had been won by the French and their allies, but at a terrible cost to both sides, and the battle in this central sector had become a sullen stalemate, with the 2nd Russian Army – or what little was left of it – east of the village of Semenovskaya, and thus south-east of the Grand Battery and in no state to support their comrades defending the threatened earthwork. The Battery was stormed eventually by Lorge's 7th Heavy Cavalry Brigade (not by Caulaincourt's 2e Cuirassier Division as Napoleonic myth has it) and by Eugene's infantry. In the south, meanwhile, the Poles and Westphalians had fought at Utitza for most of the day but achieved little.

The battle ended at evening as a stalemate, with the Russians standing firm on the hills to the east of the captured works and the *Grande Armée* too shattered to fight on. The Russians lost about 43,000 men, the Allies some 28,000. Each side also lost about twenty guns.

Napoleon, not knowing what else to do in his predicament, pushed slowly on to Moscow, and thus further into the Tsar's trap. The rest is history.

BIBLIOGRAPHY

Baden, Wilhelm Hochberg, Markgraf von, *Denkwuerdigkeiten* (Heidelberg, 1906).

Bogdanowitch, Generalmajor M.I., *History of the Campaign of 1812* (Leipzig, 1836).

Chandler, David, *The Campaigns of Napoleon* (London, 1967).

Clausewitz, General Carl von, *Hinterlassene Werke* (Berlin, 1832–7).

Ditfurth, Maximilian, Freiherr von, *Die Schlacht bei Borodino am 7 September 1812* (Marburg, 1887).

Duffy, Christopher, *Borodino: Napoleon Against Russia* (London, 1972).

Gerdes, A., *Die Geschichte der Truppen Bergs und Westfalen 1812 in Russland* (Langendreer, 1914).

Gerhardt, O., *Die Wuerttemberger in Russland 1812* (Stuttgart, 1937).

Hohenhausen, Leopold von, *Biographie des Generals von Ochs* (Kassel, 1827).

Holzhausen, P., *Die Deutschen in Russland* (Berlin, 1912).

Kraft, Heinz, *Die Wuerttemberger in den Napoleonischen Kriegen* (Stuttgart, 1865).

Lossberg, Friedrich von, *Briefe in die Heimat Geschrieben Waehrend des Feldzugs 1812* (Berlin, 1912).

Pivka, Otto von, *Armies of 1812* (Cambridge, 1977).

Roth von Schreckenstein, Freiherr, Generalleutnant, *Die Kavallerie in der Schlacht an der Moskva am 7 September 1812* (Muenster, 1855).

Smith, Digby, *The Greenhill Napoleonic Wars Data Book* (London, 1998).

Württemberg, Eugen Herzog von, *Erinnerungen aus dem Feldzuge des Jahres 1812 in Russland* (Breslau, 1846).

THE RACE FOR THE BORISOV BRIDGE

BY JONATHAN NORTH

On 19 October 1812 Napoleon's *Grande Armée* began its evacuation of Moscow and, after the bloody stalemate of Malojaroslavets, resumed its retreat towards Smolensk along a route devastated during the summer advance. Struggling along bad roads in worsening weather, harried by keen-eyed Cossacks and vengeful peasant bands, and reduced to eating horse-flesh, the steadily dwindling army pushed through a Russian attempt to bar its way at Viazma and on to Smolensk. The first snow fell on 6 November and, three days later, Napoleon and his Guard entered the burnt-out ruins of that once-great city. Over the next few days the remains of the army struggled into the city, pillaging, looting and hoping for a respite and an end to their woes. Yet as the French emperor took stock of the situation he realised that he could not winter in Smolensk, a city ravaged by shells in August and still not recovered. The retreat had to go on.

As Napoleon examined his options Russian troops were in motion. Kutuzov's army, far from chasing the French into Smolensk, circumvented the city and prepared to cut the French retreat at the little town of Krasnoi a few kilometres to the west. To the north, Russian troops from Finland – released by a peace settlement with Sweden – joined forces with troops under Wittgenstein and attacked the French II, VI and IX Corps, defending the *Grande Armée*'s northern flank. On 9 November, just after entering Smolensk, Napoleon ordered Victor and his IX Corps to take the offensive against Wittgenstein and sweep the Russian general out of his way.

Minsk in danger

Even more worrying for the unhappy French emperor were developments to the south, where in August a veteran army, hardened by six years of war with the Turks, had marched out of Bucharest under Admiral Chichagov. As summer turned to autumn, this force had made its way through the western Ukraine and, joining with other Russian troops in the region, had begun to play games of cat and mouse with Napoleon's Austrian and Saxon allies, who had been entrusted with guarding the French lines of communication. After delaying at Brest Litovsk for the last two weeks of October, Chichagov – commanding 65,000 Russians – had finally resolved to march upon the massive French base at Minsk and thus fulfil Tsar Alexander's

127

order, communicated to Chichagov in September, to 'capture Minsk and then occupy the line of the Beresina in conjunction with Wittgenstein'. Thus, on 29 October Chichagov quit Brest Litovsk, leaving 30,000 men under Sacken to occupy the Austrians under Schwarzenberg and Saxons under Reynier, and advanced with his remaining troops towards Minsk.

Trusting to Sacken to keep the Austrians busy – which he did by energetically attacking the Saxons and requiring Schwarzenberg to aid Reynier – Chichagov made his unhurried way northwards. He reached Slonim on 3 November, with Lambert leading, Sabaniev and Voinov following, and Chaplitz bringing up the rear. Meanwhile, with Napoleon withdrawing and likely to have to continue to retreat, Minsk had suddenly become of vital strategic importance. Seizing Minsk would not only deprive the French of the vast stores which might enable them to pass the winter in some comfort, but it would also allow the Russians to move northwards and take the bridge at Borisov, the point where the Moscow-Warsaw road crosses the Beresina, and sever the French from the rest of Europe. However, as Chichagov was unaware that Napoleon had left Moscow, the Russian admiral – a political protégé of the Tsar rather than a capable field commander – was also unaware of the importance of his role. He therefore hesitated at Slonim, just as he had at Brest Litovsk, more concerned with keeping an eye on the Austrians to his rear than on the prize of the vast magazines at Minsk.

The French garrison of Minsk was commanded by a forty-two-year-old Pole, General Mikolaj Bronikowski. Bronikowski, who had spent the winter before among the palms and myrtle groves of Valencia, was troubled both by the chill autumn weather and by rumours of Russian movements to the south. Throughout the summer the French had stockpiled a vast reserve of food in Minsk's magazines, totalling some 3,600 quintels of flour, 22,000 bushels of oats, 6,000 quintels of hay and 200 firkins of brandy. The town was also a major hospital, 5,000 wounded being housed in the Bernadine convent and Peter and Paul church. For its defence, Bronikowski could call upon a garrison of two battalions of French infantry (from the 95th and 46th Line), a Württemberg battalion (7th Regiment), and – consisting of newly-raised Lithuanian levies of dubious quality – the 22nd and 23rd Regiments of the Grand Duchy of Warsaw, two battalions of the 2nd Lithuanian Chasseurs and two squadrons of the 18th Lancers. Bronikowski also had 300 French dragoons and 70 Lithuanian gendarmes employed in a police capacity, fending off the bands of marauders who still infested the area for miles around (six Portuguese, ten Spaniards, twenty-five Frenchmen and a Croat had been arrested and shot in the last week of October alone) and containing the bands of insurgent peasants who, profiting from the absence of their landlords, were robbing and pillaging on their own behalf. For artillery he relied on a small number of Germans and a contingent of

French artillerymen who had been destined for IX Corps but had stayed on in Minsk for fear of partisans.

On 2 November Bronikowski received a vague report from Schwarzenberg about Russian movements. He put the garrison on the alert, forbade the departure of detachments passing through Minsk (forming a provisional battalion from these), drew up plans to fortify the place, alerted Maret at Vilna, and ordered General Kossecki to defend the bridge at Novi Svegen.

Matters came to a head when, on 11 November, Chichagov's vanguard, commanded by the dashing French emigré Count Lambert, attacked the village of Nesvizh and chased out the depot squadron of the 18th Lancers. The Russians took sixty-two prisoners for the loss of just two men wounded, but some dozen Lithuanians escaped and, riding through Kossecki's detachment, reached Minsk the following day. Bronikowski received news of their arrival just as he sat down to a lavish dinner that evening. He drew up urgent appeals for help to Maret, Dombrowski (then blockading Bobruisk a little to the east with his Polish division), Oudinot's corps (which lay beyond Bobr) and Schwarzenberg. Unfortunately, the Austrian commander – who had been marching in pursuit of Chichagov and reached Slonim on 12 November – was forced to turn back and aid his Saxon allies against Sacken's spirited aggression.

However, Bronikowski was well supported by Dombrowski, who, as soon as he received Bronikowski's message, called in all his available forces (1st, 6th, 14th and 17th Polish Regiments, 2nd, 7th and 15th Polish Lancers) and marched for Minsk. He arrived on 16 November and was greeted enthusiastically, in German, by Bronikowski.

Oudinot reacted more slowly to Bronikowski's appeal, only moving his corps to Borisov on the 18th, placing his infantry in the *tête du pont* on the western bank and keeping his artillery and Doumerc's cavalry in the town itself. Maret in Vilna could do little.

Bronikowski also began improving Minsk's defences. Throughout the 13th and 14th (the day Napoleon left Smolensk and continued his weary way westwards), the energetic Polish general oversaw the building of earthworks. These were directed by an engineer captain who had been a convalescent at Minsk and whose name only subsequently came to light.[1] Bronikowski also demolished a number of dwellings along the Svislach river, to improve the field of fire from the citadel should the Russians penetrate his outer defences.

Surprised at Novi Svergen on the 11th by the fleeing remnant of the 18th Lancers, Kossecki pushed his cavalry across the bridge and encamped his infantry and one gun on the northern bank. On the 15th his cavalry scouts returned with reports that the Russians, 25,000 strong, had just quit Nesvizh, and, after looting Prince Radziwill's chateau and enjoying the fruits of an aristocratic cellar, were advancing. Realising that his position was hopeless, Kossecki burnt the bridge and retreated.

The destruction of the bridge halted Lambert and the Russian vanguard in their tracks. Chichagov came up as darkness fell and, following a brief conference with Lambert, he decided to wait for daylight before making any attempt to get his army across. The next morning he sent his cavalry over the partially frozen river and oversaw the construction of a trestle bridge for the infantry and artillery. Getting the artillery across took time, despite the heroic exertions of nervous and frozen men. Chichagov's infantry – 'veterans of ten campaigns, in good health, well fed, well armed and well equipped' according to General Langeron, who commanded a division in the admiral's army – only joined the cavalry before Minsk on the morning of 18 November.

The siege begins

Minsk was now isolated. The Russian cavalry, ably commanded by Lambert, had cut the roads to Vilna and to Borisov. Oudinot, encamped at Borisov with the 9,000 infantry of II Corps (II Corps' cavalry, commanded by Corbineau, were on their way back to rejoin Oudinot after being detached to VI Corps) and Doumerc's cuirassiers, was seriously concerned by events to the south-west but felt himself too weak to act. Besides, he knew the importance of holding the long, vulnerable bridge at Borisov.

Chichagov had to disperse his infantry in the handful of hamlets that huddled round Minsk. The cold was intense and food and forage were hard to come by. Langeron, in his memoirs, bitterly reproached the admiral for this delay, thinking that the élan and bravery of the Russian troops made a sudden, daring assault the best tactic to adopt.[2] Yet Chichagov was no doubt right to await the arrival of his artillery rather than risk an escalade – a tactic which had worked for Suvorov but had failed miserably at Rustchuk only two years before.[3] By the afternoon of 18 November the big guns had still not come up and Chichagov had been persuaded by two of his divisional generals, Langeron and Sabaniev (who had gone down on his knees, according to Langeron), to attempt to storm Minsk that night.

By midnight those troops intended for the first wave of the attack were gathered in makeshift trenches (dug with considerable effort in the frozen earth by men of the 14th and 27th Jägers) just out of range of the city's defences. Langeron chose the Vitebsk and Koslov Regiments to form the centre column, supported on the right by the 13th Jägers and on the left by the Kourin and Kolivan Regiments, in all some 3,500 men. There was no moonlight and the city was deathly quiet as, at exactly four in the morning, the Russians climbed out of the trenches and began to run silently forward towards the French defences in three dense columns. They mounted the earthworks before the alarm had been properly given; barely a shot had been fired and everything seemed to be going well. Captain Schubert, a German officer in Russian service, took part in the storming party and his account relates the drama of that solemn night as the Russian soldiers fanned out over the defences and scented victory as their coup seemed to have been pulled off: 'They could have paused here, put themselves into order and awaited the arrival of the main reserve, but who can stop troops – especially at night – when they have just pulled off an extraordinary feat of arms, when they believe the battle is won, and when they have set their hearts on putting a rich city to the sack?'

Dombrowski, initially surprised that the Russians should attempt such an assault, had only placed three companies of Lithuanian troops in the earthworks. The vast majority of the garrison was asleep. Yet, as the first muskets went off, he responded quickly, forming his 1st and 6th Polish regiments in the open space by the Svislach and advancing at the double. Bronikowski followed close behind with a battalion of the 7th Württemberg Regiment and a battalion of the 95th.

The Russians, disorganised by their initial success, were taken completely by surprise by the sudden appearance of the Poles. These remained silent until, just 100 paces from the swirling mass of Russians, they cheered and rushed in with the bayonet. The Russians did not wait for the shock, but reeled back over the defences and took to headlong flight. Rochechouart, an emigré in Russian service, relates that the Russian troops were 'panic-stricken and drunk with fear, they shouted *frantsusyi! frantsusyi!*, being quite unable to say anything else'.[4] One battalion of the Vitebsk Regiment was completely destroyed after being cornered between the 1st Polish Regiment and the French 95th. Losses generally appear to have fallen on Langeron's division,[5] and the blow to Russian morale was tremendous – their entire gain consisted of one gun, which had been spiked as it proved impossible to drag it away.

The Poles did not issue far from the defences but their artillery opened up and shelled the Russian positions for the rest of the evening, adding little injury to tremendous insult. The bombardment continued throughout the following morning, which was bitterly cold, grey and desultory. Dombrowski repaired his earthworks and pushed on with the construction of a second line of defences consisting mostly of barricaded houses. He also sent his cavalry to Borisov to join Oudinot, and that evening, after a day spent watching the Russians move their artillery into position, the French dragoons, Polish lancers and Lithuanian gendarmes cut their way through the Cossack patrols and rode off to the north-east.

As the siege of Minsk intensified and Russian artillery at last began to open up on the city at dawn on the 20th, the *Grande Armée* was streaming into Orsha, only some 40 miles from Borisov, having fought its way through the Russian troops around Krasnoi. The first elements to arrive –

the wreck of Eugene's IV Corps – found plentiful supplies in Orsha and despatched a warning to Oudinot and Victor from Berthier of the approach of the Moscow army: 'The long marches this army has had to make, together with the numerous and glorious combats it has delivered, make rest and food imperative.' In reply, Oudinot passed on the shattering news that Minsk, with its vast and essential magazines, was under siege by '45,000 Russian troops'.

The Russian bombardment of Minsk did considerable damage. The citadel, in particular, had to endure a torrent of Russian shell. The troops manning the defences also suffered, even though the thick snow absorbed a good number of Russian missiles. Numbers of Lithuanians deserted during the day, most falling into the hands of the Russian light cavalry posted to the north of the city.

Chichagov launched a second assault on the afternoon of the 20th, spurred on by his churlish commanders and wounded pride. The Russians first sent a diversionary assault against the western side of the city, the Vilna suburb, three regiments of Jägers breaking cover (the 13th, 14th and 27th, commanded by Prince Troubetzkoy), advancing rapidly across the open ground and assaulting the French entrenchments before retreating and reforming to repeat the ruse. Three cannon shots gave the signal for the main attack, launched against the south-eastern corner of the city. Rushing forward with flags unfurled, drums beating and greatcoats swirling in the wind, four Russian regiments in three dense columns made a determined and spirited attempt to storm the defences. Casualties were heavy, as the columns were swept by canister and suffered the galling fire of two French battalions, General Engelhart being amongst those killed. At one point the Russians broke into the defences and bitter hand-to-hand fighting ensued until Dombrowski rushed his reserves forward and cleared the Russians from the corpse-strewn defences.

A second assault followed, the original regiments being joined by three battalions of Langeron's Combined Grenadiers. Russian artillery, commanded by Buzhuchev, was manhandled forward and, despite heavy casualties, opened a destructive fire on the defences. The attempt met with better success and the Russian troops, showing uncommon bravery, burst over the defences and swept the French back into the city. The defenders, inspired by Dombrowski's heroic example, rallied behind some barricaded houses and, before more Russians could be poured in the city, Bronikowski counter-attacked, personally leading the élite companies of the Lithuanian regiments and two battalions of the 17th Polish Line into a well executed flank attack. The Russians were again forced to retreat, disorganising a fresh wave of reserves that was advancing to their support. This time, however, the French and Poles pushed their pursuit too far and two companies – some 120 men – of the 46th Line were captured. As the French, Poles and Lithuanians resumed their place in the earthworks the Russian artillery opened a vengefully effective bombardment, their position batteries slamming shell into the elated defenders. As darkness fell at 5 pm the defenders' own artillery returned a spluttering and noisy reply.

The same performance was repeated the next day, troops from Voinov's division hurling themselves over the earthworks until they were beaten back by the well-directed defence. The Russians gained a small advantage, dragging two guns away and setting fire to the Vilna suburb, but no lasting gains had been made by the end of the day.

Chichagov was utterly demoralised by the failure of these assaults – although he sent a despatch off to Moscow trumpeting the capture of two guns and 1,000 men – and, fickle by temperament,[6] called a halt to the operation. His commanders insisted that he continue, as Minsk could hardly be starved into submission, but the admiral was not to be swayed. That evening he decided to leave Voinov's division, supported by Chaplitz's cavalry, to blockade Minsk while he marched for the Beresina crossing at Borisov to await Wittgenstein's arrival. Whilst unwilling to leave enemy troops to his rear, he felt the Minsk garrison was unlikely to attempt field operations, as it was weak in cavalry and artillery.

Preparations for departure were made throughout the night and most of the following morning. However, the French made a determined sortie at 11 am, bursting out of the city and penetrating the first line of Russian trenches, doing considerable damage in the process. Only in the early afternoon of the 22nd did Chichagov finally lead his men off in a north-easterly direction, marching at a steady pace for three hours until darkness fell. Most of the army encamped in the snow, and suffered heavily in the sub-zero temperatures, less than a thousand fortunates managing to secure billets in the little village of Zhodzhina. By dawn on the 23rd the admiral's force had been reduced by 2,000 effectives.

A similar situation pertained in the ranks of Napoleon's once brilliant army, only on a larger scale. His troops were now approaching Bobr, only some twenty-five miles from Borisov. The Emperor had ordered Victor's IX Corps to withdraw to Borisov, keeping Wittgenstein's army at bay and covering the army's northern flank. He did not expect Victor to reach the Beresina before the 26th. His concern for the Borisov bridge had abated since Oudinot had established himself in that town and as Napoleon reached Toloczin he was met by Corbineau's troopers, sent forward by the French marshal more as a gesture than as practical assistance. The Russian pursuit of Napoleon had slackened somewhat after Krasnoi, Kutuzov being content to send Yermolov and Miloradovich, and hordes of Cossacks, forward while he himself rested in Kopys with the main army.

The battle for the Borisov bridge

23 November was, by all accounts, a bitterly cold day. Chichagov completed his march and, at 3 pm, appeared before Borisov's defences on the western bank of the Beresina.[7] His arrival was no surprise to the French, but Chichagov, who knew there were enemy troops at Borisov, had no idea how many or to what corps they belonged. General Aubry, commanding Oudinot's artillery, had placed his guns well and opened a lively fusillade against the Russians as soon as they came into view. Chichagov's artillery replied – mostly firing high but causing havoc in the town itself, now filling with masses of troops streaming in from the direction of Bobr – and Russian skirmishers advanced to duel with the defenders safe behind the *tête du pont*. Fighting continued for the rest of the day.

On the 24th, the Russians scored a significant advantage when a body of Cossacks, locating a ford north of the town opposite the miserable village of Studianka, crossed the river and pushed towards the main road. They raided II Corps' trains, burnt several wagons and took a number of prisoners.

The prisoners were brought before Chichagov and, to his absolute astonishment, revealed that they were part of the Moscow army (infantrymen from Junot's corps) and that the *Grande Armée* was already moving into Borisov. Shaken by this revelation, Chichagov, who thought Napoleon hundreds of miles to the east, was almost stupefied by the thought that, in less than twenty-four hours, he might have to fight the French emperor and his mighty host. He issued orders to Voinov to rejoin the main body at Usha, fifteen miles to the south, and hurried his own army in that direction.

As Chichagov moved southwards, the first elements of the Moscow army began to stream over the Borisov bridge. There was considerable congestion and Oudinot directed General Eblé to construct a second bridge, suitable for infantry, to ease the pressure. Vaudancourt recorded that the following troops crossed on the 24th: Oudinot's artillery protected by Corbineau's and Doumerc's cavalry and the Polish lancers of Dombrowski's division (some 3,000 men); Junot's VIII Corps (1,000 men); Zajonczek's V Corps (2,500 men), reinforced by the Mohilev garrison; Ney's III Corps (2,000 men); and some 2,000 dismounted and exhausted cavalry. Napoleon arrived in Borisov the next day with the Imperial Guard and, with a sudden flash of energy, for so long lacking in this unfortunate campaign, sent a flurry of orders off to Maret and Dombrowski and drew up plans to isolate and crush Chichagov before the main Russian army entered the fray. Learning that Victor's corps had come up, he sent orders back to hurry up the remnants of the *Grande Armée* – which crossed the Beresina in the next few days under the direction of the 'Iron Marshal' Davout and were pushed on to Minsk – and directed that strenuous efforts should be made to hurry on the 50,000 stragglers.

Attempts to instil order at the Borisov bridge – carried out by the élite gendarmes and II Corps' gendarmes under Ravier -were partially successful

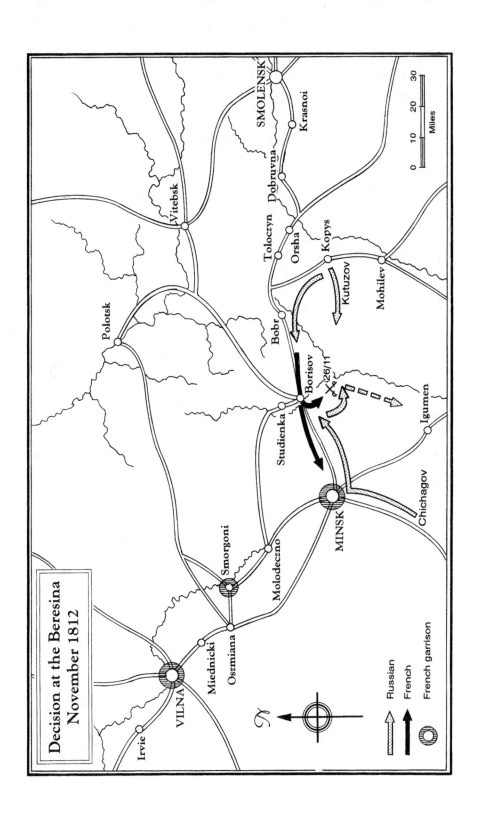

Decision at the Beresina
November 1812

SMOLENSK
Krasnoi
Dobrovna
Toloczyn
Orsha
Kopys
Kutuzov
Mohilev
Vitebsk
Bobr
Polotsk
Borisov
×26/11
Igumen
Studienka
MINSK
Chichagov
Smorgoni
Molodeczno
VILNA
Miednicki
Oszmiana
Irvie

0 10 20 30
Miles

Russian
French
French garrison

and the French streamed across until the morning of the 28th, when Victor's corps, now established in the town of Borisov, began its famous rearguard action to hold Wittgenstein and Yermolov at bay, and fear of being cut off drove the last of the stragglers across the Beresina.

Napoleon strikes back

Napoleon sent Oudinot's corps down the Minsk road, Dombrowski's Polish lancers and Lagrange's division leading, with orders to march in the direction of Minsk and then wheel about and strike eastwards towards Usha on the Beresina. Napoleon himself took his Guard south on the 25th, supported by Zajonczek, Ney, Doumerc and Corbineau, commanding some 14,500 infantry and 3,200 cavalry in all. These prepared to face Chichagov's 20,000 men and 150 guns, encamped at Usha.

Chichagov, abiding by the order to hold the line of the Beresina, was sending patrols across the river, frantically searching for any sign of the Russian main body. Late on the 25th his pickets were driven in by Kessel's Chasseurs of the Imperial Guard and the village, in which he had placed his headquarters, was shelled by Sorbier's artillery. Chichagov drew his army up in a line with his right wing resting on Usha. His left, however, was in the air, although it was partially protected by the Minsk forest and a small knoll. The admiral hoped that Voinov would appear, but that commander, having quit Minsk that very day, ran into Oudinot. Voinov turned his troops south and marched for Igumen, while Oudinot, after shepherding the remains of the *Grande Armée* on to Minsk, brushed Voinov aside and, his troops marching hard after weeks of inactivity, and guided by Polish peasants along bridle-paths and byways, arrived just south of Chichagov's position before dawn on the 26th, just as Napoleon's vaunted Guard launched a tremendous assault on Usha, the key to the Russian right wing.

Hearing that troops had appeared to his left, Chichagov, thinking that they must herald the arrival of Voinov and Chaplitz, ordered his left wing forward, which, supported by a massive battery, made progress against the depleted troops of Ney and Zajonczek. On the Russian right, the fighting in the village itself was horrendous. Sergeant Bourgogne, the campaign's ablest chronicler, was present and describes the scene:

> We found that a great number of foot soldiers had filled the houses, which were partly in flames. We now fought desperately hand-to-hand. The slaughter was terrible, and each man fought by himself for himself. We were close to a farmyard filled with Russians, and blockaded by our men. By the lurid light of the fire it was a dreadful scene of butchery, Russians and Frenchmen in utter confusion, shooting each other muzzle to muzzle.

The Imperial Guard, overcoming all resistance, drove through the village, pushing all before it at the points of their glistening bayonets. The Russian assault on the left, disorganised by its own success and exhausted by its struggle through the deep snow, began to run out of steam just as it was taken from behind by Lagrange's division. Simultaneously Napoleon launched his guard cavalry, led by Murat, and Doumerc's cuirassiers against the front of the hesitating mass. The Russian flank broke and fled in every direction, only the Zitomir and Kinbourn Dragoons resisting and, in a gallant charge, sweeping away the Polish Lancers of the Guard.[8] The Russian centre under Langeron, disorientated by the collapse of both flanks, began to withdraw, harried by the French cavalry and a stream of stragglers making for the rear. The Combined Grenadier battalions, so shamed at Minsk, covered themselves with glory here, and, repeating the feat of the Ismailov Guards at Borodino, even bayonet-charged a body of French cuirassiers. Supported by almost suicidally brave Russian artillery, these troops steadily withdrew, gaining some respite for the remainder of the army. The artillery stuck to their guns and were sabred or bayoneted, the French dragging fugitives out from beneath the guns to butcher them in vengeful fury.

Napoleon had his cavalry pursue as far as they could, which was not far considering the state of the horses. The majority of the Russians ran for Igumen as fast as the snow would allow, whilst a number of their cavalry units swam the Beresina to safety.

The emperor was overjoyed by the success and, indeed, he had won his first true victory of the campaign. The French captured some 100 Russian guns, a vast number of wagons and 3,200 prisoners. They seem to have inflicted about 5,000 casualties, mostly wounded,[9] for the loss of 1,500 of their own troops (the Guard suffering the most). A particular boon for the French was the number of horses captured, and the cavalry and artillery of the Guard quickly reserved these for themselves. Chichagov's army, reduced to about 10,000 effectives and abandoning more guns on the way, streamed south to Igumen and reunited with Voinov.

That morning Napoleon drew up his famous 29th Bulletin, which told of his heroic retreat to the Beresina through terrible conditions, and triumph over the Russian field armies and their vain attempts to impede the onward march of France. He ordered those Russian guns that could be moved to be taken on to Minsk, throwing the rest into the Beresina, and despatched a triumphant letter to Maret and the international diplomatic community at Vilna, Schwarzenberg and Macdonald (with X Corps, to the north near Riga). He ordered bells rung throughout the Empire and instructed a solemn *Te Deum* to be sung in Paris. From the snows of Russia, the old Emperor had emerged.

Sending Oudinot and Corbineau south to watch Chichagov and ensure that the Army of the Danube did not rally, Napoleon, riding in a sleigh and accompanied by Murat and Caulaincourt, made for Minsk. His spirits had revived; throughout the journey he teased Caulaincourt about how 'your friend Alexander will react now he and his commanders have been outwitted'. Pinching the Duke of Vicenza's cheek, Napoleon promised that Russia would be finished by 1814. Caulaincourt also recorded the Emperor's views on Poland and his pronouncement that he was considering the re-establishment of the Polish state: 'The time has come for Poland to drive the Russians home'.[10]

The French recover

Minsk had been somewhat overcome by the torrent of unfortunates pouring into its streets. Placards had been placed throughout the city, directing stragglers to their relevant units, and Dombrowski had ensured that sufficient formed troops had been placed at the magazines and gates to maintain a level of order. Nevertheless the sheer scale of the problem meant that a number of stores were looted and houses pillaged. For a time chaos reigned, but the arrival of Napoleon on 27 November led to a tightening of discipline throughout the army, Davout, who arrived the same day, showing particular energy in this task. Rations were distributed, the sick were collected in the hospitals under the able management of Larrey and Desgennettes, and a measure of order was restored. Civilians, Russian prisoners of war and a number of wounded generals (Poniatowski and Nansouty among them) were sent on in the direction of Grodno, escorted by a Lithuanian regiment, and preparations were made to get the army back on a war footing.

With the return of the vast majority of stragglers to the ranks, Napoleon had the following troops available: The Imperial Guard (14,500 men) including Claparède, the remains of I (6,500 men), III (4,000 men), IV (5,000 men), V (5,600 men) and VIII (2,000 men) Corps and the Cavalry Reserve (3,000 dismounted troops) were at Minsk. At Vilna Maret had gathered some 1,500 cavalry and had a number of Westphalian regiments, some Neapolitan guards and a few march battalions and, in addition, could call upon Loison's 15,000 men at Smorgoni. Wrede with the Bavarians of VI Corps and Coutard's and Franchesci's brigades (some 10,000 men in all) covered Vilna from the north. Victor with 10,000 men had burnt the bridge at Borisov and pulled back to Zhodzhina on the Minsk road. Oudinot, with the 12,000 men of II Corps and Dombrowski's Lancers, was approaching Igumen, pushing Chichagov before him. Despite the disaster that had befallen the French army, Napoleon could still call upon some 100,000 men. In addition, the Emperor ordered Schwarzenberg to leave the pursuit of Sacken to Reynier and Durutte and march with all haste for Slonim to cover his southern flank. He also directed Heudelet to link up with Macdonald's X Corps as that marshal fell back on Tilsit, and to secure Danzig and the Niemen.

In the first few days of December Napoleon left Minsk with his Guard, the dismounted cavalry and IV and VIII Corps and marched on Vilna to take up winter quarters. Before leaving he announced Bronikowski's promotion to general of division.[11] Passing through Loison's division and Bangowski's provisional cavalry regiment at Molodeczno, the Emperor arrived at Vilna and set up residence in the Bishop's Palace. Napoleon interviewed Maret at length on the state of Poland and news from France and gave orders to speed Grenier's movement from Italy and the inducement of the National Guard into service abroad. He also called a levy of the four classes and another Senatus Consultum. This, he hoped, would give him a further 300,000 conscripts for service in Russia and Spain.

The Russians, who had been suffering as much as the French from the cold and lack of food, had not been idle. Kutuzov, who had just learnt of the disaster that had befallen Chichagov, reached the Beresina on 30 November with 30,000 men. Cautious, and suspecting Napoleon had set a trap for him, he did not cross the river, but merely pushed a few Cossack detachments over to scout and harry the French. Benningsen, his chief of staff, was furious and, with Sir Robert Wilson, held an angry interview with Kutuzov on 2 December. Shaking with rage Benningsen accused Kutuzov of treachery and resigned. Kutuzov responded that if Benningsen returned to camp he would have him hanged. Wilson too was furious and wrote an urgent appeal to the Tsar to come from St Petersburg and take command of the army 'in its time of greatest need'. Kutuzov ordered Chichagov to rally at Bobruisk, sent Yermolov northwards, brought Wittgenstein's troops down from Borisov and reunited them with his own.

Lack of provisions forced the Russian army to retreat on Kopys on the 7th, a manoeuvre which sent Wilson into a fit of rage, but Yermolov scored a minor success against Wrede in the second week of December and, pointedly, was lavishly rewarded by Alexander (although upon Alexander asking him how he could be rewarded, Yermolov replied 'Sire, I wish to be appointed to the rank of German').

Despite appeals from St Petersburg and the fact that the Beresina had now frozen over, Kutuzov refused to advance and, worried by signs of unrest in his own ranks,[12] feared that his army would not survive the winter. On 16 December he sent Ostermnn-Tolstoy across the Beresina on a reconnaissance in strength. This was beaten back by Victor and Oudinot, the Russians losing 4,000 men and six guns. This put an end to Russian operations in the centre and Kutuzov withdrew most of his troops to Orsha, where considerable supplies had been assembled. In the south Chichagov was kept at bay by Schwarzenberg's Austrians operating out of Slonim. Yermolov pushed Wrede back to Vilna but could do no more as he was outnumbered and conditions had worsened.

The Polish question

Napoleon profited by this impasse by quitting the army on 15 January and moving to Warsaw. Staying in the Hotel d'Angleterre, his energy was poured into bringing more troops up to the front.[13] Moreover, he began drawing up plans for the re-establishment of the Polish nation, hoping that this would inspire the Poles to raise vastly more troops for his armies. He also summoned the kings of Saxony and Prussia to Warsaw (keeping the unfortunate Frederick with him for the rest of that year), interviewed Poniatowski at length, and despatched a long memorandum on the subject to Emperor Francis and Chancellor Metternich at Vienna. By February Napoleon was decided. He first informed the king of Saxony (who had been Grand Duke of Warsaw) that he would compensate him with territory taken from the Saxon Ducal houses.[14] To allay Austrian fears over Galicia, Napoleon offered to cede his Illyrian provinces and a strip of territory on the river Inn. With this generous offer, backed by Metternich, Francis gave his consent in principle to the resurrection of the kingdom of Poland. Napoleon then sealed the bargain with a firm promise that he would aid the Austrians in an attack on the Serbs, then rebelling against the Turks, and turn a blind eye to the annexation of the Balkans.

And so, with Russia isolated and Austria won over, Poland was at last about to be restored as a kingdom. On 1 March 1813 Napoleon, escorted by the Polish Lancers and the Chasseurs of the Guard, made his way to the Polish Diet. Baron Gros, in his celebrated painting, depicts a true scene of grandeur, with Napoleon in imperial velvet robes sweeping through the assembled grandees dressed in their traditional costumes. The reality was somewhat different: Napoleon, in his snuff-stained chasseur uniform and escorted by 100 grenadiers, abruptly announced the re-establishment of the Polish kingdom and promptly left to see his mistress Marie Walewska and his illegitimate son Alexander.[15]

Poniatowski was crowned king later that month and ruled over the territory that had formed the Grand Duchy of Warsaw and that part of Lithuania still occupied by French troops. He began calling up more troops through a conscription paid for by an issue of copper coinage. Despite Polish enthusiasm and a rush to defend Greater Poland the provision of a further 50,000 men broke the precarious finances of the new kingdom[16] and Poland was to struggle with poverty for the next sixty years.

The situation in Lithuania was also dire. Here peasants, having found that emancipation left them even more vulnerable to rapacious Polish nobles, or profiting from absent landlords, began a wave of unrest fanned by food shortages (what little of the 1812 harvest that had survived the French invasion had been used up), cholera, typhus and poverty. Sizeable bands of dissidents had swept through the province throughout 1812 but by April 1813 the situation had worsened and parts of Lithuania now rose in open revolt. On 10 April a mob murdered Prince Radziwill's intendant, Baron de Korsak, at Nesvizh in protest at Radziwill's rents and the onerous burden of conscription. The revolt spread throughout Podolia and Volhynia, and an insurgent army numbering around 35,000 men was established in the Pripet marshes. Recent studies have estimated that more than 4,000 landlords and their families were murdered and government officials fled for their lives.

The 'Time of Troubles'

Kutuzov's army had meanwhile experienced a spate of mutinies in December 1812. The mutineers proved persistent, demanding that the serfs be emancipated as a reward for liberating Holy Russia. Kutuzov, distracted by Alexander's deranged messages about the righteousness of absolute monarchy, suppressed the initial trouble. Even so, fresh outbreaks occurred amongst militias and replacements moving to the front, and in Smolensk a running battle was fought between rebels and the Ekaterinberg Regiment. Partisans refused to go home and, fearing that the nobles were plotting with the French for the removal of the Tsar, instigated an open revolt in the province of Mohilev in March 1813. It was here that, in May, a sporadic movement was given impetus by the death of Kutuzov, the defeat of the Russian spring offensive (launched by Wittgenstein, the new commander), and the emergence of a true leader amongst the rebels, Mikhail Gordachov. Gordachov soon gathered a massive following, promising to reward them with 'ownership of the land and forests, without purchase and without dues in money or kind, and [to] free peasants from the burdens imposed by wicked nobility'. By June his army had grown to more than 60,000 men as it swept through the Smolensk district, even defeating a regular force under Uvarov. The rebels devastated vast swathes of territory, ensuring that Gordachov's observation that 'Many lords and princes have I hanged, and many unjust people throughout Russia' was no idle boast, destabilising Russia to such an extent that Persians were able to roam with ease throughout the Caucasus.[17] By June units of the regular army could no longer be relied upon – infantry units, protesting at being paid in worthless assignats,[18] disbanded themselves, while the Asperon Regiment murdered the unpopular Arakchev, Alexander's Minister of War.

Europe in turmoil

Napoleon would have dearly loved to take advantage of this instability in 1813 but his troops, badly reduced by epidemics in Minsk and Vilna and unsettled by the Lithuanian rebels and by uprisings in Prussia and West-phalia, only succeeded in pushing on as far as Smolensk. His new Polish levies seemed more concerned at Schwarzenburg's activities in the Ukraine. The Emperor's attention was largely absorbed in subduing Spain and the rash of rebellion in Germany (Prussia had risen in uncoordinated revolt in March).

In Spain, Joseph Napoleon and Suchet had managed to defeat Wellington at the second siege of Burgos and pushed the Duke south towards Cadiz. Napoleon, hoping to divide and rule, returned Ferdinand VII to Spain and promptly saw opposition to Joseph split in two. Fighting continued until 1819, with Spanish royalists, backed by the British, finally being overcome by the French and Spanish Liberals at the Battle of Almeida, although Joseph Bonaparte did not live long after this triumph, dying of malaria in the unhealthy town of Marbella. The royalists promptly took ship for Mexico and Wellington, deeply humiliated, saw his country sue for peace.[19]

As Western Europe found a measure of peace Eastern Europe was plunged into ever darker chaos. In Russia the Tsar, increasingly deranged by his defeat at the hands of Napoleon, withdrew ever more into a shadowy world of religious mysticism, until, in June 1814, he died in mysterious circumstances whilst attending a church service in St Petersburg. Gordachov blamed the nobles and the nobles blamed the rebels. Whatever the case – and historians have been unable to throw light on the episode – from that time on Russia ceased to function as a cohesive entity. Alexander's brother Constantine ruled for a time but he was chased out by rebels and fled into exile in the Russian province of Alaska along with 25,000 loyal followers.

As Russia fell apart and split into an anarchic bundle of provinces and principalities – later to be termed Eurasia – its neighbours homed in for the kill: the Turks, pushing up from the Crimea, joined forces with the Persians in terrorising Russians all the way to Moscow. They were joined by the Tartars, who now rose in revolt. Not until 1824 would the Eurasian princes manage to restore some semblance of order in the Russian hinterland, briefly joining forces with the Austrians; their recovery was temporary and they were destined to spend the next century as pawns of the Habsburgs.[20] The Poles recovered most of the territory they had lost in 1772 and ruled their eastern provinces from Smolensk after the French withdrew in 1817. Even the Swedes, once allies of Alexander, turned on their former friends, reclaiming Finland, taking the Baltic states and Kourland under their protection for good measure, and sending their fleet into St Petersburg in 1815.

The Austrians took advantage of the anarchy to establish themselves in the Ukraine (despite this being officially part of Poland). Archduke Charles' conquest of Serbia was also successful and they took Belgrade, although Charles had an epileptic fit and had to be replaced by Ferdinand. Unfortunately, Archduke Ferdinand was hit by a sniper's bullet just outside Sarajevo in August 1814 and died instantly, marring the Austrian triumph.

Their conquest of the rest of the Balkans was less problematic and they soon dominated the entire Danube basin. With Prussia cowering and subject to rebellion and spiralling internal anarchy, and losing territory to Saxony, Poland and Sweden in 1813, 1815 and 1819 – episodes now known as the Partitions of Prussia – Austria emerged as the dominant German power, master of central and south-eastern Europe and economically, if not yet politically, dominating the Confederation of the Rhine. Franco-Austrian domination was to be cemented in the most astonishing way by one of history's greatest matrimonial alliances in 1827.

The new order

Napoleon, having seen peace restored in the West just as Central and Eastern Europe collapsed in turmoil, died in 1820 of cancer of the liver. His son, aged ten, succeeded him, with the empress as regent. With a Habsburg mother it was inevitable that the new emperor chose to ally with the Austrian empire and, with Metternich as mentor, he did so most enthusiastically. For seven years Napoleon II – Emperor of the French, King of Italy and Protector of the Confederation of the Rhine – ruled his father's empire, until, in 1827, Europe saw the houses of France and Austria again united by marriage when Napoleon II married Princess Maria in Vienna amidst euphoric celebrations.[21]

Thus it was that, after the humiliation of Pressburg, Campo Formio, Luneville and Schonbrunn, it was an Austro-French partnership – with France in control of Western and Central Europe and Austria dominating eastern and south-eastern parts of the continent – which emerged from thirty years of war as the new order, ruling a dual empire of size, scope and ambition unseen since the days of Charles V.

The Habsburgs had come a long way since the dark days of 1792, the death of Marie Antoinette and the first damning shots of total war.

NOTES

1. For the officer's surprising – in the light of his subsequent and more famous career – identity, see *Proceedings of the Historical Association of the Upper Garonne*, vol.XXIXb, January 1876.
2. Langeron's bitterness is understandable. Many of Chichagov's officers resented serving under this inexperienced commander. See Langeron, *Memoires* (Paris, 1902), pp.362–3.
3. A night attack on the city of Rustchuk (now Ruse in Bulgaria) in August 1810 went badly wrong and cost the Russians 12,000 casualties. See F. von Schubert, *Unter dem Doppeladler: Erinnerungen eines Deutschen im Russischen Offiziersdienst 1789–1814* (Stuttgart, 1962), p.212.
4. See Antony Brett-James, *1812: Eyewitness Accounts of Napoleon's Defeat in Russia* (London, 1966), p.123.

5. Martinnien lists two Polish officers wounded and one officer of the 95th killed. It is likely, however, that he is incorrect when he states that two officers of the 6th Polish Regiment were wounded 'at Molodechno' on this date; there was no battle there and the officers were certainly casualties at Minsk. Russian losses numbered about 500 according to Dombrowski's official report.

6. 'His brain was like a volcano: every minute it produced some new project, and this project, which was either absurd or impractical, had to be followed instantly' wrote the disgruntled Langeron of his commander. Brett-James, *op.cit.* p.126.

7. These had been constructed by the Russians themselves at the start of the campaign.

8. Interestingly, both Chlapowski and Zalusky gloss over this incident, stating that the Dutch Lancers were driven back until rescued by the Poles. See Chlapowski, *Memoirs of a Polish Lancer* (Chicago, 1996), p.165.

9. Left on the battlefield in sub-zero temperatures, the vast majority of these died.

10. Armand de Caulaincourt, *Mémoires du général Caulaincourt* (Paris, 1933), Vol. III p.224.

11. Minsk honoured Bronikowski with a magnificent statue in St Dukhawski Square. Unfortunately this monument was destroyed by Austrian troops in 1822 as they took Minsk during the Austro-Polish War.

12. In particular by a mutiny of three line regiments, suppressed after ten days of disorder. The mutineers had been militia drafted into the infantry, who were demanding the abolition of serfdom as recompense for the nation's sacrifice.

13. In the first week of January some 50,000 men passed through, including a regiment of Voltigeurs, one of Tirailleurs, the 4th Regiment of the Vistula Legion and Grenier's division.

14. In 1814 Saxon troops took over the duchies of Saxe-Gotha and Saxe-Weimar. The occupation of Weimar was marred by the accidental death of the poet Goethe at the hands of Corporal Schiller, a drunken Saxon grenadier.

15. The life of Alexander is fully covered in Pzjerjeyzukowolwski's *The Polish Napoleon* (London, 1863). Alexander infamously acted as pretender to the Polish throne in the great revolutions of 1834.

16. Marshal Davout also raised the issue that there was insufficient equipment for the new recruits, writing to Napoleon: 'There are not the necessary arms to equip the new recruits for the Polish regiments'. Davout, *Correspondence*, no.475.

17. Taking Batin in June 1812 and slaughtering some 36,000 Russians and Georgians. This was outdone by the Turks the following year, when they sacked Odessa killing 45,000 and impaling the governor, General Richelieu, in the town's main square.

18. A paper rouble was only worth 25 kopeks by the summer of 1813.

19. For details of this epic campaign students should of course refer to Sir Charles Oman's *A History of the Peninsular War, vol.VI: From the Battle of Toledo to the Peace of Lisbon, July 1817–January 1819* (Oxford, 1930). Ferdinand crowned himself Emperor of Mexico in 1817 and, funded by gold discovered in his province of California, embarked upon a career of expansion into Louisiana and the Mississippi delta. See Richard Nixon's somewhat tedious *Southern Storm: A Day-by-Day Analysis of the True Implications of the Mexican Threat, 1810–1960* (New York, 1972), vol.XXXIX.

20. This period has gone down as the second time of troubles in Eurasian history. Some

historians have estimated that the period between 1812 and 1826 cost the Eurasian (Russian) people more than a million killed.

21. The pair were happily married in a lavish and expensive royal ceremony. For details of the debauched honeymoon which followed see A. Morton's *The Harrod's Book of Royal Scandals* (London, 1998).

THE REALITY

Napoleon was, of course, utterly defeated in Russia. Bronikowski played a central role in the disaster, abandoning Minsk to the Russians under Chichagov on 21 November and depriving Napoleon of a vast store of essential supplies.

Even though Napoleon managed to raise a new army in the spring of 1813, the Russians seized the initiative, rescued the Prussians and turned the tables on the Corsican emperor. Austria, waiting in the wings to see which side would triumph, only joined the Allies in August 1813. The Habsburgs had based their empire on opportunism, and had things 'gone the other way' it would have been entirely in keeping with Habsburg tradition to find the Austrians on the side of France.

BIBLIOGRAPHY

Brett-James, Antony, *1812: Eyewitness Accounts of Napoleon's Defeat in Russia* (London, 1966).

Britten Austin, Paul, *1812: The Great Retreat* (London, 1996).

Caulaincourt, Armand de, *Mémoires du général Caulaincourt* (3 vols, Paris, 1933).

Oman, Sir Charles, *History of the Peninsular War* (7 vols, Oxford, 1902–30; reprinted London, 1995–7).

Tolaff, Ivan, *The Time of Troubles: The Fall of the Russian Empire, 1812–1830* (Anchorage, 1989).

Zalusky, Joseph-Henri, *Souvenirs du général comte Zalusky* (Paris, 1897; reprinted, Paris, 1998).

VICTORY AT KULM: THE 1813 CAMPAIGN

BY JOHN G. GALLAHER

The French army was in a shambles in January 1813. The once mighty war machine which had invaded Russia the previous summer had been reduced from hundreds of thousands of men to mere tens of thousands; and it was retreating to the west through Germany with an also weaker, but persistent, Russian army on its heels. Napoleon was back in Paris, not only consolidating his political position as news of the extent of the disaster in Russian reached France, but also creating a new army in readiness for the coming spring campaign. Italy was still firmly in the hands of the French, but the war was not going well in Spain. Two hundred thousand French veterans were struggling – and not very successfully – with Arthur Wellesley, Duke of Wellington, who was advancing through northern Spain towards France at the head of an Anglo-Portuguese army. France was war weary, as was all of Europe. Nevertheless, despite growing reluctance on the part of French mothers to send their sons to war, Napoleon was able to muster some 200,000 men in western Germany by April 1813, when the new campaign began.

In the spring of 1813 the Allied army was predominantly Russian, supported by Prussian units. The Russian army, like the French, had suffered enormous losses during the 1812 campaign. It is true that reinforcements continually flowed west to bolster its number, but the new troops were poorly trained and unaccustomed to the difficulties of prolonged campaigning. Furthermore, winter and endless marching had taken its toll. It was only on 13 March that Prussia, having abandoned its alliance with France, joined the Allies. Although Napoleon had allowed Prussia to keep just 42,000 men under arms following its defeat in 1806–7, the country had nevertheless built up a substantial reserve of trained men, from which, in the spring of 1813, it energetically set about rebuilding its army, so that by April it was already able to field about 80,000 men. Sweden too, under the leadership of an ex-French Marshal, Jean Baptiste Bernadotte, was assembling a modest force in Swedish Pomerania, which would eventually number some 28,000 menu[1]. Austria, although leaning in the direction of the Allies, was reluctant to again declare war on France. She had already done so four times in the past twenty years and each time had been defeated and forced to accept punitive peace treaties. Prince Klemens

Metternich, who was shaping Austrian foreign policy, wanted to negotiate a European settlement that would restore lands taken by Napoleon and prestige that had been lost on previous battlefields.

England continued to be France's oldest and most persistent enemy. While others had been forced to make peace with Napoleon, England had been continuously at war with France since the rupture of the Treaty of Amien in 1803. Although she contributed little in the way of troops to the continental struggle – Portugal being the exception – the English navy had remained unrivalled at sea since the battle of Trafalgar off the coast of Spain in 1805. Furthermore, English money had stiffened the back of Austria, Prussia and Russia at various times over the past ten years and was flowing on to the continent once again in 1813 to support the financially pressed Allied armies.

In 1813, Napoleon's stepson Eugene Beauharnais commanded the Army of the Elbe, consisting of some 50,000 men. Although he held bridgeheads over the Elbe at Wittenberg and Magdeburg his position was weak and precarious, because Allied armies had crossed the river both north and south of his concentration at Wittenberg. Napoleon nevertheless ordered him to hold a line along the Elbe and Saale rivers.

General Mikhail G. Kutuzov, who had commanded the Russian army since August 1812, was near death, and General Ludwig Wittgenstein would soon replace him as nominal commander of the Allied forces. However, a problem of unity of command existed among the Allies, and to some extent their forces were commanded by committee. Both Tsar Alexander I and the Prussian king, Frederick William IV, were present with the Allied army, accompanied by their respective advisors. Thus in reality the Russian Wittgenstein actually commanded the left of the army while the Prussian General Gebhard von Blücher commanded the right, neither being prepared to take direct orders from the other. In this respect the French had the great advantage of unity of command in the person of Napoleon.

Napoleon was displeased with Eugene for retreating so far west in Germany. He had hoped that the French army could have held along the Oder river; when this was not possible, he had ordered his stepson to hold the left bank of the Elbe. But the Allied army, superior in numbers, was dominating the course of events, and Eugene could do little more than slow its advance. By early April he was struggling unsuccessfully to hold a line along the left bank of the Elbe and Saale rivers. At this juncture, however, the Allies received false intelligence that Napoleon himself had joined the French army with reinforcements, and, believing that they would be out-numbered and would be facing the Emperor, the Allies decided to halt their advance and fall back to a defensive position.

Napoleon actually joined Eugene on the Elbe/Saale with 120,000 men – referred to as the Army of the Main – in late April. His grand strategy for the campaign was to divide his army and advance simultaneously against both Berlin and, through Leipzig, Dresden. The movement on Dresden was designed to cut the Allied lines of communication and supply and thus to force a decisive battle west of the Elbe. It was a classic Napoleonic movement *sur le derrière*. The movement on Berlin had two purposes, one political and the other military. Politically, it would punish Prussia for deserting him and joining his enemies. Militarily, the northern advance would hopefully draw Prussian forces from the main Allied army south of the Elbe, and thus weaken its ability to withstand the main French army. Moving on beyond Berlin to the Vistula, it would then relieve Stettin, Danzig, Thorn, and other besieged cities, these having been left with strong garrisons as the French had retreated out of Russia via Poland and eastern Germany, in anticipation of a return in the spring.

Operations began favourably from a French point of view. Napoleon left Saint-Cloud (Paris) on 15 April, spent several days at Mayence to attend to last minute affairs, and reached Erfurt on the 25th to take personal command of the two armies. Marshal Louis Davout had already been sent to the lower Elbe with 20,000 men to recapture the city of Hamburg, which had been abandoned to the enemy on 12 March. Upon retaking Hamburg, Davout would then protect the French extreme left flank and act as a reserve to the army that would march on Berlin. Eugene's Army of the Elbe, now comprising some 58,000 men, was made-up of the corps of Marshal Jacques-E. Macdonald (XI Corps), General Jacques-J. Lauriston (V Corps), General Jean-L. Reynier (VII Corps), Marshal Claude Victor (II Corps), and Joseph Latour-Maubourg (Cavalry Corps). With his left anchored on Magdeburg, Eugene would take Halle and Merseburg in preparation for crossing the lower Saale. Marshals Michel Ney and Auguste-F. Marmont, with III and VI Corps respectively, would cross the Saale and advance on Leipzig. General Henri-G. Bertrand's IV Corps would support them on their right and Marshal Nicolas-C. Oudinot with his XII Corps would move north through the Thuringer forest behind and in support of Bertrand and would form the army's extreme right flank.

East of the Saale, the Allies concentrated their forces south of Leipzig, protecting their communications back to Dresden and hoping to strike at the French right flank as it came across the river. With the corps of Blücher, Yorck, Berg, and Winzingerode, as well as the cavalry commanded by Tormassov, Wittgenstein could mass 73,000 men. If he could catch one, or even two, French corps beyond reach of the main body, he would have an excellent chance of destroying at least a portion of Napoleon's army.

The battle of Lutzen

Within a few days of reaching the Elbe, Napoleon had his armies on the march. On 1 May the Army of the Elbe was ordered to cross the Saale at

Merseburg, and the Army of the Main – led by Marshal Ney and supported by Marshal Marmont – was despatched towards Leipzig. General Bertrand and Marshal Oudinot would support Ney on his right and form the right wing of the advancing armies. While Napoleon was preparing his advance on Leipzig, the Allied commanders were busy concentrating their own forces south of the town of Lutzen and sending out strong reconnaissance forces in an effort to determine the enemy's strength and intentions. In one of the serious clashes that took place on 1 May, Marshal Jean-B. Bessières was killed near Poserna. Nevertheless, Ney occupied Lutzen and pushed his outposts south of the town, making firm contact with Wittgenstein's main force.

Neither Ney nor Wittgenstein was ready to engage in a full scale battle on the morning of 1 May: Marmont had not yet arrived in support of Ney, and Wittgenstein was still waiting for the rest of his forces to move into position. Fortunately for Ney, it was almost noon before the Allies were ordered forward. By that time Napoleon – who had been informed that a major battle was shaping up south of Lutzen – was rushing to Ney's assistance and Marmont and Bertrand were approaching from the west and the south-west. Ney's III Corps was hard-pressed throughout the afternoon, but generally held its position until help began to arrive once Napoleon reached the battlefield with units of the Imperial Guard. Then Macdonald's IX Corps began to move into position on Ney's left and Marmont arrived on his right. Wittgenstein was forced to commit his entire command: the corps of Blücher, Yorck, Berg, Winzingerode and the Prussian Guard. At 6 pm Napoleon decided that the time had come for the *coup de grâce*. He launched the Young Guard at the centre of the Allied line with the Old Guard in close support. At the same time Macdonald on the left and Marmont and Bertrand on the right threatened to crush the Allied flanks. Under pressure from every direction the Allies began to give ground. Wittgenstein's army was saved only by the onset of darkness, which enabled it to retreat east in the direction of Dresden, leaving the left bank of the Elbe and the city of Leipzig to the victors.

The battle of Lutzen had been hard fought on both sides. Casualties were roughly equal, comprising some 20,000 men for the French and perhaps a thousand less for the Allies, but once the smoke and dust had cleared, it was apparent that Napoleon had won a major victory. Lutzen had provided his new recruits with their baptism of fire and had renewed the entire army's confidence in the Emperor's ability, if not his invincibility. For the Allies, it was a serious setback that lowered the army's morale. Even so, the corps commanders were able to regroup their forces as they withdrew to the east in preparation for the next phase of the campaign.

The battle of Bautzen

Allied grand strategy now became a problem. Frederick William wanted to withdraw to the north to cover Berlin and Prussia, but the Russians wanted to retire to the east along their own lines of communication to cover Warsaw and Poland. The Russian plan had the added advantage of maintaining contact with Austria, which the Allies hoped would soon join them in the struggle against France. Being the dominant partner in the alliance Russia had its way, but concessions were made to the Prussians. General Friedrich Wilhelm von Bülow, with a corps of 30,000 men, would form a shield to protect Berlin, while the main Allied army would fall back on Dresden and, if necessary, to the Oder river.

Napoleon for his part made only slight modifications to his original strategy, adhering to his decision to divide his forces and send one army group towards Berlin while the main army pressed on to Dresden in pursuit of the Allies. To this end, Ney was given the corps of Victor (II), Reynier (VII), and Lauriston (V), along with his own III Corps and Sebastiani's cavalry corps, a total of some 84,000 men. Ney moved through Leipzig and in a general north-westerly direction across the Elbe, thereby threatening Berlin. At the same time Napoleon, with the rest of the French army, 115,000 strong, converged on Dresden. The Allies did not dispute the capital of Saxony, although they did put up at least a nominal defence along the Elbe. Nevertheless, by 10 May the French had succeeded in crossing the river in the vicinity of Dresden, following which the King of Saxony was coerced into placing his modest army at the Emperor's disposal. Alexander and Frederick William decided to make a stand west of the Oder. The site they chose was Bautzen on the right bank of the River Spree, where their engineers created a number of artillery earthworks to strengthen the position's natural defences. When Macdonald came upon the Allied army here on 16 May it was immediately obvious that it intended to give battle. Napoleon therefore dispatched orders to Ney to move south with his III Corps and Lauriston's V Corps while the main army moved into position along the left bank of the Spree. It was the Emperor's intention that Ney should leave Victor and Reynier in the north to maintain the threat to Berlin, but Ney misunderstood his orders and started south with his entire force.

On 19 May Wittgenstein was informed that Lauriston was moving south to join the main French army. Not knowing that Ney was in close support of Lauriston, he sent the corps of Yorck and Michael Barclay de Tolly – the latter having recently arrived from Russia with 14,000 men – to intercept and destroy what he believed to be an isolated French corps. But when Lauriston handled Yorck rather roughly and Ney's lead divisions attacked Barclay, the Allies fell back upon the Bautzen position and resumed their place in the line.

By the morning of 20 May, Napoleon was moving his corps into position for an attack across the Spree. He had at his disposal four army corps plus the Old and Young Guard. This force was positioned along the Spree from north to south, with Oudinot on the right flank, south of Bautzen; Macdonald opposite the town itself; Marmont north of Bautzen; and Bertrand's corps now commanded by Soult on the left flank. The Guard was in reserve behind the centre of the line. Napoleon then ordered Ney to cross the Spree downriver from the two opposing armies and, with Lauriston, to take the enemy in their right flank and right rear. If all went well, Ney would cut the enemy's line of retreat to the east and force him back against the Austrian border. The Allies intended to do somewhat the same thing to Napoleon, by turning his left flank and forcing him to retreat south towards the Austrian border.

The Allied position on the right bank of the Spree was reasonably strong, with high ground in the centre and marshes along the river on their left. Blücher's corps formed the right flank with the corps of Kleist, Yorck, Berg, Miloradovich and Gortschafoff extending in order southwards through Bautzen, with Prince Constantine in reserve. Barclay was positioned on the extreme right, to meet Ney should he cross the Spree and threaten a turning movement.

Napoleon, believing that it would be a two-day struggle, opened the battle at noon, intending to pin the Allied forces. As Ney could not be in position until the following day, the fighting took place north and south of Bautzen. The French were able to force their way across the river all along the front and by nightfall they were firmly entrenched on the right bank. The Allied corps fell back to a prepared second line of defence and remained in good order to continue the battle on the 21st. The fighting was bloody on both sides on the second day, as Ney and Lauriston came into position and threatened to turn the enemy's position. Outnumbered, and threatened on both flanks – Oudinot and Macdonald were advancing against their left – the Allies began to withdraw. Successfully holding out against Ney on his right, Wittgenstein was able to retreat to the east. Napoleon lacked adequate cavalry and his young recruits were exhausted, so that a full-scale pursuit was impossible. Consequently when a heavy rainstorm turned the roads and fields into mud, the Allied army was able to extricate itself in fairly good order and to fall back towards the Oder. Losses on both sides had been heavy, amounting to about 20,000 each.

The armistice

In the aftermath of the battle of Bautzen, Wittgenstein resigned his command as a result of profound disagreements as to how the battle should have been fought. Alexander had virtually assumed command on the field, with unfortunate results. Barclay was nominated to replace Wittgenstein, and the army retreated into Silesia, with the French following. Napoleon's lead corps occupied Breslau on the Oder on 1 June. Meanwhile, Marshal Davout had driven Allied forces out of Hamburg on 1 May and had consolidated the French position on the lower Elbe.

Shortly before the battle of Bautzen, Napoleon had sent General Armand Caulaincourt – his former ambassador to Russia – to negotiate directly with Tsar Alexander. However, in mid-May the Russian monarch still believed that an Allied military victory was possible, and he abruptly sent Caulaincourt back to Napoleon empty-handed. Defeat at Bautzen and the French occupation of Breslau rendered the Allies' military situation considerably less promising. Austria seemed daily less likely to declare war on France, the Allied position on the Oder was precarious at best, and after two major defeats the army was in desperate need of reorganisation, re-supply, and rest; an armistice was now a tempting proposition.

Despite two victories in three weeks, Napoleon was equally interested in an armistice. The French army was also in need of a respite: its young conscripts had been pushed to the limits of endurance in the two months since their departure from France. Sickness, fatigue, stragglers and heavy battle casualties had combined to reduce the effective strength of the army considerably. The lack of cavalry had rendered reconnaissance and pursuit difficult or even impossible. Supply and communication lines were overextended and in great need of reorganisation, and Cossack raiding parties were causing havoc from Hamburg to Dresden. Thus when Austria offered to act as mediator in the negotiation of peace between the warring parties both quickly accepted, and on 2 June an armistice was signed.

Neither Napoleon nor Alexander agreed to its terms with any sincerity. They simply needed time to prepare for the next phase of the campaign. Negotiations for a permanent peace were held at Prague with Prince Metternich acting as intermediary, but since neither side was prepared to make any concessions there was little progress. Then, in early July, Sweden made a firm commitment to join the Allies, while England provided substantial financial aid (£2 million) to both Russia and Prussia. The English government also promised £500,000 to Austria if she would declare war on France, which resulted in the Reichenbach Convention of 19 July by which Austria promised to join the Allies if Napoleon would not come to terms. It was also during the armistice that news of the Duke of Wellington's victory at Vitoria on 21 June reached Eastern Europe. The resumption of hostilities was now inevitable, and the wheel of fortune seemed to have turned against Napoleon and France.

The resumption of hostilities

In July the armistice had been extended to 16 August. However, by the 13th Blücher could no longer contain himself, and, in order to catch the

French off guard, he began to advance west. The second phase of the campaign had begun.

The Allied forces were divided into three very separate armies. In the north, in the vicinity of Berlin, Bernadotte was given command of 110,000 Prussians and Swedes. He was to protect the Prussian capital, watch Davout on the lower Elbe, and manoeuvre against Napoleon's left. Blücher commanded the Army of Silesia – some 96,000 Prussians and Russians – south of Breslau. The principal Allied army was the Army of Bohemia, 240,000 strong, made up primarily of Austrian troops but including perhaps 100,000 Russians and Prussians. It was massed in staging areas between Prague and the Erzgebirge mountains that formed the boundary between Bohemia and Germany. The Austrian Prince Schwarzenberg commanded this army, but both the Tsar and King of Prussia were with him and looking over his shoulder, giving advice that he could not always ignore.

The Allied overall strategy was to wage a war of attrition against Napoleon. For the first time in the Napoleonic Wars the Allies were united and all working together, and they had superior resources in men and materiel. Since it seemed to be impossible to defeat Napoleon on the field of battle, they adopted a strategy that came to known as the Trachenberg Plan. Their three armies would converge on Napoleon from the north, the east and the south, but they would refuse to give battle when Napoleon himself was present with the French army. Whenever an Allied army faced the Emperor in person, that army would withdraw while the other two continued to advance and give battle to whatever French marshal was at hand. The Trachenberg Plan was not spelled out in any detail, but its general concept was agreed and understood amongst all the Allied monarchs and generals.

Napoleon, like the Allies, had made good use of the summer armistice. His army was rested and supplies of every kind had been brought forward. Dresden had become a principal supply depot. The Emperor had formulated a new plan for resolving on the battlefield those political problems which he had been unable to settle at the negotiation table in Prague. His army would be divided into three parts. Marshal Oudinot was given command of the Army of the North, made-up of 46,000 men in two corps (Bertrand's IV and his own XII) and Arrighi's III Cavalry Corps. In addition, Marshal Davout, on the lower Elbe, would co-operate with Oudinot by threatening Berlin from the west with 25,000 men of his XIII Corps. The task of this Army of the North was to hold Bernadotte in check so that he could not threaten the main army in Saxony or the French supply lines back to the Rhine. Knowing the extremely cautious nature of the Swedish Crown Prince and former French marshal, it could be assumed that there would be no aggressive advance on Bernadotte's part.

A second army was given to Marshal Macdonald to hold Blücher's Army of Silesia in check between the Oder and the Bober rivers. As well as his own XI Corps he was given those of Marmont (VI), Lauriston (V), and Sebastiani's cavalry corps. In all he commanded a total of more that 75,000 men. The third army was the principal French force, and was commanded by Napoleon himself. It consisted of the army corps of St-Cyr (XIV), Vandamme (I), Victor (II), Ney (III), Reynier (VII), the Guard (Young and Old), and four cavalry corps, in all about 165,000 men.

Napoleon's grand plan was for Oudinot and Davout to contain Bernadotte in the north, Macdonald to contain Blücher in the east, and St-Cyr to hold Dresden, while he, with the rest of the army, invaded Bohemia by way of the Elbe through the mountains to the south. This differed from his earlier plan to strike aggressively at Berlin at the same time as he attacked the main Allied army. Berlin, after all, had only psychological significance, and was not particularly important from a military point of view. Furthermore, if Napoleon defeated the main Allied army while the other two armies held their positions, Bernadotte's situation at Berlin would become untenable. Oudinot would be reinforced, and the Allied army in the north, if it did not withdraw, would be driven from the Prussian capital.

Blücher's premature advance against Macdonald in Silesia caused Napoleon to proceed east with the Guard. In accordance with the Trachenberg Plan, the Prussian General therefore halted his advance on 20 August as soon as he received intelligence that Napoleon had assumed command of Macdonald's army, and withdrew behind the Oder. Macdonald was then ordered to take up a strong defensive position and contain Blücher. Schwarzenberg, under the influence of Tsar Alexander and his advisors, had meanwhile advanced north through the mountains to threaten Dresden. When St-Cyr informed the Emperor that the entire Army of Bohemia was forming to attack him in Dresden, Napoleon quickly returned to the Elbe.

The battle of Dresden

Prince Karl von Schwarzenberg commanded the Allied Army of Bohemia as part of the Trachenberg agreement. Its field strength was 180,000 men, although on paper – which included various detachments and support units – it was much stronger.[2] On 21 August, accompanied by Alexander, Frederick William and the Emperor of Austria, Francis I, the Allied army began a general advance on Dresden. It moved north against the French right flank in five columns commanded by Generals Wittgenstein, Kleist, Hessen-Homburg, Gyulai and Klenau. Making their way through the Erzgebirge mountains, these began to arrive in the Elbe valley south of Dresden on 25 August. St-Cyr quickly recognised the threat to his position and informed Napoleon that the entire Army of Bohemia was descending upon him.

Reacting to this confirmation of the Allied advance, Napoleon ordered II

Corps (Victor), VI Corps (Marmont), and Latour-Maubourg's I Cavalry Corps to Dresden, and, with the Imperial Guard (58,000 men), set off himself to take command of its defence. At the same time he ordered Vandamme (I Corps) and Reynier (VII Corps) to move up the Elbe to Pirna, his plan being to hold Dresden while Vandamme and Reynier threatened Schwarzenberg's left flank and rear. It was a classic Napoleonic movement.

Schwarzenberg opened the battle for Dresden in the early hours of the morning of 26 August, but the careful Austrian did not press his great numerical advantage. Napoleon arrived in Dresden at 10 am with the advance units of the Imperial Guard and took command of the battle. Although a continuous flow of fresh troops poured across the Elbe to join the struggle the French were nevertheless hard-pressed throughout the afternoon, and their outposts were steadily driven back beneath the protection of the city's guns.

Although Schwarzenberg's troops were able to drive the French out of the Gross Garten and most of their redoubts, they were unable to get into the city. When night brought an end to the fighting, the Army of Bohemia – fighting without Klenau's corps of 24,000 men[3] – was, nevertheless, in a good position to launch a final assault on Dresden the following morning, so long as the situation remained unchanged overnight.

Unfortunately for the Allies, the situation did change. French reinforcements continued to arrive throughout the hours of darkness, and on the morning of 27 August it was Napoleon, commanding 120,000 men, who was ready to take the offensive. The Allied left, under General Bianchi, became isolated from the rest of the army when Victor's II corps captured the only bridge over the rain-swollen Weisseritz river that ran south to north across the battlefield. This gave Murat the opportunity to fall upon Bianchi with General Marie-Victor Latour-Maubourg's cavalry corps supported by Victor, to drive the enemy's left back towards the mountains. At the same time, on the French left, marshals Ney (who had arrived at Dresden and been given a hastily formed corps) and Mortier, with two divisions of the Guard, turned the Allied right. When the French centre – Marmont, St-Cyr and the rest of the Guard – moved forward in the centre of the line, Schwarzenberg and the Allied monarchs had had enough. In a swiftly convened council of war they decided on a general retreat back into Bohemia.

The Allies had missed the opportunity to press home their attack on the first day of fighting, when they were in control of the battle with superior forces. This gave Napoleon the time he needed to concentrate his own forces and drive Schwarzenberg's army back into the mountains.

The retreat

The Allied army began its withdrawal under cover of darkness on the night of 27/28 August. Napoleon had believed that the battle would be continued for a third day, and as a result the French pursuit only began at mid-morning, once it had become clear that the enemy was indeed retreating. Schwarzenberg had only three roads leading south from Dresden on which to move well over 110,000 men, while Bianchi, west of the Weisseeritz and no longer in contact with Schwarzenberg, withdrew to the south-west. Some of the passes were too narrow to move troops, artillery and wagons at the same time, making the operation extremely slow and difficult. Murat, supported by Victor, led the pursuit south-west to Freiberg and then south to Zetau in pursuit of the shattered Allied left and Klenau's corps, which had joined the retreat after the battle. Marmont, St-Cyr and Mortier moved south behind the bulk of the enemy army. While Marmont followed Schwarzenberg and Barclay to Dippoldiswalde, Falkenhayn and Zinnwald, St-Cyr and Mortier pursued Kleist in the direction of Pirna. But Vandamme had already reached Pirna on the morning of the 28th, and Kleist was forced to turn south into the mountains, to Maxen, Dittersdorf and Liebenau.

When Napoleon realised that the battle had been won and that the Allied army was retreating, he had placed General Jean-Louis Reynier's VII Corps[4] under Vandamme, and ordered the two corps south from Pirna on the main road to Teplitz by way of Peterswalde. It was Napoleon's intention that Vandamme's I Corps (strengthened to 38,000 men by the addition of the 42nd Division) and the 20,000 men of VII Corps should reach Teplitz before the retreating Allied columns, thereby trapping the enemy. To this end Vandamme drove General Ostermann-Tolstoi's Russians south from Pirna on 28 and 29 August. Though Ostermann had been ordered to prevent any French attempt to move on the Allied flank and rear by way of the Elbe, the Allied strategists had not anticipated so strong a French force as that commanded by Vandamme.

Early on the morning of 29 August Napoleon also directed Marshal Mortier to Pirna with his two divisions of the Imperial Guard, in order to provide support to Vandamme should he have need of it. On the 29th Vandamme reached Kulm while Reynier was just south of Peterswalds, with Mortier passing through Pirna on the road to Gerriggeshubel. Ostermann was then ordered to hold Vandamme at Kulm at all cost, to enable Schwarzenberg and Barclay to retire through the mountain passes and reach the relatively flat lands of Bohemia. But at noon of the 29th Vandamme, with superior numbers, launched an aggressive attack on the Russian position and Ostermann was forced back to Teplitz, where he was reinforced by the lead units of Schwarzenberg's column emerging from the mountains along the Zinnwald road.

When Reynier's lead division arrived at Teplitz at about 6 pm, Vandamme pushed his right flank – the 1st Division, commanded by General Armand Philippon – forward, so as to take control of the Zinnwald/Teplitz road and block the enemy's retreat in the narrow mountain pass. When darkness brought an end to the fighting, Ostermann was still hanging on desperately to Teplitz, but Vandamme had cut off the retreat of the main Allied force.

Napoleon had moved his headquarters to Pirna late on 28 August, and on the 29th was scolding Berthier because he had so little information about Vandamme's position or condition, while news from St-Cyr and Marmont was slow in arriving and consequently out of date. Because he was concerned about the situations of Macdonald and Oudinot he remained at Pirna on the 29th, at which time he received news that all was well south of Berlin but that Blücher had made solid contact with Macdonald and had pushed back the French outposts. Macdonald was asking for reinforcements, as he believed that Blücher would attack on the 30th. The marshal was told to hold his position as long as possible and then to fall back fighting. Napoleon needed the time to complete his destruction of the Army of Bohemia.

The battle of Teplitz

On the morning of 30 August the narrow streets of Teplitz were jammed with the wagons, carts and carriages of the Allied army. Although Ostermann had been reinforced by one of Schwarzenberg's divisions before the French had cut the road from the north, he was still at a substantial numerical disadvantage. Reynier's 2nd Division had arrived by 7 am, and Vandamme was now ready to drive the enemy from the town.

In the very early hours of the 30th, Vandamme had reinforced General Philippon astride the Zinnwald road so as to prevent Schwarzenberg from breaking out into the open field. At 7 am he opened the battle by moving his left forward to cut the Teplitz/Lobositz road to the south-east. This was followed by an all-out attack on the town itself.

In the early hours Ostermann, who had been joined by the Austrian emperor and the Prussian king, had received orders from Schwarzenberg to attack northwards on the Teplitz/Zinnwald road at 8 am. Schwarzenberg would simultaneously attack southwards, and together they would reopen the road, enabling the two trapped columns to pour south and engage Vandamme. However, when Vandamme began the battle Ostermann was instead forced to fight a defensive battle, so that when Schwarzenberg attempted to break through the French blockading divisions at 8 am the Austrians were met with a withering artillery fire of canister and ball. With no support from Ostermann, and with very little artillery of their own in action, the Austrians were driven back into the pass after suffering heavy casualties. By noon Ostermann was no longer able to withstand the French onslaught, despite the fact that he had handled his command with great skill and courage in the face of the determined Vandamme. At 1 pm he ordered a general retreat to the south, in an attempt to save what he could of his command.

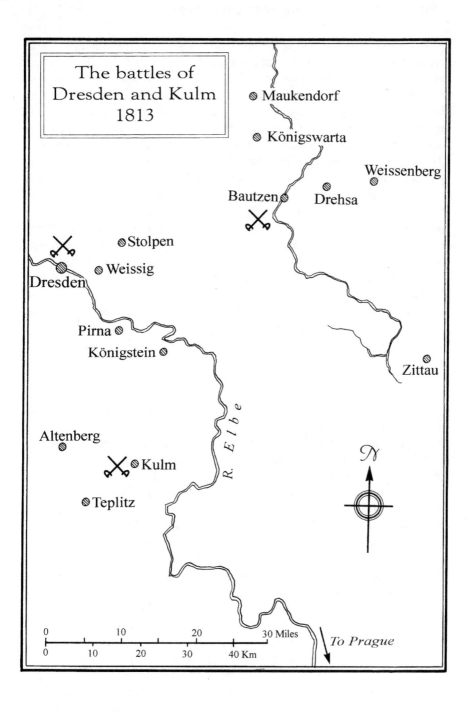

The battles of
Dresden and Kulm
1813

Maukendorf

Königswarta

Weissenberg

Bautzen Drehsa

Stolpen

Weissig

Dresden

Pirna

Königstein

Zittau

R. Elbe

Altenberg

Kulm

Teplitz

N

0   10   20   30 Miles
0   10   20   30   40 Km

To Prague

Retreating south through the mountains by way of Liebenau, General Kleist was informed on the morning of the 30th that Vandamme had already reached Kulm. His line of retreat had therefore been cut; and although St-Cyr was not pressing hard on his heels, he was nevertheless to his rear and advancing steadily. Kleist saw only one option open to him: to march across Vandamme's rear. From Furstenwalde, Kleist therefore turned east to reach the Peterswalde/Kulm road at a point between the two towns. The Prussians reached it just before noon, only to find Mortier's advance guard moving south from Peterswalde and Reynier's rearguard just two miles to his right on the same road. With St-Cyr closing on his rear, Kleist had to choose between surrendering his entire column of 20,000 men or fighting his way between Mortier and Reynier. He opted for the latter course, and, in a battle that lasted the entire afternoon of 30 August, was able to turn south and fight his way to Kulm, pushing Reynier's rather weak rearguard before him while holding Mortier at bay to his rear. But when Vandamme, at Teplitz, was informed of Kleist's presence in his rear he sent a detachment to support Reynier's rearguard, and Kleist's advance to the south was halted by heavy fighting. With Mortier increasing pressure from behind him, and unable to break through to the south, Kleist instead turned east and retreated along the road to Aussig on the Elbe. If he could cross the river and destroy the bridge behind him, he could still save what was left of his army.

By nightfall on 30 August the situation of the Army of Bohemia was a disaster. In the west, Murat was pursuing Klenau; the columns of Schwarzenberg and Barclay were trapped in the mountains north of Teplitz; and the remains of Kleist's column were fleeing to the east. When, on the afternoon of 30 August, Napoleon had learned of the appearance of Kleist on the main road to Teplitz, he immediately rushed south to take personal command of Mortier's troops. Late that evening he also received news of Vandamme's success, and before dawn on the 31st the Emperor arrived at the latter's headquarters to take personal command of the army at Teplitz.

As the sun rose on the 31st, Mortier was in pursuit of Kleist; Vandamme's entire I Corps was drawn up facing north on the Teplitz/Zinnwald road cutting the line of retreat of the bulk of Allied army; Reynier's two divisions were following Ostermann south of Teplitz; and units of the Guard were in reserve at Teplitz ready to support either Vandamme, Mortier or Reynier. Schwarzenberg and Barclay found themselves in an impossible situation. Trapped between Napoleon and Marmont on a narrow road in the mountains, their only hope was to break through the French position to the south while holding Marmont at bay behind them. They had superiority in numbers, but it was of no avail. The pass from which they were trying to emerge was only wide enough to deploy one brigade, and Napoleon, in command of the French, had massed his artillery to pour a deadly fire on the Austrian troops as they tried to advance. Schwarzenberg was unable to bring forward his own artillery because the road was clogged with troops, wagons and carts.

The fighting continued throughout the day, with the Allies mounting attack after attack, first by the Austrians and then, in the late afternoon, by the Russian Imperial Guard. As Schwarzenberg became more desperate, Napoleon brought up the Old Guard from Teplitz to bolster Vandamme's weary 1st Division, which had born the brunt of the fight. When darkness brought an end to the fighting, both armies were in the same positions as they had held that morning. The French had made no effort to advance north into the pass, and the Allies had been unable to break out to the south.

On 1 September Alexander, Schwarzenberg and their senior advisors held an emergency council of war. The situation was hopeless. To prevent the capture of the Russian Tsar, it was decided that, accompanied by a small escort, he should use a mountain trail to escape west and then south to Prague. The army had lost its supply train when Vandamme took Teplitz, and was rapidly exhausting what food it carried. Munitions were also running low after two days of heavy fighting before Dresden and the unanticipated fighting on 30–31 August. Militarily it could hold its position in the mountains for days, for while it could not break out of the mountains, neither could the French dislodge it. However, without food or any hope of relief, it was calculated that it would have to capitulate on 2 or 3 September. Napoleon was also aware of the plight of the Allied army, and had only to dig in and hold his position until the enemy asked for terms.

With great difficulty, Alexander made good his escape. Then, on 3 September, Schwarzenberg opened negotiations to surrender some 70,000 men and 120 cannons. The French victory was near complete. It is true that Klenau, with 30,000 men – most of whom had not taken part in the battle of Dresden – had escaped in reasonably good condition; and that Kleist, who had suffered heavy casualties fighting his way through the French, was able to cross the Elbe with 7,000 weary Prussians and burn the bridge behind him.[5] But Kleist had lost most of his artillery and supply train in the process.

Austria sues for peace

Napoleon had ordered Reynier's VII Corps to move aggressively against Ostermann on the night of 2/3 September. Then, when Schwarzenberg requested terms on the 3rd, he ordered St-Cyr (who had reached Teplitz early the day before) to join Reynier and push towards Prague. He wanted to reach the principal city of Bohemia before Klenau. The Emperor had all but lost contact with Murat and Victor, who were pursuing Klenau, because their line of communication ran north-east back through Dresden, then to

Pirna, and south to Teplitz. Klenau, who was not aware of the plight of the rest of the army, had meanwhile turned south across the mountains and made for Prague. Marching from the west, he met Ostermann, retreating from the north, at Schlan. Alexander had joined Ostermann, and the combined Allied force of some 50,000 men retired to Prague, where it arrived on 5 September. Napoleon took personal command of the corps of Reynier and St-Cyr early the same day, and by nightfall Murat, followed by Victor, had also arrived. With three corps, the Guard and Murat's cavalry under his command, Napoleon marched on Prague and laid siege to the remnants of the enemy army. Needless to say, all three Allied monarchs departed before the French sealed off the city. Although Prince Metternich wished to continue the war, Francis was ready to make peace with his son-in-law. He did not want the French army in Vienna for the third time in less than ten years, and there was no Austrian army capable of preventing Napoleon from reaching the city within a week to ten days. Reluctantly, Metternich opened negotiations to end the hostilities.

Back in Germany the war did not initially go quite so well for the French. Pushed into action by the audacious General Frederick William Bülow, Bernadotte began to move south towards Wittenberg on 30 August. Oudinot, whose forces had been weakened by the despatch of Reynier's VII Corps to reinforce Vandamme, was too weak to give battle in the open field. He therefore retired behind the Elbe with the city of Wittenberg as his headquarters. At the same time he informed Marshal Davout of his plight. The 'Iron Marshal', with 27,000 men, immediately advanced against Walmoden, with some 25,000 men, who withdrew to the south-east and informed Bernadotte that he could not stop Davout without immediate reinforcements. Bernadotte gave up all plans of crossing the Elbe and sent two divisions to support Walmoden, while Davout moved aggressively down the east bank of the Elbe and made firm contact with Oudinot's left at Magdeburg. However, the reinforced Walmoden was able to halt Davout's advance, and by 4 September the northern theatre of operations had sta-bilised along the Elbe. Bernadotte had meanwhile learnt of the destruction of the Army of Bohemia and had no intention of undertaking any further offensive operations.

When news reached Blücher that Napoleon had taken the Imperial Guard to Dresden on 25–26 August, he decided to move against Macdo-nald in support of the Army of Bohemia. On 29 August he made firm contact with Macdonald along the Boder river. The latter, who already knew of the victory at Dresden, informed Napoleon that Blücher was advancing and requested new orders and reinforcements. Late on the same day Blücher learned of Schwarzenberg's defeat, but was told that the Army of Bohemia was withdrawing in good order. With 87,000 men under his command, the Prussian general therefore decided to attack Macdonald while Napoleon was preoccupied with Schwarzenberg, and on 31 August forced a crossing of the Boder north of Bunzlau. However, rather than offer battle against a force larger than his own, Macdonald retreated behind the Queiss river and again took up a defensive position. It was not until 2 September that Blücher was ready to force his way over the rain-swollen river. Once again Macdonald withdrew to the west, while repeating his urgent appeal for support. Napoleon was unwilling to part with any troops until Schwarzenberg had surrendered, and Macdonald was therefore instructed to hold for as long as he could, and then to retire as slowly as possible. Consequently when Blücher attacked across the Queiss the French put up a stiff fight before falling back in good order to Gorlitz on the Neisse river (3 September). Then, on the 4th, Macdonald received news from Napoleon informing him that Mortier, followed by Vandamme, were finally on their way north to support him.

On 4 and 5 September Macdonald continued to retreat under aggressive attack by Blücher, intending to await the arrival of Mortier and Vandamme before giving battle. By 6 September Blücher had learnt of the extent of the disaster that had befallen the Army of Bohemia. Only General Kleist, safe on the east side of the Elbe and no longer pursued, remained at large, making his way south towards Prague. On 7 September Mortier made contact with Macdonald, who was at Bautzen preparing to defend the Spree river. Blücher, who was aware of the arrival of Mortier, now became concerned that his left flank could be exposed to French units moving back north, but was reassured when he received news that Napoleon was marching on Prague. He believed that the French Emperor was moving south with his entire force and that he would therefore have only Macdonald, reinforced by Mortier, to reckon with.

The second battle of Bautzen

It was 8 September when the Prussian army took up a strong position on the east bank of Spree. Mortier had joined Macdonald the night before with 15,000 men, bringing the French army up to a strength of 90,000 while the Prussians now stood at about 92,000. Vandamme's I Corps, now without the 42nd Division, was meanwhile some twelve miles south-east of Bautzen. The French plan was clear. Macdonald would attack Blücher across the Spree and Vandamme would attack his rear. Macdonald opened the battle on the morning of 9 September with a heavy artillery barrage, which was answered in kind by the Prussians. This would give Vandamme time to move on the enemy's rear.

At 9 am General Jacques-Alexandre Lauriston's V Corps, on the French left, stormed across the river, while XI Corps (under Macdonald), VIII Corps and Mortier feinted a crossing in the centre and III Corps (now under General Joseph Souham) held the left and Prince Joseph-Antoine Ponia-

towski's VIII Corps was kept in reserve. V Corps succeeded in gaining a
foothold on the east bank of the Spree, but at noon Blücher sent part of his
reserves to bolster his weakened right flank and at about 2 pm the French
advance was halted. It was at this point that Vandamme's 1st Division
appeared on the Bautzen/Hochkirch road. The noise of gunfire directly to
their rear quickly spread panic in the ranks of the Prussian army, and,
taking his cue from the sound of Vandamme's guns, Macdonald ordered a
general attack all along the line. Blücher sent the last of his reserves (one
brigade) and a full division pulled from the centre of the line to meet
Vandamme, while at the same time desperately trying to break off the fight
with Macdonald. Vandamme's 1st Division was about to be overrun when
his 2nd Division arrived on the battlefield and stabilised the situation. By 3
pm the bulk of the Prussian force was fleeing to the north-east in disorder,
but its left wing, consisting of some 20,000 men, was surrounded as
Lauriston swung south-east and made contact with Vandamme. The victory
was complete, General Horace-Francois Sebastiani leading his cavalry in a
pursuit that lasted until dark.

On receiving news of Macdonald's victory at Bautzen, Napoleon left
negotiations with Metternich in the hands of Armand-Augustin Caulaincourt and, on 10 September, set out on the road back to Dresden, taking
with him the Imperial Guard and Marmont's VI Corps. He was determined
to finish the campaign in northern Germany and Poland, where Bernadotte
still commanded more than 100,000 men and Blücher had escaped to the
north with another 50,000. If these two armies were to join forces, they
would present a formidable enemy, particularly with the shrewd and
capable Blücher directing their movements.

As Macdonald pursued Blücher to the north, he coincidentally threatened Bernadotte's left. This caused the latter to begin a general withdrawal
back to Berlin. Oudinot's and Davout's forces were united and, in accordance with orders from the Emperor, Davout assumed command of the
85,000-strong army on the Elbe, consisting of XII Corps (Oudinot), IV
Corps (Bertrand), his own XIII Corps, and Arrighi's cavalry corps.

It was also in mid-September that Tsar Alexander and Frederick William
met General Bennigsen with 59,000 Russians marching south-west from
Posen to bolster the Allied armies. With news of Blücher's defeat and
retreat to the north, it was decided to unite the three Allied armies –
potentially more than 200,000 men – in Prussia, and to try to hold Berlin,
or, if that was not possible, to fall back behind the Oder.

On 17 September Napoleon caught-up with Macdonald and assumed
command of the army, which, including VI Corps and the Guard, numbered 180,000 men. The Emperor pushed this force aggressively down the
left bank of the Oder and on 20 September relieved the besieged city of
Kustrin with its garrison of 5,000 men. It was now, as the French

approached Kustrin, that Bernadotte, fearful that his line of retreat to the east would be cut, abandoned Berlin and retreated in all haste north-east, to cross the Oder before Napoleon could cut him off from the rest of the Allied army. It was only General Bülow's insistence that Berlin be defended for as long as possible that had prevented him from abandoning the Prussian capital earlier.

Davout's orders from the Emperor, to slow the enemy's retreat by pressing hard on his heels, resulted in Napoleon reaching Stettin before Bernadotte could cross the Oder. The Swedish Crown Prince therefore turned north and fled into Swedish Pomerania, with Davout still in close pursuit. 35,000 Swedish and 25,000 Prussian troops were evacuated from Stralsund by the Swedish and British navies, but General Bülow – who would not abandon his command – and the remaining 40,000 Prussians remained blockaded there. Napoleon then recalled Davout and XIII Corps to join the main army at Stettin, where it was preparing to march to the relief of General Jean Rapp at Danzig. Oudinot and Bertrand were left to maintain the blockade of Stralsund.

The Allied position had changed dramatically for the worse. Without Bernadotte's 100,000 men Alexander could not give battle to the superior French army. He therefore began a general retreat to the Vistula, which enabled Napoleon to relieve Danzig and add yet another 20,000 men to the more than 200,000 he already commanded. There was a sense of *déjà vu* at Allied headquarters. The 1807 campaign in Poland that had culminated in their defeat at the battle of Friedland and the French advance to the Niemen river was still vivid in the minds of both Alexander and Frederick William. Once again Napoleon seemed to be invincible. Alexander could try to repeat the campaign of 1812, but while that had cost Napoleon an army – which he seemed to have replaced all too quickly – it had also laid waste to central Russia, and the Tsar was reluctant to inflict such suffering on his people and his army again. Better to sign a second treaty[6] and wait for a future opportunity to reshape Europe. Although Blücher still commanded 50,000 troops, the Prussian king, who had lost his country, could do little without Russia. The Allied monarchs therefore decided to negotiate with Napoleon from a position of some strength while they still had an army of 150,000 men in the field.

The French army of 225,000 men in Poland was not itself in the best condition. It still lacked an adequate cavalry contingent, its men were exhausted by prolonged periods on the road, major battles, and constant skirmishes, and its supply system was breaking down as the army moved through Poland to the Niemen. The weary officers and men could not face another invasion of Russia – indeed, it was already too late in the year to even contemplate such folly. Napoleon, who was himself fatigued and in poor health, was ready to bring the campaign to an end and to go into winter quarters, having re-established his reputation and control of Europe as far as the borders of Russia.

The fact that all three parties were therefore amenable to peace led to Napoleon, Tsar Alexander and King Frederick William agreeing to meet at Tilsit for a second time soon thereafter, where a treaty was signed which was not unlike that of 1807.[6]

NOTES

1. Russia had taken Finland from Sweden, and the Swedes hoped to be compensated for their loss by taking Norway from pro-French Denmark once Napoleon was defeated.
2. On the strength of the Army of Bohemia see George Nafziger, *Napoleon's Dresden Campaign: The Battles of August 1813* (Chicago, 1994). He gives its overall strength as 237,770 men (pp.142–3). Vincent J. Esposito and John Robert Elting, *A Military History and Atlas of the Napoleonic Wars* (New York, 1964), put the strength of the Allied force at 240,000 (p.133). David Chandler, *The Campaigns of Napoleon* (London and New York, 1967), gives the figure of 230,000 (p.901).
3. Klenau had crossed the mountains well to the west of Dresden and, although called to the battle by Schwarzenberg, did not arrive in time to take part in the fighting.
4. Reynier was still en route from Oudinot's command on the morning of 27 August, when he was ordered to move south to support Vandamme.
5. Vandamme had sent a battalion to Aussig to secure the bridge, but Kleist surprised the French and captured the bridge intact.
6. In 1807 Napoleon and Alexander had signed the Treaty of Tilsit. This treaty had given Napoleon control, or a free hand to deal as he pleased with all of Europe west of the Niemen River. East of the river would be under Russian control or influence.

THE REALITY

After the summer armistice Napoleon continued his original grand strategy of ordering Oudinot to attack in the north and occupy Berlin. To this end he left General Reynier's VII Corps under Oudinot. Consequently following Napoleon's victory at Dresden, Vandamme moved south from Pirna without any support. The result was that at the battle of Kulm on 30 August he was not supported by Reynier. As a result, when General Kleist arrived behind Vandamme at about noon on the day of the battle, I Corps found itself surrounded and greatly outnumbered, with no help available. Vandamme and half his corps were taken prisoner. Furthermore, Oudinot suffered a setback at Gross Beeren on 23 August, and Macdonald, advancing to the east rather than going on the defensive, was defeated at the Katzbach river on the 26th. Thus, although Napoleon won a major victory at Dresden, the Allied Army of Bohemia, having gained a victory at Kulm, was able to retreat to the safety of Bohemia and regroup. The campaign ended with the battle of Leipzig on 16–18 October, where Napoleon was defeated and forced to retreat west of the Rhine.

BIBLIOGRAPHY

Chandler, David, *The Campaigns of Napoleon* (New York, 1967).

Duval, Jules Celestin X.A., *Napoleon, Bulow, et Bernadotte, 1813* (Paris, 1906).

Esposito, Vincent J., and Elting, John R., *A Military History and Atlas of the Napoleonic Wars* (New York, 1964).

Gallaher, John G., 'Political Considerations and Strategy: The Dresden Phase of the Leipzig Campaign', *Military Affairs*, vol.XLVIII, no.2, April 1983.

Nafziger, George, *Napoleon's Dresden Campaign: The Battles of August 1813* (Chicago, 1994).

Pelet, Jean Jacques, *Des Principles Operations de la Campagne de 1813* (Paris, 1827).

Petre, Francis Loraine, *Napoleon's Last Campaign in Germany, 1813* (London, 1912).

Rousset, Camille Felix M., *La Grande Armée de 1813* (Paris, 1892).

Thiry, Jean, *Leipzig* (Paris, 1972).

— *Lutzen et Bautzen* (Paris, 1971).

WHAT IF CONSTANT REBECQUE HAD OBEYED WELLINGTON'S ORDER OF 7 PM, 15 JUNE 1815, AND ABANDONED QUATRE BRAS?

BY PETER HOFSCHRÖER

The outbreak of hostilities

Before dawn on 15 June 1815, Napoleon's *Armée du Nord* set out for its jump-off positions. There was some delay and confusion, but at sunrise – about 4 am – its vanguard attacked the Prussian positions at Thuin, southwest of Charleroi, the location of an important crossing of the Meuse river, and forty-five kilometres south of Brussels. A battery of Reille's Corps opened fire on the 2nd Battalion of the 1st Westphalian Landwehr (militia) Regiment, part of Generalleutnant von Zieten's I Army Corps. The Prussians, anticipating the French attack, were already under arms. The warning cannon were fired and Zieten's men assembled in their designated positions to make ready for the day's rearguard action. The noise of the firing could be heard in Charleroi, Zieten's headquarters, and woke the Prussian general from a few hours' snatched rest. He then rose and wrote messages to both Field Marshal Prince Blücher von Wahlstatt, commander of the Prussian Army of the Lower Rhine, and to the Duke of Wellington, commander of the Anglo-Dutch-German Army.

The news arrives in Brussels

Zieten's two messengers rode off with their despatches. The first, Major Graf Westphalen, arrived at Blücher's headquarters in Namur at 8.30 am after covering thirty kilometres or so along country lanes. The second, *Kolonnenjäger* (supply train provost) Merinsky, arrived in Wellington's headquarters in Brussels by 9 am after a journey of about fifty kilometres, mainly along cobbled roads. Zieten also sent a third officer, a Major von Arnauld, to Mons, close to the French frontier, where, after some unavoidable delays, he arrived in General Wilhelm von Dörnberg's headquarters at 9.30 am.

Merinsky delivered his message directly to Wellington, as ordered. Presumably because he anticipated the Duke passing the news on to Generalmajor von Müffling, the Prussian liaison officer in Brussels, Zieten did not send a report directly to him. However, Wellington kept the news to himself, and other than a few trusted companions at headquarters, nobody else was told. Expecting messages from his informants in Paris, and

169

believing the French offensive to be a bluff to cover a withdrawal into the interior of France, Wellington did not react. What the Duke did not yet know was that Napoleon had sold him a dummy.

As the day passed, it was business as usual in Wellington's headquarters. In the morning he continued with his paperwork; at 1 pm he wrote a memorandum on the issue of the proposed renumbering of his divisions; and before lunch he replied to a letter from Tsar Alexander of Russia. However, as the Duke was sitting down to his meal, the Prince of Orange burst in with news of the outbreak of hostilities. The Prince had just received a report sent by Major-General Behr, the commandant of the fortress of Mons. However, Wellington still did not react. Next Müffling disturbed lunch, Zieten having sent him a message at 11 am announcing the fall of Charleroi to Napoleon's forces. As this was the first Müffling had heard of the outbreak of hostilities, when he reported this to Wellington he failed to emphasise the fate of Charleroi. Instead, he merely passed on the news of the French attack on the Prussian positions. Again, Wellington did not react. The day continued.

At about 5 pm, a message arrived in Brussels from Blücher. The Field Marshal informed the Duke that he was implementing his part of the plan agreed between them by moving his entire army into the Sombreffe position. Wellington still did nothing. Finally, at about 6 pm, confirmation of Zieten's first message to Wellington arrived from Lieutenant-Colonel Sir George Berkley, Wellington's representative in the Netherlands headquarters in Braine-le-Comte. Only now did the Duke feel obliged to react. He issued his first orders of the day, doing so between 6 and 7 pm. The messengers rode off with haste from Brussels to their various destinations.

Wellington now realised that his chances of concentrating his forces in sufficient time to move to support the Prussians, in accordance with the written promises he had made to Blücher, were drastically diminished. The promises had been sent both to Blücher, via Oberst von Pfuel, one of his staff officers, and directly to Zieten, whose headquarters was in Charleroi. Wellington now realised that he needed to ensure that Blücher would hold his ground long enough for the Duke to complete his concentration. Wellington called Müffling into his headquarters. The Duke sat him down, gave him a sheet of notepaper and told him to write to Blücher informing the Field Marshal that Wellington's forces would be moving to support him that night. A waiting British despatch rider was told to take the message to Blücher with all haste.

The bad news did not stop there. Just before 10 pm, another message arrived from Blücher's headquarters. As well as informing Wellington that the Prussians were moving to concentrate in the Sombreffe position, it mentioned the fall of Charleroi, the first time the Duke had heard of this. It was now becoming clear to Wellington that his earlier view – that the French offensive was merely a bluff to cover their withdrawal into the interior of France – was incorrect. The Duke therefore issued a further set of orders, instructing his army as a whole to move east, nearer to the Prussians. Despite this, his earlier order to the 2nd Netherlands Division to move on Nivelles, thus abandoning Quatre Bras on the direct line of communication with the Prussians, was not countermanded.

Müffling returned to his office to await further information from Wellington that he would then pass onto Blücher. The Duke was well aware that the situation was worse than he had originally thought. It would now be vital for Blücher to make a determined stand, to hold off enough of the French army to enable Wellington to complete his delayed concentration. Shortly before midnight, the Duke told Müffling he had ordered all his forces to Nivelles and Quatre Bras. The Prussian then reported to his master that by 10 am the next morning, Wellington would have 20,000 men at Quatre Bras, a promise Wellington knew he would not be able to keep. However, having been told that all four of Blücher's army corps would be at Sombreffe the next day, the Duke was sure the Prussians could hold on until 17 June, when Wellington's forces would complete their concentration.

Prince Bernhard holds his ground

Meanwhile, the French had pushed back the Prussian positions and were beginning to thrust a wedge into the hinge between Wellington's and Blücher's forces, Napoleon's strategy being to divide the armies and defeat them individually. A French reconnaissance party rode up the main road from Charleroi towards Brussels until, at Frasnes, just south of Quatre Bras, it encountered two battalions of Prince Bernhard of Saxe-Weimar's Brigade of Nassauers. Saxe-Weimar was already aware of the French moves. Lacking any orders, he had used his initiative and ordered his brigade to concentrate at this vital crossroads, where the Nassauers were just moving into position as their pickets clashed with the 'Red Lancers' of the Imperial Guard. Lefèbvre-Desnoëttes, commanding the French vanguard, realised that his cavalry could not force this position by itself, so he called for infantry support. All that was available was Bachelu's 5th Division, part of Reille's Corps. However, its 4,000 men were exhausted after having marched forty kilometres that day, as well as having fought almost continuously in the burning sun. Darkness fell after a brief exchange of small arms fire. The Nassauers held their ground.

Considering this development to be important, the Netherlands chief-of-staff, Jean-Victor de Constant Rebecque, at Braine-le-Comte sent off one of his junior staff officers, Lieutenant Henry Webster of the 9th Light Dragoons, to deliver the news. Webster left Braine-le-Comte at 10 pm.

Wellington's order arrives

At 10.30 pm, Wellington's orders issued at 7 pm arrived at Braine-le-Comte, headquarters of 1st Corps under the Prince of Orange. As his master was absent, Constant Rebecque opened and read them: 'The Prince of Orange is requested to collect at Nivelles the 2nd and 3rd divisions of the army of the Low Countries.'[1] The 3rd Division was already at Nivelles, but the 2nd was at Quatre Bras. Aware that Saxe-Weimar's Brigade of Nassauers was in contact with the French at Quatre Bras, Constant Rebecque hesitated a moment, pondering the wisdom of the decision. However, not wanting to risk Wellington's wrath, he then penned an order to Saxe-Weimar ordering him to use the cover of darkness to withdraw. This order arrived just after midnight.

Prince Bernard – a young, daring man – was outraged. Aware that abandoning Quatre Bras to the French would divide the two Allied armies, he rode to Braine to protest in person. Constant Rebecque heard his argument calmly. Asked by Saxe-Weimar if he was aware that his orders would result in the Prussians being cut off from getting any support from Wellington's troops in Brussels, Constant Rebecque merely shrugged his shoulders, saying 'Lord Wellington's orders must be obeyed'. Moreover, the Nassauers were low on ammunition, and could not have held their positions for long anyway. Prince Bernhard got back to his troops just before 2 am, leaving him with two hours of darkness to complete his withdrawal. The French outposts heard some noise as the Nassau brigade pulled out, but were too exhausted to investigate.

Webster arrives in Brussels

Thanks to a change of horses and a sense of urgency, Lieutenant Webster arrived in Brussels at midnight, having ridden at break-neck speed all the way from Braine-le-Comte. Covered in dust, he entered the Duchess of Richmond's ballroom and slipped his message to the Prince of Orange, who discretely passed it on to the Duke of Wellington. He read the news: 'At this instant [i.e. at 10 pm], Captain Baron Gagern has just arrived from Nivelles with a report that the enemy has already pushed as far as Quatre Bras.'[2] The Duke did not want to believe his eyes. When, late that afternoon, he became convinced that the French offensive was more than a bluff, he had been sure that the main thrust was going to come via Mons, the shortest route to Brussels. Wellington had considered the assault on the Prussian positions in and around Charleroi to be a mere diversion. Now the Duke did not know what to think, but realised he was in danger of being cut off from the Prussians, whose support he needed. Wellington spoke to Picton, telling him to have his division ready to move off at 2 am instead of 4 am. He needed to move down the Charleroi road to block any French thrust towards Brussels.

Ney takes Quatre Bras

When dawn broke on 16 June, Lefèbvre-Desnoëttes' patrols reported the crossroads at Quatre Bras free of the enemy. He had Bachelu move his infantry up to secure the position quickly and immediately reported the good news to Marshal Ney, commander of this wing of the French forces. Ney rode in person to Napoleon, whose headquarters was in Fleurus. The Emperor was overjoyed, telling the marshal that his deception of Wellington had worked and boasting that they were going to dine in Brussels that evening. Bonaparte then drew up his plans for the day. He decided to have Grouchy keep on the heels of the Prussians, who were now surely going to fall back further. Ney was to secure the narrow bridge at Genappe immediately, as well as to scout in the direction of Nivelles, pushing back any of Wellington's forces he found there. Meanwhile, Napoleon himself was going to take the main part of his troops and march up the Brussels road. If he was to meet serious resistance, then Ney could move to his support. It was now time to drive his wedge home.

Blücher decides to fall back

Early that morning, from his headquarters at the windmill of Busy at Brye, Blücher could see that he was facing the bulk of Napoleon's forces. He had already received news of a mix-up in the delivery and execution of his orders to General von Bülow, and now knew that his IV Army Corps – one-quarter of the total Prussian force – was not going to arrive at Sombreffe that day. Blücher needed to have confirmation of Wellington's immediate plans before deciding what to do next. He therefore sent Major von Brünneck of his staff to establish what the Netherlanders were doing, and awaited news from Wellington.

Next, Müffling's report of midnight arrived. It contained the news that Wellington's army was going to march via Nivelles and Quatre Bras and that 20,000 of his troops would be at the latter place at 10 am. This reassured Blücher, and he could now prepare to do what he enjoyed most: fighting the French. However, the arrival of another report at 10 am spoiled his breakfast. Brünneck returned, bleeding from a wound to his arm. The French had ambushed him close to Quatre Bras, which was very firmly in their hands. As Saxe-Weimar's Nassauers had been there the previous evening, Blücher started to wonder what had happened to them and why he had not been told. Generalleutnant Graf Neidhardt von Gneisenau, Blücher's chief-of-staff, raised an eyebrow. Generalmajor von Grolman, another of Blücher's senior staff officers, muttered under his breath. Their chief did not normally allow them to express their true feelings about their ally's reliability, but Gneisenau and Grolman could no longer restrain themselves. Wellington had apparently abandoned them, and was probably already well on his way to Antwerp and the Channel ports. They would now

have only three of their army corps available that day and were facing the
entire French army.

Blücher's itching hand moved away from his sabre. He called for pen and
paper and dictated his orders for the day. There was no way he could face
Napoleon without both Bülow and Wellington. Zieten was instructed to
fight a rearguard action in and around Sombreffe. Generalmajor von Pirch
and Generalmajor Freiherr von Thielemann, commanders of II and III
Army Corps respectively, were ordered to alter their line of march towards
Gembloux, to the north-west, where Bülow would arrive the next day.
Once his army was concentrated there, Blücher would take stock of the
situation and then decide what to do. Blücher also moved his own headquarters to Gembloux.

Wellington decides to stand at Brussels

It was still dark when Picton's Division formed up to march out of Brussels.
Spirits were high, but there were some sad farewells. Following their orders,
his men moved down the Namur road, halting just south of the Forest of
Soignes, where they started to cook their breakfast. At about 9 am,
Wellington and his staff rode up. After a brief conversation with Picton, the
Duke continued down the road towards Quatre Bras. From the heights
opposite Genappe he saw that they French had taken possession of this town
and its vital bridge. There was now no way he could get through to aid the
Prussians. At 10 am he reported the situation to Blücher. The Duke had to
choose his words carefully, for he did not want to admit the full seriousness
of his position. Wellington feared that the Prussians might turn for the
Rhine, leaving his scattered forces to bear the brunt of the French attack. He
wrote:

> On the heights behind Genappe,
> 16th June 1815, at 10 [am]

> My dear Prince!

> My army is situated as follows. The Army Corps of the Prince of Orange is
> at Nivelles. The Reserve has arrived at Waterloo. The English cavalry will
> be at Nivelles at midday. Lord Hill's Corps is at Braine le Comte.
>   I do not see much of the enemy before me, and I await news from Your
> Highness and the arrival of troops to decide my operations for the day.
>   Nothing has appeared near Binche, or on my right.

> Your obedient servant
> Wellington.'

Wellington presented certain of his positions as being much more advanced
than they really were. The Cavalry was not going to be at Nivelles at
midday, and Hill was certainly not at Braine. The Duke knew that part of

the information he was giving his ally was incorrect, but he wanted to say nothing that might lead Blücher to turn tail and head for home. Taking a circuitous route to avoid the French at Quatre Bras, the despatch rider reached Blücher's headquarters at midday. The Field Marshal's mood changed immediately. His friend Wellington had not abandoned him after all. Blücher scowled at Gneisenau and Grolman. Pen and paper were again called for.

The Field Marshal's reply to Wellington stated that he was facing the entire French army at Sombreffe, but, as Bülow had been delayed, Blücher was now falling back to join the latter at Gembloux. From here, he would march with his entire army to support Wellington on 17 June, when he was sure that they could defeat Napoleon together. This letter reached Wellington at 1.30 pm at the village of Waterloo, where he had just set up his headquarters. On the basis of the incorrect information that the Duke had just sent him, Blücher was sure that the Duke had enough troops concentrated to look after himself. Wellington's deception had backfired.

Wellington's orders

A glum Wellington pondered the content of Blücher's letter. The Duke was very much aware he could not fight his way through to his ally. Also, since the Prussians were now withdrawing he was likely to have to face a substantial part of Napoleon's forces alone that very day. Whatever Wellington did, stopping the French marching into Brussels was his priority, so he first ordered Picton to take up positions along the ridge of Mont St Jean to fight a delaying action. He then sent a rider to Nivelles to order the Netherlanders to withdraw slowly to Halle, delaying the French for as long as they could. Hill was ordered to join the Prince of Orange there, with the 4th Division marching towards Brussels via Ninove. The Reserve Cavalry was ordered to Brussels. Once Hill was at Halle, the Netherlanders were to withdraw towards Brussels.

Napoleon's moves

The day had begun with Napoleon's forces organised in two bodies. Ney was on the left, with Reille's Corps and the Guard Light Cavalry, while Napoleon commanded the rest of the army, comprising the Guard and the corps of Vandamme, d'Erlon, Gérard, and Lobau, with the Reserve Cavalry under Grouchy. However, seeing only one Prussian corps in and around Ligny from the vantage-point of the Tombe de Ligny, Napoleon considered that Blücher would be continuing his withdrawal that day. He therefore reorganised his forces, placing Grouchy in command of his Right Wing. The newly appointed marshal was given Gérard's and Lobau's Corps, while Napoleon took charge of his four cuirassier divisions. Gérard's Corps was ordered to assault the village of Ligny. Grouchy left Lobau in reserve around

Fleurus and moved Pajol and Exelmans towards the Prussian left. Meanwhile, Napoleon took the Guard, Vandamme and d'Erlon to join Ney, with Reille's Corps, at Quatre Bras. The sun rose and a smiling Emperor encouraged his men with talk of the 'sun of Austerlitz'. Supported by Kellermann's III Cavalry Corps, Lefèbvre-Desnoëttes pushed up the road towards Brussels. At 2 pm, Reille's infantry moved off, having breakfasted and cleaned their muskets. D'Erlon advanced towards Nivelles. The Guard and Vandamme followed Reille. It was a sunny day, and spirits in the *Armée du Nord* were high.

The day of 16 June

Grouchy now moved against the Prussian positions. Zieten staged a determined defence against Gérard's assaults on Ligny, which began at 2.30 pm. The Prussians were largely untried militia and raw recruits, held together by a hard core of experienced officers and NCOs. Although the previous day's fighting had exhausted them, these young recruits had been too nervous to rest well that night. What little food they had – the already inadequate supply system had broken down under the pressures of combat the previous day – was devoured. Drinking water was in short supply, so thirst was a major problem. The muddy water of the marshy Ligne brook was used to clean their muskets after a fashion. Some attempt was made to prepare the buildings of the village of Ligny for defence. Zieten did not want his poorly trained men to be caught in the open by the French veterans he was facing. Instead, he obliged Gérard's men to commit themselves to a costly street fight in which their experience would not be so great an advantage.

Zieten held his ground with great determination, the attacking French making little headway against the village. His companies of Silesian *Schützen* (trained marksmen) picked off French officers whenever they could. Gérard, leading his men against Ligny for the second time, was shot in the chest and badly wounded, command of his corps falling to Pêcheux, his senior divisional commander. More brave men fell in the bitter street fighting, where no quarter was asked and none given. Enemy soldiers often butchered the wounded found seeking shelter in the cellars when a house fell. Those lucky enough to escape such treatment could not flee the fires that started to spread in the village. Casualties were high.

The *History* of the 19th Regiment, part of Henckel von Donnersmarck's Brigade, describes the scene:

> The right flank column of the enemy moved towards the northern entrance to Ligny, towards the skirmishers under Kapitain von Glasenapp. It went over to the attack, a battery of artillery to the fore. Our brigade battery replied.
>
> The enemy skirmishers concentrated their attack on Glasenapp's

positions, but were repulsed. Their second attempt to take the garden up the hill was equally unsuccessful.

For the next half an hour, the enemy sent forward small detachments to try to dislodge Glasenapp from his positions, but they were repulsed by volley fire from the 2nd Battalion. Finally, the enemy moved up larger forces and established themselves after a violent firefight. From here, the enemy engaged in frontal attacks on our positions, while their skirmishers tried to outflank the battalion.

One enemy column now attempted to storm the road towards the church, while another moved towards the western entrance.

The first attack, forceful though it was, was driven off. After considerable effort, the enemy gained a foothold. As they pushed into the village, every house and every cellar was contested in bloody hand-to-hand fighting.

Major von Schouler rallied three companies on the road to the rear of Ligny and led them in a counter-attack towards the church that was still held by Rex's Landwehr battalion. He reached as far as the Ligne brook before receiving a severe head wound. The attack faltered while Kapitain von Borcke replaced him.

An exchange of artillery fire now took place. Meanwhile, Lieutenant Kessler moved up his skirmish platoons. Once they were in place, a general counter-attack took place, driving the enemy out of the village. The regiment regained its starting positions.[3]

Zieten's Reserve Artillery was deployed along the crest of the slope rising towards the village of Brye, from where it deterred the French from outflanking him from the right. Realising that forcing the Prussians from their positions by means of a frontal attack was costing him too much time and too many men, Grouchy ordered his cavalry to start moving around Zieten's left, teasing him and threatening his line of retreat. He hoped this manoeuvre would encourage the Prussians to fall back out of Ligny.

Zieten's I Army Corps Reserve Cavalry fought off the first French attempt to work their way around the Prussian left flank. However, the Prussian cavalry was in the throes of reorganisation, and Zieten's troopers were little match for Pajol's and Exelmans' well-disciplined veterans. At 4 pm, Thielmann's Reserve Cavalry from III Army Corps was sent in to hold off the masses of French cavalry long enough for Zieten to withdraw his infantry.

II and III Army Corps reached Gembloux that evening unhindered, but Zieten's Corps, after two days of hard fighting, was exhausted and decimated. The Sombreffe position was in French hands by 5 pm, though the Reserve Cavalry of the Prussian I and III Army Corps delayed the advancing French well into the evening. By nightfall, the Prussians had concentrated their forces at Gembloux. With the arrival of Bülow that night, Blücher had three fresh corps to hand for the next day's fighting.

From the ridge of Mont St Jean, Wellington saw his worst fears realised: four divisions of crack French heavy cavalry were coming up the road from Genappe. He had insufficient mounted troops of his own available to oppose them. Moreover, the Duke had too little infantry to hand to make a determined stand. At 4 pm, when Lefèbvre-Desnoëttes and Kellermann's troopers drew up opposite his positions, Picton's men started their fighting withdrawal into the Forest of Soignes. The squares of redcoats held out all the way, and thanks to the cover offered by the trees the French cavalry were unable to press home their advantage. Pack's Brigade formed the rearguard. The 42nd Highlanders were the last to seek cover, doing so only after seeing off several charges by Lefèbvre-Desnoëttes' Guard Light Cavalry. However, the main road to Brussels was now open.

The two Netherlands divisions at Nivelles fell back to Halle in good order, although d'Erlon did not press them too hard. Outnumbering their enemy two to one, General Collaert's division of Netherlands Cavalry had little problem holding off d'Erlon's light horse. On the way, Alten's Division joined the Netherlanders. They found Cooke waiting for them at Halle. The 2nd Division joined them that evening, while Colville arrived during the night. The Reserve Cavalry had already ridden through Halle on its way to Brussels. Wellington thus managed to extricate his forces from a potentially disastrous situation. He had kept his cool in very difficult circumstances.

The evening of 16 June

That day, Wellington had managed to salvage something of the situation. Napoleon had reached the outskirts of Brussels, but had been unable to keep his boast of dining there that evening. The Duke was now close to concentrating his entire army and his losses had – thanks to his skilful tactical handling – been relatively light.

Blücher had suffered heavier casualties, but now had his entire army concentrated at Gembloux. However, his forces were more than a day's march from Wellington, and Napoleon lay between them, able to strike in whatever direction he wanted.

D'Erlon was outside Halle, Grouchy was facing Gembloux, and the Emperor himself was just south of Brussels. The situation was still in the balance. However, Napoleon was about to play his next card.

Bonapartist sympathisers in Brussels spent that night getting organised. Arms from secret caches were distributed and preparations were made for a demonstration the next morning. News of this reached Wellington, who started to get nervous, doubting that he could hold on to the city. He was unwilling to risk a battle with his line of retreat so threatened. Only Blücher could provide relief, so the Duke rode to Wavre that night for a conference with his ally.

The midnight conference at Wavre

Wellington went to the meeting at Wavre hoping to be able to persuade the Prussians to move in the general direction of Brussels the next day. Expecting the revolt in Brussels to spread to the ranks of the Netherlands forces, the Duke planned to move them out of the way to Antwerp first thing in the morning. He had considered detaching the Netherlanders from the remainder of his army, sending them to Antwerp alone. However, he believed the risk of Bonapartist officers gaining the upper hand to be too high. If they were to obtain control of even part of the Netherlands army, he would find himself with hostile troops astride his one safe line of retreat. That would mean the end of his army, and was a risk that Wellington could not take. The Duke therefore decided that he had no choice but to have his more reliable troops accompany them. This left him with so few men that all he could contemplate now was a rearguard action. However, even that was in danger of being overwhelmed by the French, so he had to ensure that Napoleon's attention was focused elsewhere.

Wellington's plans started to firm up. Picton was to hold Brussels for as long as he could. The remainder of Wellington's infantry was also going to retire towards Antwerp the next day. The Reserve Cavalry would cover this move, so Napoleon would be subjected to some delay before following up from Brussels. A messenger was already on his way to Louis XVIII at Ghent, telling him to make for Ostend immediately, where he could embark for England. Wellington was not going to tell Blücher any of this. Müffling, having his office in a separate building to Wellington's head-quarters, and not being able to speak English, was to be kept in the dark.

Wellington and Blücher met in the town of Wavre at midnight on 16/17 June. They discussed what they intended to do next. High on Blücher's agenda was the union of their forces to fight the battle necessary to defeat Napoleon. Top of Wellington's secret agenda was to ensure that the Prussians would attract enough of Napoleon's attention to allow him to slip away to Antwerp relatively unmolested. The Duke maintained he would be able to hold Brussels that day, while Blücher agreed to march towards the city via Louvain. Both commanders left the meeting satisfied with the result. Gneisenau and Grolman muttered to each other, doubting their ally's sincerity. Müffling assured them that their suspicions were groundless.

Morning of 17 June

First to leave Brussels was Wellington's 1st British Division. It was followed by the 2nd Netherlands Division. Then came the 3rd British Division, followed by the 3rd Netherlands Division, which, in turn, was followed by the 2nd British Division. Troopers of the Reserve Cavalry lined the road. That way, Wellington hoped to get the Netherlands troops to Antwerp relatively intact, by not giving any unreliable elements the opportunity to cause disruption. The Netherlanders had done their duty until now, but circumstances had changed, and Wellington had to ensure that nothing occurred which might destabilise the newly founded kingdom. The British 5th Division held on in Brussels for as long as it could, while Uxbridge's cavalry tried to keep the streets clear of demonstrators. Barricades went up in the southern, francophone quarters of the city, and shots were exchanged. To avoid being caught up in any fighting, the 4th Division and Prince Frederik's men circumvented the city, skirting around its northern perimeter and marching towards Vilvoorde.

Just before he set off, Wellington called Müffling into his headquarters. The Duke explained to him that the situation in Brussels had suddenly deteriorated so much that he could not risk staying there. A letter with this news was sent to Blücher, but to avoid French patrols, the messenger had to take a circuitous route. It would therefore be some hours before Blücher knew what the situation actually was. This time Wellington's ploy was going to work and Müffling was quite unaware that he had been duped.

Napoleon's forces were now organised as follows: the Right Wing under Grouchy comprised Pêcheux (replacing Gérard), Pajol and Exelmans; the Left Wing, under Ney, consisted of Reille, d'Erlon and Kellermann; and the Reserve under Napoleon was made up of the Guard, Vandamme, Lobau and Milhaud. As the French did not start out until late that morning, having taken time to cook breakfast and clean their muskets, Wellington was able to get his men well on their way to Antwerp before Napoleon started to threaten Brussels. At 10 am, Vandamme moved into the south of the city to the jubilation of the local population. After a brief exchange of fire, Picton fell back. Uxbridge's troopers, drawn up outside the northern perimeter, then took over the rearguard duties. It was now 11 am, and Napoleon had a late breakfast in the Palais Royale. At noon he addressed the crowds that had gathered in the street outside, and news of his success started to filter out to the rest of the world. Louis XVIII was already sailing towards England.

Meanwhile, Blücher's II Army Corps, commanded by Pirch, had started towards Louvain, followed by Zieten and then Thielmann. Bülow stood his ground at Gembloux, taking up the rear, while Grouchy's men started fights with the Prussian pickets.

Once he had addressed the cheering masses in Brussels, Napoleon considered what he should do next. He was not going to be able to overtake Wellington before he reached the safety of Antwerp's walls, so the defeat of Blücher became his first priority. He therefore sent Ney, with Reille's and d'Erlon's Corps, supported by Exelmans' cavalry, to follow up Wellington. He then left Lobau to hold Brussels and set out with Vandamme, the Guard and his cavalry to join with Grouchy. As the Prussians were moving north, apparently attempting to join up with Wellington, Napoleon took his

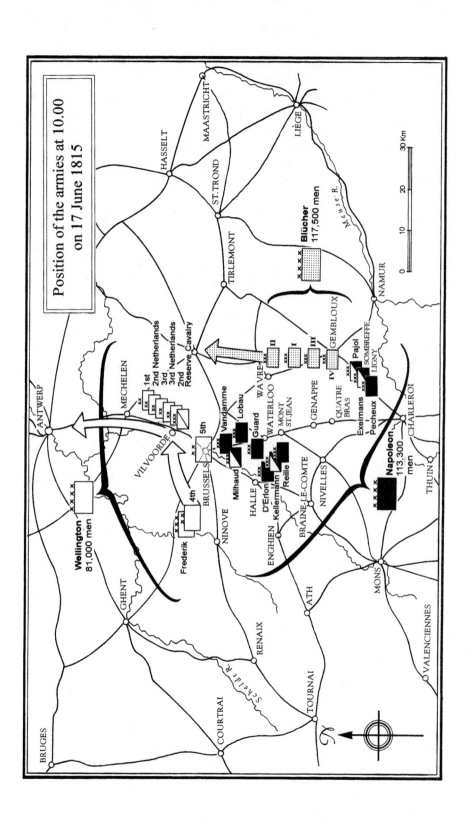

Position of the armies at 10.00 on 17 June 1815

forces along the road from Brussels to Louvain to head them off. Blücher was going to find himself caught between two fires.

That afternoon, Wellington's messenger arrived with news of the fall of Brussels. Despite the reservations expressed by both Gneisenau and Grolman, Blücher decided to throw caution to the wind and continue his move towards Louvain. If he could get close to that town by evening, he had a good chance of linking up with Wellington north of Brussels on 18 June. The Field Marshal still did not appreciate his ally's real intentions.

The evening of 17 June

By evening, much of Wellington's infantry had reached Antwerp. His cavalry held Michelen. The afternoon's heavy rain had prevented effective use of any French infantry in pursuit of the Anglo-Dutch-German Army. It may have been too damp for firearms to be used, but Uxbridge's troopers, their sabres unaffected by the rain, had given Milhaud's cuirassiers plenty to think about.

Pirch's vanguard of the Prussian II Army Corps had clashed with French pickets south of Louvain. On one occasion, the Prussians managed to drive off Vandamme's chasseurs à cheval and follow up into his infantry, forcing them to halt their march and form square. The Brandenburg Hussars came close to breaking the square of the 23e de ligne, but a counter-attack by the 12e chasseurs à cheval into their flank had forced the Brandenburgers to withdraw. Once again, the French cavalry had shown their superiority and the Prussians had been repelled. Pirch reported his situation to headquarters. Furthermore, Grouchy was following hard on Bülow's heels, whose rearguard of hussars and uhlans was proving an inadequate match for the veteran French cavalry.

Napoleon had established a line of communication with Grouchy from Brussels via Wavre. The various wings of the *Armée du Nord* were acting in co-ordination under the control of their master. The Emperor was using the strategy of the central position with consummate skill.

A despondent Blücher now knew he had no chance of getting to Louvain unhindered. A message then arrived from Müffling reporting Wellington's move on Antwerp. Gneisenau and Grolman nodded to each other knowingly, but said nothing to the Field Marshal for fear of upsetting him even more. Without Wellington's support, Blücher knew he could not force his way through and link up with his ally. He would now have to move east the next day, towards the Rhine, or face a crushing defeat.

The morning of 18 June

Louis XVIII arrived in Dover and an express containing his news was sent to London. This was to have serious consequences.

Wellington completed his withdrawal behind the walls of Antwerp.

However, his Netherlands troops showed greater signs of unrest, and the Duke began to feel unsure that he could even hold Antwerp. Ney positioned Reille's Corps to observe the fortress. D'Erlon and Kellermann were recalled by Napoleon, who now took command of Grouchy's wing. Along with his own force, the Emperor moved eastwards on the heels of the Prussians.

Blücher's forces withdrew in the direction of Tirlemont. Considering himself too weak to achieve a link-up with Wellington, the Field Marshal resolved to fall back on Maastricht and Liège. Here, he would await the Russians and Austrians, who should be ready to move against France at the end of the month.

Events in London

Following the arrival of the express from Dover, Lord Liverpool, the Prime Minister, called his cabinet together that evening. Arguments over policy became bitter as evening darkened into night. Vansittart, the Chancellor of the Exchequer, protested about the drain on national resources that a long war would cause. Britain's debts were already high, and further loans could not be obtained. Viscount Sidmouth, the Home Secretary, warned that any increases in domestic taxation would lead to social unrest. The old dispute between Earl Bathurst, the Secretary for War, and Viscount Castlereagh, the Foreign Secretary, over the suitability of the Duke of Wellington as commander of the Allied forces in the Low Countries, broke out again. With a divided government and empty coffers, it was clear to Liverpool that a continuation of the war was going to be difficult.

The next morning, Liverpool met with the Russian and Austrian ambassadors. The Prime Minister informed them that Britain would not be sending more troops to the Low Countries and that he had doubts if his government could raise the necessary loans to meet the promised subsidies in full. The ambassadors reported the situation to their respective governments. The political situation for the Allies was grave.

Napoleon's overture for peace

By 20 June, the Prussians had fallen back to a position behind the Meuse. The fortresses of Maastricht and Liège were in their hands. From here, they would be able to hold their ground for the time being and protect Northern Germany from a French invasion. Blücher wrote to his king requesting that additional forces should be sent to him. A further three army corps were available at home, and these included the royal guard, the heavy cavalry and a number of veteran infantry units. The Prussian General von Kleist's North German Army Corps was already on its way from the Moselle. Blücher was sure he could soon renew the fight.

Wellington held Antwerp, but he was concerned about the loyalties of the population and was beginning to consider disarming the Netherlands troops. That decision would be fraught with consequences, so he delayed for a while, hoping for a positive turn in the course of events.

Napoleon moved his army to observe the garrisons of Antwerp, Maastricht and Liège. As he lacked the strength to advance further, Napoleon put on his politician's hat. His informants in London had passed on the news of Liverpool's impasse. Bonaparte sent messages of peace to Wellington, Blücher, Tsar Alexander and Emperor Francis I of Austria. Napoleon had not wanted this war, and he was anxious to end it. The population of Belgium was behind him and called him their liberator. As Emperor of the French, he had no other territorial ambitions. Recognising the status quo would save much bloodshed.

Events in Heidelberg

On 22 June, the reports from London arrived at Imperial Headquarters in Heidelberg. The Tsar and Emperor Francis were already in a meeting when news arrived that the Saxon Army, disgraced by its rebellion against its Prussian commanders at the beginning of May, had now sworn an oath to Napoleon. Kleist also reported unrest among some of the contingents of his North German Army Corps. On its march to join Blücher, the rate of desertion had increased substantially and Kleist now considered his men unreliable. Some of his contingents came from territories that had, until recently, either spent several years under direct French rule, or had been Napoleon's close allies. Added to all this was the general war-weariness that particularly affected younger conscripts.

Without a firm guarantee of funding from the British, the Austrians considered themselves unable to continue the fight. Metternich and the Emperor started to moot the question of recognising Napoleon's new regime. After all, he was married to an Austrian princess by whom he had had a son. Both mother and child were under the protection of the Austrian court. An Austrian Bonaparte on the French throne after his father's death would not be a disadvantage.

That evening, Napoleon's overture for peace arrived. Metternich persuaded the Tsar to offer Napoleon an armistice while the situation was discussed. As, in any event, it would be another ten days before the Russian and Austrian armies could move against France, would that not be a wise thing to do? Friedrich Wilhelm III, the King of Prussia, knew he could not go it alone. He was the Tsar's junior partner, so he fell in line. The king then wrote to inform Blücher that he would agree to a cease-fire. This news was greeted with outrage in Blücher's headquarters. The Field Marshal's hopes of putting right the wrongs of the politicians with military force faded. The old war-horse wrote back to his king in Berlin tendering his resignation.

Napoleon, seeing the cracks in the Allied coalition beginning to grow, agreed to their offer of a cease-fire and replied by offering talks. He believed that what he could not gain by force of arms, he could now gain by force of argument.

News of Napoleon's success reached Dresden. In public, the King of Saxony condemned his army's actions. In private, he hoped their actions would strengthen his demands for the retention of all his territories. Berlin followed events within this neighbouring state with some concern. Troops were moved to the Saxon border and placed on alert, rendering them unavailable to support Blücher at the front.

From Dresden, the news went to Warsaw. Polish patriots considered it opportune to stage an uprising against Russian rule, hoping for a return to the few short years of independence they had enjoyed during the heyday of Napoleon's Empire. Arms were distributed; barricades went up in the streets of the city and the rebellion spread throughout the countryside. The line of communication between the Russian army in Germany and the motherland was now threatened. Until then, the Tsar had not been certain of his course of action. Now events were dictating it to him. Alexander arranged to move part of his forces from Germany to deal with the uprising in Poland. A Russian intervention in France now seemed unlikely.

The uneasy peace

On 1 July, Napoleon met with Allied representatives at Maastricht. Seeing little chance of removing Napoleon in the short term, they agreed to accept the status quo. Wellington insisted that Antwerp should have a British garrison. Napoleon agreed on the understanding that the port was not to be the territory of the House of Orange. King Willem was left ruling only Dutch-speaking territories. An embarrassed and humbled Wellington returned to England and withdrew from public life, his ambition to become a politician thwarted by his failure in the Low Countries. The sullen Prussians agreed to recognise Napoleon as Emperor of France. Their requirements to maintain garrisons in Maastricht, Liège and Luxembourg were accepted, but in return Prussian demands for the annexation of all or part of Saxony were dropped. Napoleon, too distant and too weak to assist the Poles, left them to their fate at the hands of the Tsar's soldiers. The Austrians, anticipating a new golden age for the Habsburg dynasty with Napoleon II's future rule in Paris, presented no demands to the Emperor. The Austrian position in Northern Italy remained unchanged. Their leading role in Germany was confirmed and the foundation of their future domination of the continent of Europe established. Only the Prussians maintained a substantial garrison on the Rhine. The rest of their army, however, continued to eye Saxony with suspicion. Louis XVIII, now in permanent exile, settled down to a life of leisure in the English countryside. He was presented with the estate of Stratfield Saye near Reading for his country seat and Apsley House for his London residence.

NOTES

1. John Gurwood, ed., *The Dispatches of Field Marshal the Duke of Wellington during his Various Campaigns* (London, 1838), vol.XII, p.473.
2. De Bas and T'Serclaes de Wommersom, *La campagne de 1815 aux pays-bas* (Brussels, 1908), vol.I, p.410.
3. This account is based on the actual regimental history, with suitable amendments.

THE REALITY

Throughout history, there are vital turning points where the actions of a relatively minor participant can play a great role in the outcome of events. The initiative shown by Constant Rebecque in actually disobeying Wellington's order to move the 2nd Netherlands Division to Nivelles from Quatre Bras was crucial to the successful outcome of the campaign. One wonders if a British officer, knowing that Wellington's authority was never to be questioned, would have acted in the same way. Moreover, without Prince Bernhard of Saxe-Weimar's decision to hold his position at Quatre Bras rather than fall back towards Nivelles, Constant Rebecque might not have been quite so bold. Wellington's success and fame owe much to these two men.

This essay, up to and including the section headed 'Prince Bernhard decides to hold his ground' is factual, with only a minimum of conjecture. This conjecture is based on probability and the balance of the evidence. Wellington's order is that actually given. However, in this fictive scenario, Constant Rebecque obeys it. The section headed 'Webster arrives in Brussels' is also fact. We then slip into the 'what ifs'. The mixture of reality and fantasy illustrate how close Wellington's order to Constant Rebecque came to causing a catastrophe. The fictive letter from Wellington written in Genappe at 10 am on 16 June is based very closely on one actually written by the Duke only half an hour later at Frasnes, just south of Quatre Bras. Only a few words have been changed. The remaining account is fictional, but hopefully close enough to what might have happened in such circumstances to be credible. As Wellington himself said, it was a close run thing.

BIBLIOGRAPHY

Chandler, David, *Campaigns of Napoleon* (New York, 1967).

Charras, Jean Baptiste Adolphe, *Histoire de la campagne de 1815: Waterloo* (Paris, 1869).

Chesney, Colonel Charles C., RE, *Waterloo Lectures: A Study of the Campaign of 1815* (London, 1907, reprinted 1997).

Clausewitz, Carl von, *Der Feldzug von 1815 in Frankreich* (Berlin, 1835).

De Bas and T'Serclaes de Wommersom *La campagne de 1815 aux pays-bas* (3 vols, Brussels, 1908).

Wellington, 2nd Duke of, *Despatches, Correspondence, and Memoranda of Field Marshal Arthur Duke of Wellington* (New Series, 8 vols, London, 1867–80).

NAPOLEON AND WATERLOO

BY ANDREW UFFINDELL

Waterloo is one of those epic battles whose fame will never fade. It was the climax of a short, bloody and decisive campaign that began on 15 June 1815, when Napoleon suddenly invaded the United Netherlands and thrust northwards on Brussels. Two enemy armies were deployed against him: firstly 117,000 Prussians under Field Marshal Gebhard Leberecht von Blücher; and secondly a composite force of 93,000 men, commanded by the Duke of Wellington and composed of contingents from Britain, the United Netherlands and the German states of Hanover, Brunswick and Nassau.

Together, these two allies massively outnumbered Napoleon, who could field only 124,000 men, but they needed time to concentrate from scattered cantonments. Before they could do so, Napoleon had a glittering window of opportunity in which to knock out one or other of them. On 16 June, he dealt Blücher a heavy but inconclusive defeat at Ligny, twenty-six miles south-east of Brussels. Wellington's still-concentrating army was unable to intervene at Ligny, being held at bay at Quatre-Bras, eight miles to the north-west, by the French left wing under Marshal Michel Ney.

17 June

Drubbed but still defiant, the Prussians fell back twelve miles northwards and rallied around the town of Wavre. Napoleon did not pursue immediately on the morning of 17 June, but waited at Ligny for the arrival of information about his two enemies and their lines of retreat. Only towards 11 am did he finally act. Informed that Wellington had still been at Quatre Bras earlier that morning, the Emperor ordered his reserves, namely the Imperial Guard and the bulk of VI Corps, to join Ney at Quatre Bras and fall on the Duke's exposed army.

Faulty intelligence had misled Napoleon into thinking that the Prussians were retiring eastwards. He turned to Marshal Emmanuel de Grouchy and told him to pursue them. Some units were already seeking to pick up the Prussian trail: these were General Count Rémy Exelmans' II Cavalry Corps, a division of General Count Claude Pajol's I Cavalry Corps and General Baron François Teste's infantry division, detached from VI Corps. In addition to these troops, Napoleon now entrusted Grouchy with General Count Dominique Vandamme's III Corps, General Count Etienne Gérard's

IV Corps and General Count Edouard Milhaud's IV Cavalry Corps. Grouchy left to give the necessary orders.

Soon afterwards, Napoleon changed his mind, clearly having realised that if he gave Grouchy so large a force, he would find himself short of troops should Wellington offer battle. He therefore dictated to his Grand Marshal of the Palace, General Count Henri Bertrand, an order for Grouchy to return both Vandamme and Milhaud and to send them westwards along the road to Quatre Bras. Grouchy was therefore left with the 20,000 men of Pajol, Exelmans, Gérard and Teste. But, since the Prussians had such a head start, he only gradually realised that they had gone northwards, rather than eastwards.

We do not know how Napoleon would have fared had he pursued his original option of giving Grouchy as many as 36,000 troops. He would have left himself with only 69,000 men and would probably have run into serious difficulties in any battle against Wellington. In any case, the die was cast. Grouchy rode off to find the Prussians, while Napoleon led his forces to Quatre Bras to link up with Ney.

It was too late to bring Wellington to battle that day. Ney had not stirred, despite Napoleon's orders to pin Wellington down at Quatre Bras with a frontal attack. Instead, the Duke had skilfully broken contact and retreated northwards up the Brussels road, while torrential rain turned the Belgian countryside into a quagmire in which the pursuit foundered.

Wellington halted and deployed his army on the ridge of Mont St Jean, two-and-a-half miles south of the village of Waterloo, where he had his headquarters on the southern edge of the Forest of Soignes. Late that evening, he received from Blücher at Wavre a promise that 'I shall not come with two corps only, but with my whole army'. Secure in this assurance of strong Prussian support, Wellington thereupon resolved to give battle next day in the positions that he occupied.

Dawn of Waterloo: 18 June

The sun rose towards 4 am. Napoleon was supremely confident of victory, but as yet had only his leading units on the battlefield, for the subsequent corps had halted the previous evening along a five-mile stretch of the Brussels road, all the way southwards to beyond the village of Genappe. Hence Napoleon postponed the start of the battle, in the hope that this would give time for his rearmost units to arrive and also allow the water-logged ground to dry somewhat, so that his artillery could manoeuvre more easily.

Meanwhile, he held a pre-battle conference with his senior sub-ordinates. He quashed their fears that the Prussians might try to unite with Wellington, for he believed that they had been too badly defeated at Ligny to recover so soon. He also ruled out an attempt to outflank

Wellington, since difficult, muddy terrain ruled out swift and compli-
cated manoeuvres, particularly to the east. In any case, Napoleon did not
want to frighten Wellington into resuming the retreat, but instead intended simply to overwhelm him with a massive frontal attack. Since he
could pit 83,000 troops against Wellington's 68,000,[1] his attitude was
hardly surprising.

At 10 am, the French army – except for III Corps, which had yet to
arrive – paraded over the soaked fields and formed up for battle in a
glittering kaleidoscope of uniforms. At 11.30 am, the battle began.
Napoleon's first move was a limited assault on the farm of Hougoumont,
Wellington's strongpoint in the western sector of the battlefield. But this
attack escalated out of control, with half of General Count Honoré
Reille's II Corps being sucked into the fighting. In vain did the French
infantry assail the farm buildings and the formidable, loopholed garden
wall. Casualties soared.

But the attack on Hougoumont was merely a preliminary. Napoleon was
about to unleash a massive assault in a bid to smash through Wellington's
eastern wing and win the battle in one, brutal stroke. A great battery of
eighty guns pounded this sector of the Allied line, to prepare for an
onslaught by the 16,000 infantrymen of General Jean-Baptiste Drouet,
Count d'Erlon's I Corps. Protected on either flank by cavalry, d'Erlon was to
break through the enemy front and then swing round to the west in order to
cut the Brussels road and drive Wellington away to the north-west.
Napoleon would then unleash his reserves and throw III and VI Corps, the
reserve cavalry and the Imperial Guard at Wellington's reeling army to
complete the victory.

The preparatory bombardment continued for a whole hour. While it was
in progress, Napoleon spotted troops on the eastern horizon and shortly
afterwards learnt from a captured messenger that the Prussian IV Corps was
bearing down on his eastern flank. He thereupon detached two light cavalry
divisions, plus VI Corps under General Georges Mouton, the Count of
Lobau, to check this threat. He remained confident that he still had enough
time and men to crush Wellington, but, just in case, sent a vague message
to advise Marshal Grouchy to bring his detachment nearer to the main
army.

Then, at 2 pm, I Corps advanced in four massive columns. At first
everything seemed to be going marvellously. Then steel flashed on the ridge
crest as British heavy dragoons, hitherto hidden from view on the reverse
slopes, charged, routed, and furiously hacked their way through the dis-
solving ranks of French infantry. Flushed with success, the British horsemen
dashed on, up to the Great Battery on the French side of the valley. There,
they came under a deadly counter-attack from ruthless French lancers, and
those of them that survived fell back across the valley.

The gathering storm

Napoleon redoubled his efforts against Wellington. The Prussians presented no immediate threat and the stout-hearted Lobau was perfectly capable of containing them with his tough VI Corps. On Napoleon's orders, French artillery fire was now raining down on both La Haie Sainte and Hougoumont. Fire broke out at both these farms and French infantry repeatedly assaulted the gates.

The impetuous Marshal Ney renewed the offensive with a series of massed cavalry charges on Wellington's centre, involving the cuirassiers of Milhaud's IV Cavalry Corps and the light cavalry division of the Imperial Guard. Napoleon thought that these attacks were premature, but since they had gone in, he prepared to support them with the available infantry, consisting of Vandamme's III Corps and those units of II Corps which had not been sucked into the struggle at Hougoumont. Towards 5 pm, after several charges, the French cavalry established itself on top of Wellington's ridge crest and, despite counter-attacks from Allied horsemen, hovered around his infantry squares. Wellington's artillery stood abandoned on the crest of the ridge, for the gunners had taken shelter within the squares. Now French infantry columns advanced inexorably across the valley to consolidate what the cavalry had won. Gun teams likewise toiled through the mud.

Soon, swarms of French infantry skirmishers, backed up by artillery, were in action along the ridge crest, pouring a deadly fire into Wellington's small, cramped infantry squares, which replied feebly from their southern faces. Wellington's cavalry commander, the Earl of Uxbridge, galloped energetically from unit to unit of his cavalry, ordering them to counter-attack. However, the Dutch-Belgians refused to budge, while a regiment of Hanoverian hussars fled the battlefield altogether. The British heavy cavalry were a wreck, which left only the British light cavalry and the Brunswick hussars and uhlans, who charged as often as they could and won temporary successes despite the French weight of numbers.

The French attritional tactics steadily wore down Wellington's front line, as canister continually blasted great gaps in the walls of his squares. A battalion of Nassau infantry counter-attacked on the Prince of Orange's orders, only to be ridden down almost instantly by French cuirassiers. And the farm of La Haie Sainte finally fell to the French, after the heroic garrison had exhausted its ammunition.

Napoleon sensed that the moment had come. After detaching the Young Guard division to help Lobau contain the Prussians, he entrusted Ney with the seven battalions of the Middle Guard and ordered him to punch a hole through Wellington's increasingly tattered centre. Through the gap he could then pour the fresh III Cavalry Corps of General François Kellermann.

The intervention of the Middle Guard decided the day. Wellington's centre was driven from the ridge crest, and this reverse loosened his army's grip on its positions to both east and west. Uxbridge flung the remains of the British heavy cavalry and some King's German Legion horsemen forward into the fray. This desperate counter-attack initially smashed a formation of cuirassiers, but then came to grief at the hands of the Middle Guard battalions, which coolly formed square and blazed away with musketry. Caught in the crossfire, horses reared and fell while others plunged forward in terror and carried their riders out into the open, where they were ruthlessly speared by French lancers.

Wellington quickly realised that if he tried to maintain contact with both Hougoumont on his western flank and the Prussians in the east, his own army would be split apart as the French advanced in the centre. He therefore evacuated what he could of Hougoumont's garrison, abandoned the rest to its fate and began to retire northwards in order to keep his army in being.

Uxbridge, meanwhile, summoned Sir John Vandeleur's brigade of British light dragoons from the far eastern flank, leaving Sir Hussey Vivian's hussars to cover that wing as it retired.[2] The Prince of Orange also reacted to the French success and sent his ADC, Captain the Earl of March, galloping to General Baron David Chassé's Dutch-Belgian 3rd Division, which stood in reserve in the west. 'The French have broken into the centre,' March exclaimed breathlessly. 'You must counter-attack at once.' The gallant Chassé flung his division into the battle and temporarily checked the French push. But it could not last, and General d'Aubremé's brigade broke and fled when suddenly assailed by French cavalry. The Prince of Orange bravely held his own against two cuirassiers before being wounded, disarmed and captured.

French gunners toiled to bring more and more pieces into action and mercilessly pounded Wellington's exposed units retreating across the plateau. Ammunition wagons exploded again and again, each sending a column of white smoke boiling furiously up into the sky to open out into a mushroom cloud. Wellington could do little to reply to this destructive fire, having lost most of his front-line artillery when it was overrun on the ridge crest. For instance, Captain Cavalié Mercer of 'G' Troop, Royal Horse Artillery, had spiked his guns and then withdrawn across the fields with his few surviving men and horses.[3]

Wellington defeated

Battered remorselessly for over six hours, Wellington's army now began to disintegrate. Most of the Dutch-Belgian cavalry and much of the infantry disappeared, and it was generally only the British and some of the German units that kept their cohesion as they fell back, defying the French at every step and striving to maintain some sort of rearguard line. A tragic little incident further slowed the French advance. One of the regiments in

Vandamme's III Corps was the 2nd Swiss Infantry, which wore its traditional red tunics. At first, the British mistook the Swiss for fellow redcoats
and held their fire, until they discovered their error. But then, in the heat
and chaos of battle, the French made the same mistake and poured repeated
volleys into the luckless Swiss, who were shot down from all sides.

A network of tracks intersected the countryside to the north of Wellington's ridge and eased his retreat. The withdrawal was easiest on the
eastern side of the Brussels road, for here the Forest of Soignes extended one
mile further south than it did to the west. Indeed, the troops in this sector
had to retreat only 2,600 yards from the ridge to the cover of the forest, and
at one point, where the forest jutted out at the village of Vert Coucou, they
had to cover only 1,800 yards. The hussar brigade of Sir Hussey Vivian,
covering the eastern flank of this withdrawal, reached and occupied the
village of Ransbèche, which anchored the eastern end of Wellington's new
position.[4]

The Brussels road itself was so clogged with abandoned carts, corpses and
debris that neither army could use it; units instead moved across the muddy
fields. Besides, as they advanced the French would encounter a chain of
strongpoints alongside the road: first the farm and then the village of Mont
St Jean, and from there onwards houses dotted along both sides all the way
to the village of Waterloo, where the road entered the Forest of Soignes.
Thus it was to the west of the Brussels road that Wellington's retreat was
most dangerously exposed. The country here was more open, although the
hamlets of Merbraine and Ménil did provide convenient rearguard points on
the way north.

From what Wellington said at the time to his staff, we can see that he
aimed to retire as best he could back to the shelter of the Forest of Soignes.
If possible, he would turn at bay there and continue the battle with the
assistance of growing numbers of his Prussian allies. Otherwise, he would
have to retire through the forest to make a stand immediately south of the
ramparts of Brussels, on the open hills of Uccle and Ixelles. This position
would enable him to cover the key approach roads from Hal, Waterloo and
Wavre. Blücher might even be able to join him here.

The forest, far from obstructing Wellington's retreat, would actually
shield it by delaying and confusing the French and enabling Wellington to
disengage. As an officer of the Royal Engineers noted, 'there is no under-
wood; it is composed entirely of beech, and intersected, in every direction,
by vistas and alleys, in which the nobility and gentry of Brussels ride and
drive. The forest is practicable for cavalry, artillery and infantry, in almost
every direction.'[5]

However, Wellington was aware that in the past, French armies intent on
seizing Brussels had tended not to go due north, but instead had sought to
avoid becoming entangled in the Forest of Soignes and had gone round it to

the west. This was one reason why, before the battle began, the Duke had left a detachment of 17,000 men nearly eight miles west of Waterloo, around the town of Hal, where the French would need to cross the River Senne in order to bypass the forest. This detachment would at the very least delay Napoleon long enough to enable Wellington to pull his army back through the forest before it was encircled.

But Wellington was worried by one consequence of his retreat: a gap had opened between himself and Blücher. Indeed, the Prussians had been forced back on to the defensive and now feared for their exposed northern flank. Fortunately, some of their battalions, plus a brigade of Wellington's Nassau troops who had become detached from their own army, firmly held the château of Frischermont and the village of Smohain, which anchored this flank. Furthermore, the French were still too much engaged with Wellington to switch their attention to Blücher, and soon General Count Hans von Zieten's Prussian I Corps would arrive to plug the gap. Indeed, by 6 pm Zieten's advanced guard was already passing the village of Ohain, just 2,300 yards east of Ransbèche, where Wellington's eastern flank now lay.

Hougoumont was isolated now. The troops in the orchard and garden had managed to fight their way out, but those in the building block had been tied down by a fierce French assault and quickly surrounded. Cannonballs were already smashing through the massive wooden doors of the North Gate, ammunition was running out, and fire had broken out once more, sending a great pall of black smoke drifting into the air. This time the Gardener's House was ablaze and the Coldstream Guardsmen were forced to abandon their firing positions above the southern gate. Nearly all the other buildings were already gutted and the courtyard was literally macadamised with corpses.

A ragged fusillade came from the farm of Mont St Jean on the Brussels road, where two battalions of Hanoverian Landwehr and the tattered remnants of Colonel Christian von Ompteda's King's German Legion brigade repelled the initial French onslaught on the main gate. But eventually the French brought up cannon, smashed their way in and poured triumphantly into the courtyard. They mercilessly bayoneted all who could not escape, including those of the wounded whom the hospital doctors had been unable to evacuate. Yet the French now faced an even more complex stronghold: Mont St Jean village was holding out 500 yards further north, and Ney was screaming for artillery to pound it into submission.

So the fight raged on, Uxbridge being among those wounded during these tense moments. As dusk fell, shells were exploding in the village of Waterloo, which stood at the entrance to the Forest of Soignes, two-and-a-half miles north of Wellington's initial position. Major-General Peregrine Maitland's 1st Foot Guards (now known as The Waterloo Guards) prepared to check the French from behind barricades of carts and loopholed houses, while other formations, including Major-General Frederick Adam's brigade, which was still in reasonable shape, held the wood to the west. To the east stood Major-General Sir John Lambert's brigade, together with the united remnants of Sir Thomas Picton's 5th Division, now commanded by Colonel Sir Charles Belson of the 28th Foot.

The brunt of the French assaults on the Forest of Soignes fell at first on Belson's men east of the Brussels road. But in this sector the houses of the village of Roussart were strung out like a chain of forts along the southern edge of the forest. Frustrated here, the French then vainly attacked the British Guards holding the village of Waterloo, before shifting the weight of their onslaughts further west. They initially had more success here and plunged headlong into the forest. But they soon became disordered in the dark, and after repeatedly falling into ambushes they broke and poured back in such haste that they nearly sparked off a general panic. A similar reverse had befallen the Duke of Marlborough's advance guard back in 1705, when it had rashly advanced into the forest at Waterloo at dusk and had been sharply repelled by a French force under the locally-born Colonel Jacques Pasteur.

The fighting died away fitfully towards 11 pm. Despite the setback in the Forest of Soignes, the French were elated. Twenty-one years previously, Marshal Jean-de-Dieu Soult, Napoleon's chief-of-staff, had helped to seize this same plateau from the Austrians during the Revolutionary Wars. He now wrote exuberantly to Marshal Louis Davout, the Minister of War in Paris:

> Once more French arms have triumphed on the glorious battlefield of Mont St Jean. Never has the Emperor been so great. Two days after beating the Prussian army at Fleurus [Ligny], His Imperial Majesty has just defeated Wellington and driven him back in disorder towards Brussels. Some Prussian units that have rallied and joined Wellington will likewise be harried throughout the night. The Emperor directs you immediately to send reinforcements to the armies defending the eastern frontiers, where he will shortly go himself after occupying Brussels. Let France rejoice.

Despite heavy losses and a longer battle than he had anticipated, Napoleon had beaten Wellington and did not doubt that the Duke would now abandon Brussels and scamper back to England. But he would have to wait until the following morning before launching a pursuit of Wellington and those Prussian corps that had reached the battlefield. Once he reached Brussels, Napoleon planned to offer peace, absorb Belgian manpower to repair his losses and also create some new, younger marshals, foremost among them General Count Etienne Gérard, who had so distinguished himself at Ligny on 16 June, and the loyal General Count Antoine Drouot of the Imperial Guard.

The duel with Blücher: 19 June

Apart from Napoleon, hardly anyone slept soundly that night. The battlefield was bathed in an eerie moonlight. Here and there, flames flickered in shattered farms and villages, while nervous sentries repeatedly fired at fleeting shadows.

Even today, we do not know exactly what happened in Blücher's headquarters that night, beyond the fact that another fierce dispute occurred between Blücher and his chief-of-staff, General Count August von Gneisenau. It was sparked off at 1.30 am when a message arrived from Wellington, asking whether the Prussians intended to continue the fight. Gneisenau, deeply suspicious of Wellington and desperately anxious for the safety of the Prussian army, feared that the Duke wanted to use the Prussians to cover his retreat through the Forest of Soignes to embark at Antwerp.

Gneisenau's nightmare was the thought of the Prussian army being forced back south-eastwards against the steep, muddy valley of the River Lasne and there destroyed. To avoid this risk, he wanted to pull back the exposed Prussian southern wing, which, during the afternoon of 18 June, had been pushed right forward, as the Prussians concentrated their efforts on trying to take the village of Plancenoit in the south. If Gneisenau had his way the army would be more balanced and, if it did have to retreat, would be able to do so north-eastwards, parallel to the Lasne rather than across it, and towards the city of Louvain, where it could unite with General Baron Johann von Thielmann's Prussian III Corps (left at Wavre as a rearguard and currently holding Marshal Grouchy's detachment at bay with ease).

But Blücher flatly rejected the idea of abandoning his hard-won gains near Plancenoit. Too much Prussian blood had been shed there and if they managed to take the much-contested village, they would be in a position to cut Napoleon's line of retreat southwards. At 3 am, after much dispute, a messenger finally left to inform Wellington that Blücher would renew the battle, in his present positions, soon after dawn.

During the night the rearmost units of the Prussian I and II Corps had joined IV Corps on the battlefield and brought Prussian numbers up to 70,000. The bulk of these troops, namely II and IV Corps, were in the south, between Smohain and Plancenoit, with 7th and 8th brigades of II Corps (a total of 11,000 men) even further south, on the southern bank of the River Lasne and in a position to press on, bypass Plancenoit and threaten to overwhelm Napoleon's southern flank. In the north, Zieten's I Corps had completely closed the gap between Wellington and Blücher, but was extended in a two-and-a-half mile arc from Ransbèche in the north to Smohain in the south.

As a result of losses suffered on 18 June, Napoleon must have now had about 55,000 men, and Wellington – after deducting both casualties and deserters – roughly 30,000 troops still in fighting order.

True to his word, Blücher heralded the second day of the battle with a fierce onslaught on the French VI Corps. A mass of Prussian cavalry had assembled in the fields north of Plancenoit and now came on in waves, with the rising sun behind them. A fierce artillery duel shattered the quiet and the smoke from the guns steadily intensified throughout the morning.

Late the previous night, Napoleon had pulled the Middle Guard back into reserve after its successful attack on Wellington. He now prepared to commit it once more to the fray, this time against Zieten. He aimed to punch right through Zieten and thrust south-eastwards in order to isolate the Prussian II and IV Corps and pin them against the valley of the River Lasne. By mid-morning all the available Guard batteries were pounding Zieten's men in preparation for the assault. The hitherto uncommitted heavy cavalry division of the Guard joined the attack, which began at 10 am.

Zieten's corps stumbled back under the impact, so much so that Blücher suspended his cavalry charges in the centre. For a moment it seemed that all was over and Baron Carl von Müffling, the Prussian liaison officer with Wellington's army, was shot dead as he tried to stem the tide. But the Prussians hurriedly collected whatever guns they could spare and brought them into action to stabilise the situation. The opportune arrival of the Prussian 9th brigade of over 5,000 men put an end to French hopes of a breakthrough. (The 9th brigade was part of Thielmann's III Corps at Wavre, but in the confusion of 18 June had become detached and had followed Blücher's march to Waterloo). Brought to a halt, the French guardsmen had shot their bolt and now had to endure an unrelenting artillery fire as they grimly held on to the murderously-exposed positions that they had won.

Lull in the north

Things had been quieter, meanwhile, along the edge of the Forest of Soignes. At dawn, French sentries had found themselves confronted by only a line of outposts, for Wellington kept the rest of his men hidden inside the forest.

Towards 5 am the Duke learnt that Blücher intended to renew the battle and therefore took the risk of summoning Lieutenant-General Sir Charles Colville from near Hal, with over 5,000 British and Hanoverian infantry, a regiment of Hanoverian hussars and six guns.[6] Receiving the Duke's summons, Colville began his march eastwards at 7 am, but would not be able to reach the battlefield before 12 noon. Another 10,000 Dutch-Belgian infantry, a Hanoverian hussar regiment and sixteen guns remained in position around Hal under Prince Frederick, the younger brother of the Prince of Orange. Some historians have heavily criticised Wellington for weakening the Hal detachment at this uncertain moment. Others, in contrast, condemn him for not calling in all the troops from Hal, including Prince Frederick's Dutch-Belgians.

Fighting suddenly flared up when the French launched a strong probe into the forest in the mid-morning, but Wellington checked the move and counter-attacked, waving his cocked hat to direct a bayonet charge by the decimated Highlanders. It was then that disaster struck. As he urged the Gordons to 'go on, 92nd, drive those fellows away', Wellington suddenly toppled from his saddle. Officers leapt from their horses and dashed to the scene, but were powerless to do anything for their commander, who had been shot through the heart.

Wellington's fall temporarily paralysed his army. ADCs galloped off to find the surviving senior officers, but inevitably it took time to get to grips with the situation. Large-scale attacks in support of the Prussians were suspended for a couple of hours and fighting in this sector petered out as the troops settled down to cook what provisions they had managed to find. The ominous silence did nothing to reassure Gneisenau and left Napoleon free to concentrate his efforts against the Prussians without any diversions on his weakly-held northern flank.

Command of Wellington's army had devolved upon Lieutenant-General Sir Rowland Hill, since both of his seniors – the Prince of Orange and the Earl of Uxbridge – had been either captured or seriously wounded.[7] 'Daddy' Hill was an unlikely hero, being so mild-mannered that he seemed more like a good-natured country gentleman than a warrior. Yet he had proved a bold and self-reliant commander in the Peninsula and he now capably organised a powerful offensive, to begin towards 12.30 pm. He sent most of his available cavalry to the western flank, to co-operate with Colville's reinforcements due to arrive from Hal. These troops were to outflank the French western wing and thrust deep into the heart of Napoleon's army. Hill's remaining units would leave the cover of the forest and advance across the plateau further to the east in support.

Hill's men were desperate to avenge the fall of their commander and comrades and would attack ferociously. Lieutenant-Colonel Sir Neil Campbell, commander of the 54th Foot on the march with Colville from Hal, had an added incentive. He had been the British commissioner on Elba responsible for keeping an eye on Napoleon while the fallen Emperor had been in exile on the island. But while Campbell had been away on a trip to the Italian mainland, Napoleon had slipped back to France, leaving the humiliated Campbell beside himself with rage.

The catastrophe unfolds

Hill's cavalry skilfully screened Colville's arrival from French observation and the assault came as an unpleasant shock. Almost instantly, Hill broke the over-stretched French I and II Corps and sparked off a panic. The French front simply collapsed. Soon afterwards, at the opposite end of the Allied line, the Prussian 7th and 8th brigades, attacking over the fields south of Plancenoit, finally overwhelmed their Imperial Guard opponents and thrust westwards across the Brussels road. The beleaguered French army began to crumble and then suddenly imploded. The stage was set for one of the greatest disasters in military history.

Since Prussian units had already cut the Brussels road, the only line of retreat now open to the French was the paved Nivelles road, running south-westwards from Mont St Jean. But hordes of Prussian cavalry were riding across the fields south of Hougoumont to link up with Hill's cavalry accompanying Colville's thrust through Braine-l'Alleud in the west. Several thousand Frenchmen escaped before the Allies completed their encirclement and others would manage to smash their way out of the trap, but Allied infantry and guns shortly arrived to reinforce their cavalry spearheads.

Soon Napoleon's army writhed in its death-throes as Prussian artillery remorselessly pounded the seething mob of fugitives. Somewhere in the chaos, Ney perished heroically in a hail of fire as he bellowed defiance and shouted at his men to 'come and see how a Marshal of France dies on the battlefield'. Marshal Soult met a more inglorious end, being captured by the Prussians, mistaken – owing to his short stature – for the Emperor and promptly shot.

Napoleon, meanwhile, had halted the two battalions of the 1st Grena-diers of the Guard on the high ground near La Belle Alliance. For a while he hoped to fight his way out, but he had left it too late. What ensued soon became enshrined in myth, but the basic facts are clear. Rather than sur-render, the gallant guardsmen fought practically to the last man to defend their Emperor. When the firing finally ceased and the smoke dispersed, not a Frenchman was left on his feet and Prussian troops searching among the corpses found that Napoleon himself had been slain.

Towards evening, the approximately 30,000 Frenchmen caught in the Waterloo pocket resigned themselves to their fate and laid down their arms.

Aftermath

At Wavre, Marshal Grouchy had tied down the bulk of Thielmann's Prussian III Corps along the River Dyle, although he was too weak to inflict a defeat. Grouchy remained unaware of Napoleon's disaster until informed of it by a captured Prussian messenger late in the evening of 19 June. He escaped from his perilously-exposed position by promptly marching south-eastwards to Namur and then moving southwards across the border into France, showing a skill and resolution that won him great renown. For this, and his subsequent service, he was in 1846 appointed by King Louis-Philippe to be a Marshal-General of France, an extremely rare honour shared only by the legendary eighteenth-century commanders Claude, Duke of Villers, and Maurice, Count of Saxe.

The effects of Waterloo were far-reaching. For the French, it was a catastrophe that eclipsed even that of Leipzig two years previously. Napoleon's life came to an abrupt but dramatic end, sparing the Allies a long drawn-out struggle that might have lasted into 1816. Blücher and Hill marched unopposed on Paris and there secured an armistice at the beginning of July, which led to formal peace by the end of the year.

In Britain, the news of the victory brought little rejoicing, for the fearsome casualties and the loss of the Duke caused much mourning. Besides, initial reports of Wellington having been defeated had unleashed a bloody uprising in Ireland, where garrisons had been reduced to dangerous levels.[8]

Only in Prussia was the outcome of the battle greeted with unreserved joy. Indeed, it had been the Prussians who had overwhelmingly borne the brunt of the campaign and the hero of the hour was Blücher. Right through the campaign, in contrast to Wellington's caution and Gneisenau's timidity, Blücher's driving determination to take on and beat Napoleon stands out supreme. However, revisionist historians in Britain have recently tried to demolish what they see as the Blücher myth. They argue that Wellington gave battle at Waterloo only because he counted on early Prussian support, which in the event arrived several hours late, partly because the Prussian high command idiotically led their advance with their easternmost corps. But for this, Blücher might have averted Wellington's defeat on 18 June and even beaten Napoleon that same day.

Today, much of the battlefield has changed dramatically, for the Forest of Soignes has largely vanished and the town of Waterloo has become a sprawling mass of houses that extends right up to Mont St Jean. But further south, the battleground remains mostly open countryside and the Prussian sector in particular is dotted with monuments. Tributes to the British fallen are mostly in the Wellington Memorial Chapel in the centre of Waterloo.

High point of any battlefield tour is, of course, the Napoleon monument near La Belle Alliance, to which pilgrims still flock in their thousands. The site assumed an even greater significance in 1962, when French President General Charles de Gaulle was assassinated there during a state visit. A granite Cross of Lorraine now towers beside Napoleon's statue and the association of these two great leaders so tragically cut down strikes a powerful chord even today. The fatal plateau of Mont St Jean will cast a long shadow over French national consciousness.

NOTES

1. Not including the detachment of 17,000 men that Wellington had left eight miles away around the town of Hal to guard against a possible outflanking move to the west.
2. An officer of Vivian's brigade had been ordered that morning to reconnoitre a line of retreat in case the unit had to make just such a move as this: H. Siborne, ed., *The Waterloo Letters* (1983), p.196.

3. C. Mercer, *Journal of the Waterloo Campaign* (1985), p.168.
4. Place-names are taken from modern maps and differ in some cases from those on W.B. Craan's famous battlefield map of 1816. For instance: Ménil/Le Mesnil; Merbraine/Merbe-Braine; Ransbèche/Haut Ransbeek; Vert Coucou/Verd Coucou.
5. J. Carmichael-Smyth, *Chronological Epitome of the Wars in the Low Countries* (1825), p.403.
6. J. Colville, *The Portrait of a General: A Chronicle of the Napoleonic Wars* (1980), p.201.
7. It is unclear who would have assumed command in other circumstances. The historian Sir William Fraser, the son of a Waterloo veteran, wrote: 'frequently as I have heard the subject discussed, I never have known it finally settled as to who would have commanded at Waterloo, if the Duke of Wellington had been killed.' The Prince of Orange, as a full general, was senior to Uxbridge, who was a lieutenant-general. However, Uxbridge himself assumed that the command would devolve upon him and on the eve of the battle had asked Wellington what his plans were, in case Wellington should become a casualty. Sir William Fraser added that 'I heard many years ago, on good authority, that a Commission was found on Picton's person, giving him the absolute command of the British forces, and their Allies, in the case of the Duke's death.' But this seems unlikely and in any case, Picton was killed early in the afternoon of 18 June. See Sir W. Fraser, *Words on Wellington* (nd), pp.1–3.
8. G. L'Estrange, *Recollections of Sir George B. L'Estrange* (nd), p.208.
9. H. Houssaye, *1815 Waterloo* (1987), pp.228–9.
10. H. Parker, *Three Napoleonic Battles* (1983), p.208.

THE REALITY

With hindsight we can see that Napoleon lost his best chance of a decisive victory on 16 June, when he failed to destroy the Prussian army at Ligny. If, in that battle, d'Erlon's I Corps had fallen on Blücher's western flank and encircled a large portion of his army, as Napoleon had intended, then there could have been no Waterloo. Wellington on his own simply would not have given battle against Napoleon and would probably have abandoned Brussels and retreated northwards to the port of Antwerp.

As it was, Napoleon's failure to destroy Blücher at Ligny left him with three options on the morning of 17 June:

First, he could personally lead the bulk of his army after the Prussians and complete their defeat.

Second, he could detach a sizeable force to shepherd the Prussians away from the campaign area, while he took the rest of his army after Wellington.

Third, he could detach a weak reconnaissance force to shadow the Prussians, and take all his remaining troops – perhaps as many as 97,000 of them – after Wellington.

In reality, Napoleon took option two: he sent about 32,000 men with Grouchy to pursue the Prussians and took only 72,000 to Waterloo. But he made that decision only after some hesitation. Initially he entrusted Grouchy with nearly 36,000 troops, namely III and IV Corps, II and IV

Cavalry Corps and a division each of VI Corps and I Cavalry Corps. Minutes later he changed his mind and took back both Milhaud's IV Cavalry Corps and the light cavalry division of General Baron Jean Domon, which was detached from III Corps. These cavalry units accompanied him to Waterloo.[9]

In our fictional account, Napoleon simply takes this change of mind one step further and also reclaims the rest of III Corps. After the losses suffered at Ligny, this corps contained a little over 11,000 infantrymen and gunners and our fictional account examines the impact that these extra troops could have had on the engagement at Waterloo.

I leave it to the reader to ponder what might have happened if Napoleon had chosen the third option and brought even more troops to Waterloo, or if he had followed the first option instead, and led the bulk of his army after Blücher instead of Wellington. It is enough here to note that these were less likely options for Napoleon to take. It is true that he later lamented that he should have sent only one cavalry and one infantry division (less than 4,000 men) to pursue Blücher, but this observation had the advantage of hindsight and ignores the peril in which such a small detachment would have been placed.[10]

Finally, remember that the actual battle of Waterloo was far less of a near run thing than the campaign as a whole. By the time he began the battle of Waterloo at 11.30 am on 18 June, Napoleon's chances were unhealthy. A frontal attack on Wellington's strong position could have succeeded only at the cost of such heavy casualties as would have rendered any French victory a hollow triumph, like Borodino in 1812. So what was really at stake was the nature and timing of the victory over Napoleon. Even if he had somehow won a meaningful victory at Waterloo, he almost certainly would have gone down to ultimate defeat under a powerful Allied invasion of France, probably that same year, but otherwise in 1816.

BIBLIOGRAPHY

Becke, A., *Napoleon and Waterloo* (reissued London, 1995).

Chalfont, Lord, *Waterloo: Battle of Three Armies* (London, 1979).

Chandler, D., *Waterloo: The Hundred Days* (reissued London, 1998).

Chesney, C., *Waterloo Lectures* (reissued London, 1997).

Houssaye, H., *1815 Waterloo* (reissued Etrépilly, 1987).

Ropes, J., *The Campaign of Waterloo: A Military History* (reissued London, 1995).

Siborne, W., *History of the Waterloo Campaign* (reissued London, 1990).

Uffindell, A., *The Eagle's Last Triumph: Napoleon's Victory at Ligny, June 1815* (London, 1994).

—, 'Could Napoleon have won Waterloo?' in *British Army Review* (April 1998).

— and Corum, M., *On the Fields of Glory: The Battlefields of the 1815 Campaign* (London, 1996).

Weller, J., *Wellington at Waterloo* (reissued London, 1998).

AMBUSH AT QUATRE BRAS

BY COLONEL JOHN ELTING

And we are here as on a darkling plain
Swept with confused alarms of struggle and flight,
Where ignorant armies clash by night.
— Mathew Arnold, *Dover Beach*

'The Emperor has need of us!'

The 7th Infantry Division came fast-striding along the darkening road from Ligny to Quatre Bras, answering the summons brought by a courier with a bullet through his shako and another in his shoulder. 'If he'd taken us along in the first place, he wouldn't be in this fix! But if those Prussian *illégitimes* need their noses wiped again, we're the little boys to do it.'

The 7th had been chewed up at Ligny two days previously. Its commander then — General Jean Girard, tiny, all-out fighting man with the sacred fire in his heart and brain — was dying in a Paris-bound carriage. The Emperor had left them to recover while cleaning up the battlefield. But its colonels knew their business. The 7th was rested, its cartridge boxes were full, and its ranks fleshed out again with odd-lot detachments left behind by other units, slightly wounded men released from the ambulances and certain reluctants plucked from cellars and thickets and quickly convinced that they *did* yearn to be heroes. Its attached artillery company still had men and horses for five six-pounders. It even had a body of cavalry, over 200 of them, built around a detached company from the 1st Hussars; its commander, Captain Jacques Merle — so gentle and soft-spoken that fellow officers called him 'Mam'selle', so stark-deadly a fighter that his troopers spoke of him with awed blasphemy — had swept together every serviceable horse and cavalryman he could find. It was a bizarre outfit, made up of every type of cavalryman, with a few horse artillerymen and supply train drivers for variety, but it would follow Merle.

Napoleon found the 7th waiting when he reached Quatre Bras.

Sight of these fresh troops brought the Emperor out of a half-daze. No sense in putting them across the Brussels highway to try to halt the flight of his defeated army — they'd be swept away. Fugitives might gasp *Vive l'Empereur*, but they'd keep running. But the 7th could ruin pursuing cavalry.

203

His orders were quick. Marshal Soult, chief of staff, would take his own staff and half of the survivors of the Guard escort squadrons and set up a rallying point between Frasnes and Charleroi. An artillery officer would find a good gun position along the highway south of Quatre Bras. The 7th's 2nd Brigade – the 12th Light and 4th Line – would line the outskirts of Bossu Woods, just west of the highway, its left flank extending north of the Nivelles road and slightly refused. Two six-pounders would take position on that road, with Merle's cavalry behind them. The 1st Brigade would be split. Its 11th Light would hold the highway, its weak one-battalion 82nd Line would barricade itself in the Quatre Bras and Gemioncourt farms.

Fugitives were beginning to dribble down the highway when the artillery officer returned: less than a mile further on a slight jog on the highway would enable guns emplaced alongside it to put raking fire down its length towards Quatre Bras. Napoleon placed the remaining three six-pounders there, reinforcing them with two twelve-pounders plucked from the retreating troops. A battalion of the 11th Light took position on either side of the battery, ready to block the highway with commandeered wagons.

Infantry and guns in position, the Emperor turned to Merle: 'When our guns stop firing, the Prussians will be running – encourage them, at least into Genappe. Then circle westward and rejoin. You already have the cross; tonight you ride for a colonelcy. Also I need thirty or so well-mounted men to create a distraction. Have you a non-commissioned officer who is brave, clever and lucky to lead them?'

'Yes, sire,' half-turning his head, Merle called, *'Maréchal-des-Logis-Chef* Gros Noir!'

Gros-Noir was long and gaunt, all bone and whipcord, sitting his horse as if he had grown out of it. A hooked, hawk's-beak nose jutted from his dark face between feral yellow eyes. The Emperor looked at him, looked again – and somehow his weary face quickened into that of the ardent young general of the *Armée d'Italie*.

'From the Islands?'

'Yes, my Emperor.'

The Emperor laughed. *'Bon!* This might be Arcola, twenty years ago. This time you can be my Hercule!'[1] Then, briskly, he added: 'Pick your men; thirty should suffice. Move out as soon as you can. Find the Prussian left flank and get behind them. Create as much uproar as you can without dying heroically. Report back by daybreak. Your epaulet awaits you.'

Gros-Noir's sabre flashed up in salute. 'Yes, my Emperor!'

He took twenty hussars from his own company, a trumpeter and a sapper of dragoons, and a half-dozen chasseurs à cheval, including another trumpeter. Then, while his corporals checked horseshoes and weapons, Gros-Noir surveyed the battered little village and – employing instincts honed by twenty-odd year's service – swooped into the cellar of an outlying cottage and extracted a trembling citizen with all the hallmarks of being the local smuggler-poacher. Gabbling protests trailed away at the sight of a gold Napoléon proffered by Captain Merle and a growl and gesture from Gros-Noir which emphasised the only alternative. The poacher saddled a rough-coated pony, shuddering somewhat as a chasseur draped a noosed rope around his neck as a guarantee of continued co-operation. Then the little party, with Gros-Noir, the guide, his attendant chasseur and two German-speaking troopers at its head and another at its tail, faded into the woods.

Sight of the Emperor, the waiting guns and the 11th Light – its drums rumbling the long roll 'Fall in' – slowed the retreating units. Those still keeping formation were praised and given a rendezvous; careering vehicles were forced off the road, and obstreperous cavalrymen dismounted. The retreat flowed steadily on but in increasing order.

The first small clumps of Prussian horsemen were polished off quickly by Guard cavalrymen. When their first formed regiments passed Quatre Bras, Napoleon gave the word. The 11th's carabiniers shoved a line of wagons across the road abreast of the guns. Then –

Gros-Noir

Cat-footing past the Prussian V Corps' happily drowsy sentries, Sergeant Gros-Noir had located an ideal target – a Prussian battery parked in a small clearing, guns pointing southwards, caissons parked close behind them, horses tied to wheels and trees. Though lighted linstocks smouldered beside each gun, the cannoneers were sleeping or clustered around small fires, intent on pans and bottles. A single nodding sentry leaned against a tree where a rough road entered the far side of the clearing. Through the trees beyond, lines of infantry campfires glimmered.

At Gros-Noir's gesture his small detachment (less the guide's disgusted escort) swung into line. A forward sweep of his sabre, and it spurred in, trumpets blaring, riders whooping. Standing Prussians were slashed down, sleepers trampled. Those who could fled. There was no pursuit. Dropping from their saddles, hussars muscled the cannon around and touched them off at those infantry campfires; horses were cut loose and sent stampeding with blows and yells. One of the caissons was rolled over the nearest campfire; while some troopers threw fresh wood under it, the dragoon *sapeur* chopped out the spokes of a front wheel, rendering the caisson immobile. Remounting hastily, the Frenchmen followed their now co-operative guide away. Within minutes they heard the 'whu-ump' of the exploding caisson and saw bits of blazing wreckage cascade down through the tree tops. Thus ignited, the other caissons exploded thunderously and almost together. There was shocked silence, then the rattle of Prussian drums as infantry regiments stumbled into formation. Scuttling artillerymen babbled of hordes of French

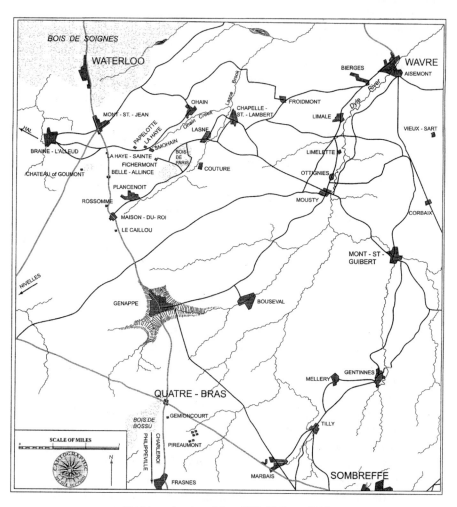

Positions for the night of 18–19 June 1815

English – Mostly west of the Brussels (Waterloo-Frasnes) highway, roughly Chateau of Goumont
as far south as Le Caillou.

Prussians – Much intermixed. I Corps: Maison du Roi and to the east. II Corps: Genappe-
Plancenot (left 23.00 hrs for Mellery). III Corps: Wavre. IV Corps: Genappe-Plancenoit.

French – Grouchy: Wavre–Limale.

cavalry; frightened horses blundered into their lines. Eventually, with much *verdammung* and tripping over roots and rocks, a couple of battalions probed gingerly into the woods. There was some shooting at stray horses and shadows; inevitably a few shots went in the wrong direction and – naturally – drew a blind leaden retaliation, giving worried colonels and brigade commanders the impression of a lively infantry skirmish.

All hell broke loose behind them along the Brussels road.

Surprise

Napoleon's orders had been imperative. The artillery would open fire on his command, each gun to fire six rounds. Infantry would join in. The six rounds fired, the infantry would clear the highway and Merle would attack. There would still be Frenchmen mixed with Prussians, but there was no help for that – hopefully, the moonlight would enable gunners and infantrymen to make some distinction.

'Fire!'

Generalleutnant Graf August von Gneisenau, Prussian chief of staff, was a man of frustrations. Born a Saxon, veteran of the Austrian and British armies, then one of those foreign officers eking out an existence in the penny-pinching Prussian service, he had clawed his way to high rank by intelligence, hard work and courage. In the process, like many converts, he had become more Prussian than any Junker in matters military. But his talent for staff work had thwarted his ambition to command troops in combat. Now, with the French at last cleared from Genappe, he saw an opportunity – the hated enemy in flight after what must be a decisive defeat – and seized it. Sending an order to Generalmajor Georg von Pirch to march his II Corps to Mellery to aid Generalleutnant Johann Thielmann's III Corps – reportedly in trouble to the east at Wavre – he had cast aside his staff functions, gathered up some 4,000 cavalry, the 15th Fusilier Regiment and some stray companies of infantry; and launched himself in pursuit. That left nobody much minding the shop at army headquarters, but glory beckoned.[2]

It was exciting, exhilarating riding down the moonlit highway, with squealing fugitives falling under Prussian sabre strokes, begging for mercy or scattering blindly from the road. There were occasional obstructions – bayonet-bristling cores of regiments formed up tight around their eagles, men who knew it was both dishonour and death to break ranks and so held together – but the Prussians flowed past these seeking easier prey. There were isolated guns and caissons, drivers vainly flogging their horses, vainly trying to defend themselves; knots of horsemen, overtaken and lanced from behind. Jena was avenged at last – a righteous judgement, heaped up and overflowing. Who knew – he might even overtake Bonaparte himself. If so, there could be no mercy for that monster who had so humbled Prussia; only, as old Blücher had put it, 'the unchallengable justice of God'.

He passed a farm at a crossroads – Quatre Bras already! Then, a mile or so beyond, the flow of flight and pursuit slowed – a patter of shots and wounded troopers dropping back. Wagons across the road, they said. Some French seemed to be trying to rally.

'Fools!' Gneisenau turned to his aide-de-camp riding at his elbow. 'Infantry to the front! We'll –'

With one obliterating crash, his sky fell in.

Cavalry, even solid regiments, could be a skittery thing, especially after dark. No competent commander used it either for rearguard or advance guard after dusk. And Blücher's cavalry, with its high proportion of Landwehr and recently reorganised units, was not solid.

In that sudden blaze and blast of short-range fire, panic gripped and maddened horses and men alike. Gneisenau's command stampeded back toward Genappe, riding down the hapless infantry that had accompanied it, troopers from the leading regiments literally sabring their way through the less damaged ones behind. French prisoners broke free, French stragglers in woods and farms along the road took heart and began firing into the tormented column. French gunners worked their guns furiously, twelve-pounder shot ricochetting down the hard surface of the Brussels road, six-pounders belching canister, until their six rounds were fired and French infantry swarmed across the highway, mopping up. Gneisenau, wounded and pinned under his horse, was captured.

Out of the shadowed Nivelles road, Merle swung his grab-bag squadron onto the fleeing Prussians, the old wolf-yell *Vive l'Empereur* ringing above the hoof-roar and tumult, trumpeters lustily sounding the charge. His 'sword point in their loins',[3] never pausing to take prisoners, Merle herded the tumbling masses into Genappe.

Blücher at Genappe

Genappe was a trap, its narrow bridge and main street still cluttered with abandoned wagons and now filled with units from all the Prussian corps, slowly fumbling their way through it. Into this jumble poured the Prussian cavalry, flogging their horses, striking at anyone in their way. They jammed the bridge; some went into the river on either side of it, splashing through the shallow water – and God help any man whose horse stumbled.

Marshal Blücher had established a makeshift headquarters in Genappe. Exhausted, bruised, jubilant with honest pride, he was enjoying a hastily-prepared meal and a large tumbler of brandy when the cannon opened at Quatre Bras. Then, louder and louder, came the uproar of retreat, yells of *Raus! Ruchzug! Raus!* until the room's walls shook. Furious, Blücher went out of the door and into the street, shaking off officers who tried to hold him back. Sword in hand, cursing expertly, he threw himself into the rout with thunderous orders to rally.

It was hopeless. The old hussar had used up his luck at Ligny. In the dark nobody recognised him – he was ridden down and trampled. The aide who had saved him at Ligny tried a second rescue, but fell under flailing sabres – whether Prussian or French, nobody knows. Spilling northward out of Genappe, the confused mob – cavalry, infantry, and what-not – rolled towards Wellington's bivouacs. From somewhere near their junction with those of Zieten's Prussian corps, artillery opened up on it.

Merle knew better than to push his luck and get embedded in the Prussian mass. He had studied a map of the area, had a chasseur who had grown up near Genappe riding at his elbow. Part-way through the town a narrow lane led westward from the main street. Reaching it, Merle brought his dragoons to the front to cover the junction with dismounted fire while the rest of his squadron thinned from an eight-man to a four-man front to squeeze into it. A quarter of an hour later he was clear of Genappe, riding freely along an empty ridge line. Across a valley Wellington's campfires gleamed.

Prisoners in the night

Sergeant Gros-Noir was finding the rest of the night rather anti-climatic. His detachment cut up a few fatigue parties, burned a few supply wagons, and stampeded the horses and orderlies of a brigade headquarters. One hussar had his horse shot out from under him and was captured by pursuing uhlans (following Gros-Noir's previous instructions, he told them he was from Grouchy's advance guard). By two in the morning they had stirred up so much Prussian ire that Gros-Noir thought it wise to shift to the east bank of the Lasne River. His poacher-guide knew of a seldom-used ford, narrow and difficult; men and horses alike were bone-weary, the water high and fast from past days' rains, and one chasseur and his mount were swept away and drowned. After that the detachment holed up in a rocky copse, half sleeping while half stood guard and wolfed stale bread.

It was still dark when a sentry reported a big column on the march to the north and east, moving away from the battlefield. Taking two German-speaking hussars, Gros-Noir coasted along the fatigue-fogged regiments; their oilcloth covered shakos and faded green overcoats indistinguishable in the dimness from those of any Prussian cavalry patrol. An occasional 'What unit, comrade?' brought some enlightenment, but finally the sergeant found what he had been looking for – a major who, accompanied by his orderly, had dropped out of the column to answer a call of nature. The orderly, entangled in the reins of two horses, could only gape at the pistol muzzle suddenly thrust into his face; the major, busy refastening his waistband and sash, began a shout but then swallowed it. Swiftly disarmed (the major's watch and wallet went with his sword and pistols), they were hustled back to the copse and interrogated, separately.

That complete, Gros-Noir considered briefly: the column was Pirch's II

Corps, en route to Mellery to rescue Thielmann's III Corps, wherever it was now. The situation back on the battlefield was obscure. Seemingly the French had rallied, the *verdammit* English weren't supporting their brave Prussian allies, and there was a surplus of confusion and a shortage of rations and sleep. Abruptly Gros-Noir extracted an impressive coin from what had been the major's purse and thrust it under the guide's nose. 'Get us back to the Emperor safely, the quickest way, and this is yours. Fail us and . . .' He ran a callused thumb along his sabre's edge.

A rallying

At Quatre Bras the Emperor was tidying up. The 7th Infantry Division dropped back to a selected defensive position, screening the movement by sending its voltigeurs toward Genappe to sweep the area for any Prussian patrols that might wish to be neighbourly. All they found were a few detachments, mostly lost and apprehensive, which promptly took to their heels, running through Bülow's IV Corps' disordered bivouac with unsettling yells of *Hier kommen der kleine manner*,[4] to the further dismay of that scrambled outfit. Riding frantically from one perceived crisis to another, General der Infanterie Graf Bülow, a stout enough straight-ahead fighter when he could see his enemy, was rapidly losing control. Blücher himself had diagnosed his raw troops as capable of only two manoeuvres – a disorderly advance or a chaotic retreat. Without Marshal Vorwärts[5] to lead and inspire it, or Gneisenau to transform the old hussar's visceral inspirations into cogent orders, that second option would take hold.

Marshal Ney, shaken out of his blind battle madness by the sight of fleeing Prussians, a dose of cognac, and an overdue curt flare of Imperial anger, was given the rearguard, consisting of the 7th Infantry Division, the twelve-pounders, three still-steady (if grievously riddled) regiments from Lobau's VI Corps, and a couple of scratch squadrons of Jacquinot's 1st Lancers. It was a task he had in his bones, and he quickly steadied to it. He was told to hold on until further orders, informing the Emperor at once of any enemy advance.

The Emperor then rode south through Frasnes to where Marshal Soult – given a mission he understood far better than being chief of staff – had reverted to his old 'Iron Hand' expertise in getting a defeated army ready to fight again. Corps and divisions found their rallying points designated and guides awaiting them. Just north of Charleroi an isolated barn had been cleared to serve as army headquarters; General Bailly de Monthion (the sorely missed Berthier's long-time assistant) already had it organised. More couriers went out – to recall Grouchy; to find the Guard (which had detoured Genappe); to bring in Piré's 2nd Cavalry Division and other units which had retired by side roads further west; to order the army trains to send forward ammunition and replacement cannon and then displace south to Philippeville. Officers and sergeants from rallied regiments lined the road, collecting fugitives for their units. Campfires began to flare; the smell of cooking proved almost as strong a magnet as the sergeants' dulcet voices.

The *commissaire-ordonateur* sent to Charleroi to move the trains was promptly interrupted by the local garrison commander who – his drunken slumbers thus interrupted – came bursting downstairs bellowing objections. Luckily, he tripped over his spurs halfway down and ended with his front teeth embedded in the bottom step. Thereafter things proceeded with order and dispatch. The garrison fell in and marched for Frasnes, while a detail of gendarmes from the train's escort set up a straggler control line at the Charleroi bridge.

It was a nervous army, glad to catch its breath, but mostly ready to break and bolt. But no attack came, and the noise of battle receded northward. The last stragglers and the 7th Division's wounded came in full of brag and swagger. 'We gave those *sacré sauerkrauts* a blessing! You should have heard the *maudits* squeal! Bet they're still running.'

Slowly, units steadied and settled themselves to eat and sleep. Their Emperor was still with them. Veterans – some still fuzz-faced boys, called up in 1814 – began to remember. 'He is full of tricks, our *Tondu*. Just wait – we'll have them in the *merde profond* before they know what hit them!'

Their Emperor had had barely twenty hours' rest in the past five days, had fought two major battles, and had endured repeated blunderings by hitherto competent subordinates. He was drawing on his last inner reserve of strength and willpower. Yet he rode through his rallying army with a confident word for old sweats and gaping recruits alike, quick to note the deserving, to reward or reprove. Back at his 'palace' – a bed of straw in a partitioned-off corner of the barn – he had a quick glass of wine and a bit of bread, dictated orders, checked the latest reports, and collapsed into his bed, a rolled up cloak for a pillow, his overcoat for a blanket.

It was almost first light, that early morning moment when you can begin to distinguish individual white hairs in the coat of a black horse, when Colonel Gourgaud, his senior *officier d'ordonnance*, awakened him.

'Sire, that sergeant's back with important news.'

Standing lance-straight, his drooping detachment behind him, Gros-Noir reported: the Prussian II Corps was heading for Mellery to help Thielmann – though it wasn't sure where Thielmann might be. It was weary and moving slowly.

The Emperor's head came up. 'You have down well, lieutenant!' Raising his voice, he spoke to the detachment. 'I am content with all of you. You deserve well of *la patrie*.' Then, to his rousing staff: 'Take care of these men. Ready my maps. Give that major some wine and really question him.' He ran a thumb across his stubbled chin. 'Send for Ali and Marchand[6] and coffee.'

Whistling off-key, the Emperor headed for the table where his maps lay displayed, lighted candles flaring at each corner. Suddenly he paused. 'Where's the *pissoir?*'

Alarums and excursions

Generalmajor Hans Joachim von Zieten, commander of the Prussian I Corps, was finding the champagne from the cellar of his farmhouse headquarters to be a decidedly substandard vintage. Lacing it with brandy from the same source didn't help, so it was with some irritation that he received a staff officer's report that fighting had flared up beyond Genappe, that it seemed to be moving nearer, and that excited fugitives from IV Corps and various cavalry regiments were beginning to filter through I Corps' bivouacs.

Zieten was an energetic, responsible officer, albeit just now somewhat obfuscated. Followed by an aide-de-camp and an orderly (both in a similar condition) he got to horse and rode westwards towards the junction of his corps and Wellington's left flank, seeking enlightenment. His escort – a squadron of the 2nd West Prussian Dragoon Regiment – being busy demolishing a nearby cottage and getting drunk, was several minutes slow mounting up and following.

The rough farm road was littered with bodies from the past days' fighting, and occasional supplicating wounded. The horses stepped nervously among them, snorting their unease. Now out in the fresh air, Zieten could grasp that something had gone seriously wrong. Fugitives brushed past him, heedless of his shouts. There was heavy firing around Genappe, and an occasional cannon shot from the high ground west of the village, apparently directed at Wellington's position. That *verfluchen teufel* Bonaparte –

'*Qui vive?*'

The French challenge rang almost under his horse's nose. In the gloom, Zieten could distinguish only flat-topped French shakos and the glint of bayonets. Instinctively the Prussians whirled their mounts, grabbing for the pistols in their saddle holsters. The aide's went off, a shako went spinning, a bayonet skewered the aide's arm, and a swinging musket butt slammed across the nose of Zieten's horse. Screaming, the animal reared, sending Zieten headlong into the road-side ditch; aide, orderly and riderless horse went careering back through the tardy dragoons.

Zieten had ridden into a sentry and some foragers of a Belgian battery on Wellington's far left flank, all so drunk and out-of-hand that nobody short of the Archangel Michael could have restrained them.[7]

Untangling themselves from aide and orderly, the dragoons came galloping with a chorus of hiccuping hurrahs. The foragers, who had only begun exploring Zieten's pockets, dived into the hedgerow. Fanning out in pursuit, the dragoons rode into the Belgian battery – and also into Captain Mercer's nearby troop of Royal Horse Artillery. Belgians dived under gun carriages and caissons, emerged with musket, rammer and handspike. The English had been collapsing into exhausted slumber; they had been shot up at the battle's end – so they believed – by Prussian artillery; and they now came up swinging anything lethal they could grab. A wounded young grenadier à cheval whom they had retrieved joined in with a whooped '*Vive l'Empereur!*' Out of the natural perversity of their race, several gunners enthusiastically echoed him. And the same defiant shout rose from veterans amongst the Belgians. A Prussian battery bivouacked south of Mercer's sent a detachment to investigate; its leader's skull caught a swinging Prussian sabre, the rest fled. A British staff officer checking troop dispositions rode up to ascertain the situation but found no friends whatever. Quickly losing his hat, one stirrup, and his equanimity, he fled for Wellington's headquarters, crying alarm and woe.

Fortunately the dragoons were too few and too drunk to master the situation. Officers and sergeants gradually regained control. For all the fury involved, serious casualties were few – drunken men usually strike clumsily and with the flat of their blades – broken arms and heads and assorted nicks and contusions being the worst of the injuries inflicted.

In the resulting sorting-out someone almost accidentally discovered Zieten, face down and half-drowned in a half-inch of water. His situation was further compounded by a dragoon's attempt to administer the military cure-all – a slug of schnapps – from his canteen. Luckily Mercer intervened and, lacking a barrel to roll him over, draped Zieten across the tube of a nine-pounder gun to drain. That approximately accomplished, the unfortunate Prussian was given a dose of British-issue rum – explosive, dark stuff that gives the uninitiated the sensation of having swallowed an irritated tomcat.[8] It was too potent for Zieten's abused system; he vomited violently, and then began a comprehensive damnation – hoarse, but sincere – of Great Britain in all its aspects, especially its military.

Clamour down-slope interrupted him – yowling French cavalrymen swept through the Prussian battery, and came crashing into the reforming dragoons. The impact was so sudden that it seemed impossible that there were only three of them. The Prussian battery was frantically firing back along their track, envisaging massed squadrons following them, but their shots hit only the landscape, Prussian fugitives, and the nervous systems of every Allied commander who heard them.

The three cavalrymen were lost souls, stragglers from Merle's column who had missed his westward turn in Genappe. Two of them had lost control of their horses; clinging desperately to their saddles, they went wailing on into the darkness. The third, a corporal '*saoul comme dix Polonais*', came slashing right and left. Halfway through Mercer's jumbled position, his gasping horse tripped over a gun trail; the corporal performed a perfect parabola, landed on his feet, brought his sabre up to the salute and dropped it. Reaching out, he plucked a rum-filled canteen from a goggle-eyed gunner, downed a three-finger slug, returned the canteen with a polite bow, then smote his chest with both hands, announcing:

'*Brigadier* Jean Danois, *La Petite Tulipe Rouge*, of the advance guard of Marshal Davout's *Armée la Seine*' – and instantly passed out, full-length. Awed beholders swore that he was snoring before he hit the ground.

'Davout!' Memory of that terrible, never-defeated marshal sobered Zieten. He would, he told Mercer, see that the corporal's words reached both Blücher and Wellington, though he doubted the latter had brains enough to understand their import – he hadn't responded to Zieten's warnings on the 15th until almost too late. Sending an officer to silence the Prussian battery, he clambered weakly into a saddle and rode off, with a few final comments which, probably fortunately, only Mercer fully understood. Enlisted men parted with expressions of comradely esteem – *Englische schwein*! – *Chiens sales Allemandes*! – *Belgier Hundsfotts*! – Copulating bastards!

Allied doubts

Jogging westward, Merle looked hungrily at those campfires. Alas, nothing could be done with his handful. He did jump several patrols and outposts of British hussars, capturing a number of excellent horses and sending fugitives galloping into Wellington's lines to report masses of French cavalry.

Then he had an unexpected stroke of luck – a French twelve-pounder, still harnessed to two exhausted horses. The sound of French voices brought several French artillerymen out of hiding; they had, for the honour of their arm, been trying to get their gun away, but British patrols had been too active. There were a dozen rounds of solid shot left in the 'coffer' on the gun's tail. It would be extreme range, but ... The horse artillerymen in his own detachment jumped to help unhook the gun from its *avant-train* and swing its muzzle around.

Again Merle's luck was in; the second round struck amid outlying campfires, sending embers high and wide. The next was as accurate. In Wellington's camp, soldiers who had stood firm throughout a day of artillery bombardment and surges of cuirassiers suddenly scrambled away from their fires and ran. Officer casualties had been heavy; some officers, believing their victory complete, had sought more comfortable quarters. Few were on hand to check the disorder. As the gun slammed again, and more hussars rode in shouting danger, flight took hold and fed on itself, cursing, shoving, running. It was long minutes before a few drums began to beat 'Assembly' and mounted officers pushed into the throngs bellowing damnation.

Merle got more horses hitched to the gun, shifted it westward a quarter-mile, and deliberately fired off its remaining rounds, while his dragoons dismounted and delivered musket volleys to add to the show. Then he went away, at the trot.

Eventually the British camp quieted, men searching for their units with much loud accusation and self-excusing. Another tide of runaways had headed for Brussels, howling destruction and defeat. A squadron of the reliable 1st King's German Legion Hussars scouted southwards, but found nothing. But nobody got much sleep.

The Duke's pre-dawn council of war at his Waterloo headquarters began badly, and rapidly got worse. Wellington himself was exhausted and mentally drained. He had been out-generalled, almost out-fought; now his desperately-won victory seemed to be slipping through his fingers. His own army was sorely battered, parts of it still in charming confusion, key subordinates dead or disabled.

The Prussians quickly proved unshirted trouble. With old Blücher and Gneisenau gone – nobody knew how or where – there was no unity of command. Their senior surviving commander, Graf Bülow, had had a rough night on top of a very rough day; the only positive reaction left in his system was an ingrained reluctance to take orders from anyone who was not both a Prussian and senior to him in the Prussian service.[9] His corps was scattered from Genappe to who knew where. Thielmann's III Corps was out of contact and apparently in trouble. A staff officer from Pirch's II Corps stated flatly that it had orders from Gneisenau to march to Thielmann's aid; until those orders were changed by proper Prussian authority, Pirch would continue his march. The Prussian Army, thought the Duke, resembled a just-decapitated chicken.

Zieten arrived late, considerably the worse for his nocturnal adventure, but sorer in mind than body. His views were immediate and unrestrained – the Duke had ignored his warnings of an imminent French offensive; he had failed to keep his promise to support Blücher at Ligny; he had mismanaged yesterday's battle and would have been damn-well beaten had not the Prussians made superhuman efforts to rescue him. Now he was trying to give them orders and he – Zieten – wasn't taking any!

The Duke regarded Zieten with the hauteur of an Anglo-Irish aristocrat considering a peasant caught raiding his poultry yard, then addressed him with that icy contempt that (so his officers sometimes whispered over their third bottle) had driven more than one unfortunate subordinate to suicide. It was a superior freeze-and-flay excoriation. Zieten didn't understand one word in ten, but the intent was obvious and left him momentarily stunned. Then he blurted something about all of England's gold not being enough to buy one Prussian's honour. He – Zieten – would go and rally Pirch and Thielmann and finish off that Bonaparte himself. Therewith he slammed out of the room. Bülow produced a few confused words and gestures and bumbled after him.

A bandaged acting aide-de-camp warily approached the Duke, sealed message in extended hand. 'By courier from Mons, Your Grace.'

Events in the north

Away to the north, the French commander of the Dunkirk area had finally brought himself to obey repeated Imperial urgings that he annoy his equally quiescent Dutch opposite number. His means were limited, but he had scraped together a sort of posse – a half-company of chasseurs, some mounted gendarmes, *douaniers* and national guardsmen, and a few ornate volunteers from local guards of honour – and sent them forth before daylight on 18 June, under a recalled-to-active-duty *chef d'escadron* of the Imperial Gendarmerie, who proudly bore the warrior name of Xaintrailles. Having an excellent knowledge of the region's back trails from his pursuit of the more iniquitous elements of its population while Belgium and Holland were part of France, Xaintrailles handily got his variegated command several miles into Netherlands territory before sunrise. Shortly thereafter he stumbled on a Dutch militia regiment on the march. Shouting 'Charge!' the major put in his spurs; the Dutch fired one spasmodic volley, mostly into the tree-tops, and then departed in every available direction. Xaintrailles reined in and regarded his command: the chasseurs, gendarmes and *douaniers* were still there, but most of their civilian comrades were only a dust cloud on the road home. Xaintrailles shrugged; his faithful handful shrugged back. Collecting an abandoned Netherlands' flag and – later – several national guardsmen whose horses had discarded them, he rode back to report his victory. Naturally, some national guardsmen and guards of honour became lost during their hurried departure. For the next few days individuals and small parties kept popping up all along the frontier, to the alarm of local commanders and the troubling of farmers' stables and hen roosts.

A report of that almost bloodless encounter now had come snowballing into the Duke's hands. Hordes of French cavalry were advancing westwards from Dunkirk. Wellington had always feared a French thrust at his right rear, aimed at cutting him off from his Antwerp base. Ordinarily he would have suspected that this report was an exaggeration of some three-shots-and-a-gallop border skirmish, and demanded competent confirmation. Now, behind his still impassive face, he was uncertain, but his orders were crisp enough: the army would prepare to move on short notice; a strong cavalry reconnaissance must be pushed toward Quatre Bras; Generalmajor von Müffling[10] must try to pound some sense into the skulls of his two compatriots; and the English community that had grown up in Brussels, and Louis XVIII in Ghent, must be warned.

That done, the Duke personally penned a letter to a Lady Francis

Webster, warning her to leave Brussels for the greater safety of Antwerp. (The Duke had a very susceptible heart, particularly – if regrettably – towards young married ladies.)

Grouchy

Marshal Grouchy found 19 June a demanding day. He had begun it by whipping Thielmann, sending him off northward in disorder. Debate with his subordinates as to what to do next was cancelled by the arrival of a staff officer despatched from Quatre Bras by Napoleon; the French had been repulsed at Mont St-Jean, but – after a successful night counter-attack – were rallying between Frasnes and Charleroi. The Emperor had need of him there.

Sending his wounded and prisoners off to Namur under dragoon escort (a wandering, half-lost Prussian cavalry brigade would glimpse them from a distance and take them for Grouchy's whole command in full retreat), Grouchy marched. The roads were poor, but his men responded willingly. They had won their fight; now they'd show the *sacré* Imperial Guard and all the rest how it was done. Somewhere along the way another courier pulled up his lathered horse: the Prussian II Corps, possibly 20,000 strong, was heading for Mellery ('Here on your map, Marshal'), very weary and moving slowly.

Ghent in turmoil

In Ghent His Most Christian Majesty of France Louis XVIII (who had, with some difficulty, been persuaded to pause there during his flight back to his long-time English asylum) was chilled by renewed apprehension. It would be a grievous error to linger and so tempt his misguided subjects into the sacrilege of laying violent hands on their divinely anointed king. Therefore benevolence and wisdom alike dictated the removal of such temptation to safety beyond the English Channel. Younger brother Artois and Artois' sons Angoulême and Berry – equally conscious of their royal blood – chorused agreement.

So there was lamentation, hurried summoning of carriages, mounting in haste, and riding off in all directions. Sensing imminent abandonment, the outer fringes of Louis' 'court' and his raggle-taggle 'Army of Ghent' began heading for the bushes, snapping up anything available and portable as they scattered into oblivion.

Allied reactions

It was mid-morning before the British cavalry reconnaissance reached Quatre Bras, after working through Genappe and the debris from the battle and the night before. Occasional Prussian units, mostly moving northward, met them – seldom with friendly greetings. Probing cautiously past Quatre

Bras, they found no French at all, and so quickened their advance. They did not see a French officer making himself small in the attic of the crossroads farmhouse.

Ney had adopted a Russian tactic – no patrols or outposts in front of his position, his troops held under cover. That lone officer in the attic, carefully keeping the lens of his telescope out of the sunlight to avoid betraying reflections, had watched the British cavalry come up out of Genappe and signalled their appearance. The English were barely 200 yards away when Ney's infantry stood up.

It was quick and messy: the crash of canister and musketry, fired almost point-blank; lancers harrying the flanks of the beheaded column; and a tumbling retreat back through Genappe.

Not long afterwards the Duke again faced his subordinates. Obviously the French were at Quatre Bras in strength, It would take a full-scale attack to move them and the past day and night had left his own army incapable of that. Blücher and Gneisenau were still missing; Zieten had gone off towards Wavre; Bülow was trying to reassemble his corps and follow; II and III Corps were out of contact; and no help could be expected from any of them.

The reports of Grouchy and Davout joining Boney? The first was to be expected, the second was dubious – but Boney would be gathering in every available man and gun. And there were those reports of a French raid toward Antwerp – probably overblown, but not to be ignored.

'By God, gentlemen, that fellow Napoleon has humbugged me again! No help for it, we must retire on Antwerp. We had to retreat more than once in Spain, yet it all came right in the end. We march at dusk, in the following order ...'

When the Duke closed with the observation that 'If Boney pursues, Brussels and the other Dutch-Belgian fortresses will delay him', heads nodded in agreement around the room. No-one voiced the common apprehension: how much reliance could be placed in those Dutch-Belgian garrisons once they saw Wellington retreating?

Beyond the Channel, anxious Londoners saw lights burning late at the Horse Guards, the Admiralty and Whitehall. The Duke was in trouble; those arrogant Prussians apparently deserting him; the Austrians had stalled along the Rhine; the Russians were still crossing Germany. There were few troops left in England; the militia could be called out, but ... Veteran regiments were returning from Canada, but it would be two weeks or more before they began to arrive. They had had little luck against those damned Yankees, but they were the Duke's old sweats of Spain. Unfortunately, there might not be enough of them, and some might not arrive in time. The Duke must keep what troops he had intact, even if that required a retreat on Antwerp. Antwerp had to be held, whether as a beachhead or bolt hole; and additional transports must be secured.

It was a certainty that England's allies would be demanding additional and larger subsidies. And England was sick and weary of war and high wartime taxes. Public unrest smouldered across the nation like fire in a peat bog, flaring into open violence at unexpected times and places.

The men who conferred by late lamplight were for the most part level-headed and cold-blooded, hardened by decades of war – patriots, yet men who could distinguish the probable from the merely desirable. It was inevitable that one of them would finally ponder, half-aloud, 'That Boney's getting fat and older; he has a son he'd like to pass his throne on to. Defeat him again, and we'll still have that greedy, fog-headed Russian and his jack-booted Prussian toady on our hands. Just possibly. . .'

Walloped by one courier of disaster after another, Berlin was an over-turned anthill. More troops were needed – well, there was Kliest's small corps along the lower Rhine; two corps along the Elbe to keep an eye on Austria and, should opportunity offer, gobble up what was left of inde-pendent Saxony; and a reserve corps near Berlin. Most were green troops, incompletely equipped; unfortunately recruits from the just-seized Saxony and Rhineland territories were not displaying appropriate gratitude for their new status as Prussian subjects. More than one *bierlokal* wall was displaying '*Hoch der kaiser Napoleon*' or even '*Vive l'Empereur!*' Somewhat more dis-tracting, with both Blücher and Gneisenau gone the cliques among the Prussian high command were at each other's throats, much to the distress of their modest king, Friederich Wilhelm III.

Of course, there were the Russians – possibly 180,000 of them, under that most un-Russian commander, Field Marshal Barclay de Tolly – on the march across Germany, shedding sick and deserters and displaying the usual great-souled Russian willingness to treat their ally's property much as they would their enemy's. But Barclay was a careful, long-headed officer, not likely to rush in until he learned what the situation really was – which just then nobody really knew.

In Vienna, the congress of Europe's rulers – who had been raucously dividing Napoleon's former empire, somewhat like a convocation of vul-tures around a dead lion – suddenly evaporated as monarchs bolted home. (Notably, the least apprehensive was Friedrich August, the thoroughly robbed king of Saxony; one observer thought he detected a certain antici-patory glint in the hitherto defected royal eye.) Tsar Alexander departed, proclaiming that the military crisis required his assumption of the com-mand of all Allied forces – an assertion that produced mutterings in several languages to the effect of 'Give an idiot child a box of eggs and a big stick. . .'

The only calm individual was the French representative, Charles Maurice de Talleyrand-Perigord, once Napoleon's faithless foreign minister, past master at influencing others without committing himself. Appraising the exodus with hooded eyes, he calculated his opportunities: Napoleon was a sensible man who seldom wasted talent. He had forgiven Talleyrand before for intrigues and treacheries. Now, if he won more battles, he would need an expert diplomat, capable of converting military success into an established Bonaparte dynasty in France. For the present Talleyrand would wait, safe in Vienna, outwardly still Louis XVIII's loyal representative. Meanwhile one would discreetly re-establish certain contacts in Paris.

One letter the Emperor had dictated before collapsing into his bed of straw in the barn near Charleroi was to Marshal Davout, his Minister of War in Paris:

> I have need of you. Transfer your office and the Paris command to Carnot.[11] I grant him full powers. Bring forward [a list of available units and replacements]. Hasten the return of the two Young Guard regiments from the Vendée. Repeat again my orders to the governors of Lille and Dunkirk to probe the enemy positions to their front. Bring me also the Marquis de Lafayette and the Duke of Otranto[12] telling them I may soon seek negotiations with the English and so have need of their services. Paris will be safer without them.

Paris would soon see not just some panicked fugitives from the battle, but also a procession, short but grimly impressive – six bandaged cavalrymen riding proud behind jubilant trumpeters, each man brandishing a captured flag.

Lafayette would answer Davout's summons. An obtusely idealistic egoist, he could already see himself as indispensable in guiding the Emperor onto the path of peace, possibly even persuading him to abdicate in favour of a renewed French Republic which would naturally hail Lafayette once more as France's mentor and saviour.

Fouché lacked both Lafayette's inner innocence and Talleyrand's aplomb. Also the Emperor might have learned of his recent correspondence with Wellington. He met Davout's messenger with apparent acquiescence and a request for a few minutes to change clothes. Thereafter, putting on a gardener's cap and blouse, he slipped out his back door. One of Davout's aides-de-camp and a file of veterans were waiting for him.

Along the Rhine frontier, the army of Field Marshal Prince von Schwarzenberg, Allied commander-in-chief, had been attacking from Strasbourg south to the Swiss border. Now, abruptly, he reined in. When some subordinates, especially the crown princes of Bavaria and Württemberg, protested, the fat Austrian leaned back in his overburdened chair and gave them a quizzical smile. 'This news from the north may change all our plans. Best we deliberate. If Bonaparte *has* beaten the English and Prussians, my gracious master, Emperor of Austria, may suddenly remember his responsibilities as the Emperor Napoleon's affectionate father-in-law.'

Next morning

Before first light on 20 June, Grouchy struck Mellery, surprising and shattering Pirch's II Corps. General Vandamme, who – atoning for his mistakes two days before at Wavre – led the attack, would get his long-desired marshal's baton.

Military historians generally agree that Napoleon's post-Waterloo 1815 campaign was possibly the most brilliant of his entire career.

NOTES

1. At Arcola Napoleon had used a small cavalry detachment under mulatto Lieutenant Hercule Dominique to dislocate the Austrian line.
2. An impulse natural to staff officers in like circumstances. Thus the author got his Purple Heart.
3. French for 'stepping on their heels'.
4. 'Little men' – German for voltigeurs.
5. Blücher.
6. Mameluke and valet.
7. Netherlands' artillery had retained French-style shakos.
8. From personal experience and the observation of two senior officers who took one slug too many.
9. Gneisenau, junior and non-Prussian, had to phrase Bülow's orders: 'I have the honour of humbly beseeching Your Excellency...'
10. Prussian representative at Wellington's headquarters; naturally, he neither spoke nor understood English.
11. Lazare Carnot, minister of war 1793–7 and 1800–1, currently minister of the interior.
12. Joseph Fouché, scoundrel extraordinary, minister of police.

THE REALITY

For reasons unknown the 7th Infantry Division did not appear at Quatre Bras. As a minor point, the Charleroi garrison commander did not fall downstairs. And so history took its recorded course.

BIBLIOGRAPHY

Genappe: Municipal Records, Carton 78, January-September 1815.
Esposito, Vincent, and Elting, John R., *A Military History and Atlas of the Napoleonic Wars* (London, 1999).
Hofschröer, Peter, *1815: The Waterloo Campaign – Wellington, his German Allies and the Battles of Ligny and Quatre Bras* (London, 1998).
—, *1815: The Waterloo Campaign – The German Victory* (London, 1999).
Huddleston, F.W. *Warriors in Undress* (London, 1925).
MacIssac, Alexander, *Diary of an officer of the North British Dragoons, appointed ADC to Wellington 19 June 1815* (unpublished).
Marbot, Marcellin, *Mémoires* (3 vols, Paris, 1892).
Mercer, Cavalié, *Journal of the Waterloo Campaign* (London, 1870, reprinted 1989).
Siborne, Herbert T., ed., *The Waterloo Letters* (London, 1993).